HEADQUARTERS
FAR EAST COMMAND
MILITARY HISTORY SECTION
Japanese Research Division

IMPERIAL GENERAL HEADQUARTERS ARMY
HIGH COMMAND RECORD.

Mid-1941 - August 1945

This Monograph may not be reproduced without the permission of the Chief of Military History

JAPANESE MONOGRAPH

4 5

Published by Books Express Publishing
Copyright © Books Express, 2011
ISBN 978-1-78039-901-0

Books Express publications are available from all good retail and online booksellers. For publishing proposals and direct ordering please contact us at: info@books-express.com

Preface

Through Instructions No. 126 to the Japanese Government, 12 October 1945, subject: Institution for War Records Investigation, steps were initiated to exploit military historical records and official reports of the Japanese War Ministry and Japanese General Staff. Upon dissolution of the War Ministry and the Japanese General Staff, and the transfer of their former functions to the Demobilization Bureau, research and compilation continued and developed into a series of historical monographs.

The paucity of original orders, plans and unit journals, which are normally essential in the preparations of this type of record, most of which were lost or destroyed during field operations or bombing raids rendered the task of compilation most difficult; particularly distressing has been the complete lack of official strength reports, normal in AG or G3 records. However, while many of the important orders, plans and estimates have been reconstructed from memory and therefore are not textually identical with the originals, they are believed to be generally accurate and reliable.

Under the supervision of the Demobilization Bureau, the basic material contained in this monograph was compiled and written in Japanese by former officers, on duty in command and staff units within major units during the period of operations. Translation was effected through the facilities of Allied Translators and Interpreters Service, G2, General Headquarters, Far East Command.

This Japanese Operational Monograph was rewritten in English by the Japanese Research Division, Military History Section, General Headquarters, Far East Command and is based on the translation of the Japanese original. Editorial corrections were limited to those necessary for coherence and accuracy.

FOREWORD

The overall preparation of Japanese Monograph No 45 was accomplished by the following former officers of the Japanese Army:

Hattori, Takushiro, ex-Colonel, and former Chief of 2d Section (Operations), Army General Staff, Imperial General Headquarters.

Takase, Keiji, ex-Colonel, and former staff member in 2d Section (Operations), Army General Staff, Imperial General Headquarters.

Nakamura, Ryuhei, ex-Major, and former staff member in 2d Section (Operations), Army General Staff, Imperial General Headquarters.

In addition, specific sections of the original Japanese Monograph were assigned and written by the following former officers:

Ishiwari, Heizo, ex-Lt Colonel, and former Chief of Japanese Army History Compilation Section, Army General Staff.

Tanaka, Koji, ex-Lt Colonel, and former staff member in 2d Section (Operations), Army General Staff, Imperial General Headquarters.

Fukaya, Toshimitsu, ex-Major, and former staff member in the Department of Inspectorate General (Army Training).

Okada, Kikusaburo, ex-Maj General, and former Chief of the War Material Section, War Ministry.

Nishiura, Susumu, ex-Colonel, and former Chief of Army Affairs Section, War Ministry.

Takayama, Shinobu, ex-Colonel, and former Chief of Sub-Section (Logistics) in 2d Section (Operations), Army General Staff, Imperial General Headquarters.

Ureshino, Michinori, ex-Lt Colonel, and former staff member in 10th Section (Shipping), Army General Staff, Imperial General Headquarters.

Shirai, Fumitada, ex-Lt Colonel, and former staff member in Sub-Section (Logistics), 2d Section (Operations), Army General Staff, Imperial General Headquarters.

In this revised edition of Monograph No 45, corrections have been inserted from the Japanese Errata on the original Japanese monograph. This had not been done in the previously submitted translation. As an editing policy, effort was directed to verifying original translation and designations, clarification of phrasing, and adding pertinent information which has become available since the original monograph was written.

TABLE OF CONTENTS

CHAPTER I -- Japanese Military Command Organization

State Affairs and "Supreme Command" Relationship	1
"Supreme Command" Independence and Direct Appeal to Throne	3
"Supreme Command" and State Affairs Concurrent Matters	3
Methods for Issuing Concurrent Affairs Orders	5
Principles in Assignment of Military Officers as War Minister	5
Imperial General Headquarters and Government Liaison Conferences	6
Legislative Characteristics of the Conference	7
Relationship Between the Emperor and the Conference	8
Conference (Council) in the Imperial Presence	8
Conference (Council) Agenda Example	9

CHAPTER II -- General Situation Before the War

Military Preparations	10
Training Programs	14
Expansion of National Defense Industries and War Materiel	16
Reserve Army Supplies Stockpile Preparations	19

CHAPTER III -- Pacific War Operational Preparations

Preparations Related to Outbreak of Russo-German War	22
Preparations Related to Economic Blockade by US, Great Britain and the Netherlands	24
Pre-War Estimate of Enemy Situation	25
Development of Southern Operation Plan	28
Southern Army Order of Battle Outline	29
Army General Staff Assignment of Objectives and Missions in Southern Operation	30
Hongkong, Guam and Bismarck Archipelago Operational Assignments and Strategy	33
Air Force Operational Assignments	34
Line of Communication (Logistical Support)	34
Proposed Southern Operation Military Administration	35

CHAPTER IV -- First Phase of the War

    PART I --- First Stage (December 1941 - June 1942) 37

        Decision as to Time and Date for Beginning War 37

        Summary of Orders Issued to Southern Army Commander 38

        Summary of Orders Issued to China Expeditionary Army Commander 39

        Alternate Plans for Malay Attack 40

        Orders for Kwantung Army and China Expeditionary Army Related to China Incidents 40

        Summary of Operational Progress During First Stage Period 40

        Java Operations Planning 42

        Burma Operations Planning 44

        Situation Review and Tentative Plans 45

        Preliminary Planning for a Chungking Operation 49

        Aleutians, Midway and Southeast Area Operations Plans 50

        New Calédonia, Fiji, Samoa Islands and Port Moresby Operations Plans 53

        Operational Conduct for Southern Army Following Completion of First Stage in Occupational Operations 55

        Army-Navy Central Agreement Regarding Southern Area Defense Responsibilities 56

        Establishment of Air Bases in Important Southern Zones 58

        Line of Communication (Logistical Support) 59

        The Chekiang-Kiangsi Operation 60

    PART II --- Second Stage (July - December 1942) 62

        Suspension of Fiji, Samoa and New Caledonia Operations 62

        Conduct of Guadalcanal Operation 63

        Situation Review and Plans (October 1942) 67

        Southeast Area Operations (November-December 1942) 69

        Changes in Other Area Operations Caused by Solomons Difficulties 72

        Miscellaneous Actions During Second Stage 73

        Line of Communication (Logistical Support) During First Phase 73

CHAPTER V -- Second Phase of the War (January -- August 1943)

    Situation Estimate Regarding Enemy Offensive Potential ... 75

    Amendments to Operational Plans for Southeast Area 77

    Orders and Operational Principles for Southeast Area 79

    General Operational Progress During Period 81

    Central Pacific Area Operations 83

    Orders and Operational Principles for Southwest Area 84

    Troop Activities in Southwest Area Operations 87

    Troop Activities in Other Areas 88

    Line of Communication (Logistical Support) During Second Phase 89

CHAPTER VI -- Third Phase of the War (September 1943 - June 1944)

    PART I --- First Stage (September 1943 - February 1944) 91

    Situation Review and Estimate of Enemy Potential Plans ... 91

    Army General Staff Operational Plan Changes 94

    Existing International and War Conditions 96

    Southeastern, North-of-Australia, and Central Pacific Areas Operational Strategy 98

    Army-Navy Central Agreement Regarding Central Pacific Operations 102

    Operational Conduct for North-of-Australia Area 103

    Efforts to Strengthen Shipping and Transportation 104

    Steps Taken to Combat Submarines 105

    Strengthening of Sea Bases 106

    Approval of Imphal Operations ("U" Operation) 107

    Instructions Concerning "Ichi-Go" (Hunan-Kwangsi) Operation 109

    Instructions for Various Other Areas 112

    Additional Construction and Maintenance Plans for Air Bases 113

    PART II --- Second Stage (March - June 1944) 114

    Situation Review and Estimated Enemy Plans 114

    North-of-Australia Area Instructions 117

    First and Second Modifications of 2d Area Army Front Line. 119

Northeastern Area Instructions 121
Formosa and Nansei Islands Instructions 122
Southern Area Command System Unification 124
Change of Mission and Instructions for Southern Army 125
Central Pacific Area Instructions 129
"A-Go" Operations in Mariana Area 130
Instructions Strengthening Homeland Defenses 134
Line of Communication (Logistical Support) During Third Phase 135

CHAPTER VII -- Fourth Phase of the War (July - December 1944)

Operations Summary for Fourth Phase 137
Development and Preparations for "Sho" Operations 138
Preliminary Actions Leading to No 1 "Sho" Operation 146
Start and Conduct of No 1 "Sho" Operation 149
Operational Conduct in Other Areas 154
Army-Navy Discussions Regarding Unified Air Forces Command 162
Measures to Facilitate Railway Transportation on the Continent 164

CHAPTER VIII -- Fifth Phase of the War (January - August 1945)

PART I ----- Operational Stage Prior to "Ketsu-Go" (January-March 1945) 166
Situation Review and Conclusions Regarding US Strategy ... 166
Attitude of Russia and Military Preparations of Chungking Nationalists 170
Appraisal of Japan's Man and Materiel Power 170
Fundamental Strategy of Imperial General Headquarters 172
Establishment of Civil Defense Plan 176
Operational Army Mobilization Schedule 178
Southern Army Operations 180
Central Pacific, Formosa and Nansei Islands Directions and Operations 185
Preparations and Disposition of Forces in Korea, China and Manchuria 188
Line of Communication (Logistical Support) During this Period 191

Conduct of Homeland Operations and Strategy	193
Air Operations and Enemy Bombing of the Homeland	198
PART II --- "Ketsu-Go" Operational Stage (April - August 1945)	205
Operational Preparations Resulting from Situation Estimate	205
Objectives	209
Line of Communication (Logistical Support) Preparations	211
Transportation Preparations	212
Communication System Preparation	214
Land Forces Concentration Plan	215
Army-Navy Strategic Collaboration	216
General Military Preparations and Disposition of Fighting Forces	217
Direction of Operations in Korea Area	219
Direction of Operations Against Enemy Invasion of Okinawa	221
Main Continental Operations	225
China Operations During the Okinawa Campaign	229
Manchuria Operational Preparations	231
Summary of Operations June 1945 to End of War	235
Homeland Operations	236
Air Operations	237
Operations After Fall of Okinawa	242
Continental Organization Revisions and Operations	244
Operational Conduct Following Soviet Entry in War	247
South Burma and Philippines Operations	249
Line of Communication (Logistical Support) During Fifth Phase	249
Termination of Hostilities	251
Chart 1 -- Regular Members of the Liaison Conference July 1941 -- August 1945	9
Chart 2 -- The Disposition of the Army Land Units (December 1941)	14
Chart 3 -- The Disposition of the Army Operational Supplies (December 1941)	14

Chart 4 -- The Disposition of the Army Air Units (December 1941) 14

Chart 5 -- Estimated Army Strength of the Enemy in the South (September 1941) 25

Chart 6 -- Estimated Enemy Air Forces in the South (September 1941) 25

Chart 7 -- Estimated Enemy Naval Forces Operating to the South (September 1941) 25

Chart 8 -- Estimate of the Enemy Strength, May 1942 48

Chart 9 -- Estimate of Possible Increases in Fighting Power of US-British Forces (May 1942) 48

Chart 10 - "Sho" Operations Air Strength 142

Chart 11 - Plan of Employment of War Materiel Reimported from Manchuria 193

Chart 12 - Source of Army Air Force Operational Strength in Case of Enemy Attacks
Planned Transfer and Allocation of Army Planes Against Nansei Islands or Formosa 200

Chart 13 - Planned Operations and Strength for Army Air Force (Homeland and China) 200

Chart 14 - Source of Navy Air Force Operational Strength in Case of Enemy Attacks
Planned Transfer and Allocation of Navy Planes Against Nansei Islands, Formosa or Iwo-Ogasawara Islands 200

Chart 15 - Planned Operations and Strength for Navy Air Forces (Homeland, Southwestern Pacific Area and Surface Escort) 200

Chart 16 - Casualties and Damages Suffered from Air Attacks 1942 - 1945 204

Chart 17 - Revised System of High Command 207

Chart 18 - Plan of the Army General Staff regarding the Maneuver of Land Forces in "Ketsu-Go" Operation 215

Chart 19 - Strength of Army Air Force (End of May 1945) 225

Chart 20 - Disposition and Utilization Plan of the Air General Army 241

Chart 21 - Disposition and Utilization Plan for the Navy Air Force 241

SUPPLEMENT I -- Chronology of Major Events during Greater East Asia War 1

SUPPLEMENT II - Chronology of Major Liaison Conferences during Greater East Asia War 5

SUPPLEMENT III -- Chronology of Major Actions & Decisions by
   the Army General Staff 7

SUPPLEMENT IV -- Guide to Designation of Units, and Their
   Purposes and Normal size 15

CHAPTER I

Japanese Military Command Organization

State Affairs and "Supreme Command" Relationship

Based upon the Constitution enacted in 1889, domestic and foreign affairs (Civil) in the Japanese Government were executed, generally, by the Emperor with the assistance of appropriate State Ministers. Responsibility for results remained with the respective ministers and did not reflect upon the Emperor.[1]

The Army General Staff regulations and the Navy General Staff regulations, developed to implement Constitutional Clause No 11[2], provided for execution of and responsibility for operational requirements necessitated in support and protection of the Emperor as Supreme Commander. To advise the Emperor in his position as Supreme Commander, the necessary assistants had been created for command responsibility to the throne in 1878 by creating the positions, Chief of Army General Staff and Chief of Navy General Staff. Their duties and responsibilities were clarified in the General Staff Regulations of 1889. As Chiefs of the respective branches for Army and Navy, these were the working "Supreme Command" authorities.

The State Ministers for Domestic and Foreign Affairs had no connection with the "Supreme Command" as Constitution Clause No 3[1] indicates. The only exception to this was in Concurrent Affairs which is explained later.

Even in war-time, the separate responsibilities to the throne were still held by the respective Chiefs of Staff for their specific branch of service. Though an Imperial General Headquarters was

---

[1] Constitutional Clause No 55 - The State Ministers assist the Emperor and are responsible for the results.

No 3 - The Emperor is sacred and inviolabe.

[2] Constitutional Clause No 11 - The Emperor has the Supreme Command of the Army and Navy

created, it did not break the basic responsibility. However, in cases of problems requiring joint action, Central Agreements arrived at by the two chiefs of staff were handled through the office of Imperial General Headquarters. It is important to emphasize that by far the major number of directives and orders issued by Imperial General Headquarters were not of the Central Agreement type. In fact, they were mostly individual Army Section or Navy Section actions covering their individual fields of responsibility to the throne.

The Emperor's non-responsibility clearly defined that the Emperor was not responsible for the entire sovereignty of the nation. This not only applied to the domestic and foreign affairs but also to the "Supreme Command". Highest responsibility of the "Supreme Command" was to organize, supervise and represent in direct access to the throne the Army and Navy General Staffs.

The Army field commanders, though directly responsible to the Emperor, could not report directly to the throne but presented their recommendations through the Chief of Army General Staff who was Chief of the Military Assistance Agency to the Emperor.

The Constitution enacted on 11 February 1899 and the Army General Staff Regulations enacted on 7 March 1889 were based in general upon Prussian laws.

In general, the laws, Imperial decrees, and other Imperial proclamations had to be endorsed by the State Ministers. This had the effect of binding their responsibility and relieving the Emperor.

"Supreme Command" Independence and Direct Appeal to the Throne

As mentioned before, the responsibility of the "Supreme Command" was entirely outside of the State Ministers' administrative power which included the War and Navy Ministers. In other words, the Chief of Army General Staff or the Chief of Navy General Staff assisted the Emperor on matters concerning strategy and operations and were privileged to appeal directly to the Emperor on such matters without going through the channels of the cabinet or the premier. This was called the independence of the "Supreme Command". Similar authorized appeals made by the War or Navy Minister, the Chief of the General Staff, the Inspectorate General of Military Training and sometimes by the Inspectorate General of the Air Force in connection with Concurrent Affairs (which were overlapping responsibilities with the "Supreme Command" in a broad sense) were customarily called the direct appeals to the throne. The procedure for the direct appeal to the throne was stated in the cabinet regulations. Reports to the Premier from the War or Navy Minister regarding such direct appeals were mandatory.[3]

"Supreme Command" and State Affairs Concurrent Matters

As for the correct methods of government procedures, the aforementioned facts should not be difficult to understand. However, there were matters of an ambiguous nature existing between the general State Affairs (domestic and foreign affairs) and the "Supreme Command" which might be confusing.

These were the Concurrent Affairs or the affairs of the "Supreme Command" in a broad sense. These were joint responsibilities in military affairs held by both the "Supreme Command" and the general State Affairs. The principle Concurrent Affairs were

---

3 The Cabinet Regulations. Clause No 7 - Matters which are appealed to the Emperor concerning Military Secrets and orders must be reported to the Premier from the War or Navy Minister, except those which are granted to the cabinet at the Emperor's discretion.

the Army and Navy organization and the determination of its standing troop strength[4].

They also included authority needed to construct and maintain military establishments such as military standards and regulations, disposition of units, supply of materials, etc.

Thus, the relation between the State Affairs and "Supreme Command" in Concurrent Affairs was an overlapping one to a degree.

The Concurrent Affairs concerning the Army were handled by the War Minister, Chief of the General Staff, Inspectorate General of Military Training, and sometimes by the Inspectorate General of the Air Force according to their authority and nature of the work. The respective chief was responsible either independently or jointly with the other chiefs. The War Minister was responsible for the execution of all matters. Regulations of each office expressed the authority of each chief in handling Concurrent Affairs. In addition to regulations, there was a mutual agreement establishing areas of responsibility for the War Ministry, General Staff Headquarters, and the Inspectorate General of Military Training.

Matters which were to be handled by the Chief of General Staff involved the use of troops for maintaining local public order; the dispatch, duty and relief of overseas expeditionary forces; wartime organizations; mobilization plan; grand maneuvers; etc.

The Inspectorate General of Military Training was responsible for establishing the military training regulations, the drill regulations and manuals for the various branches of service, etc.

The War Minister would handle matters concerning the standards and design of weapons, finance, sanitation, veterinary and judicial affairs, etc. Also handled by the War Minister was the peace-time system concerning military training and national defense, special inspection, etc. To clarify peace-time operations it is pointed

---

[4] Constitutional Clause No 12 - The Emperor decides the Army and Navy Organization and their standing troop strength.

out that the Chief of the Army General Staff was responsible for drafting the organization of each unit, offices and schools under his jurisdiction. The Inspectorate General was responsible for schools under his jurisdiction. The War Minister was responsible for other offices, schools, depots, etc.

Methods for Issuing Concurrent Affairs Orders

The methods for issuing orders on Concurrent Affairs were in accordance with the Military Order No 1 of 1907; they were in forms of Army or Navy announcements over the signature of the War or Navy Minister and treated as Military Orders which the War or Navy Minister was responsible for executing. This system of Military Orders was developed to cover matters resulting from concurrent interests of "Supreme Command" and State Affairs in items affecting the Armed Forces.

The Military Order No 1 of 1907 included: Clause No 1 - Regulations concerning the "Supreme Command" of the Army and Navy will be the Military Orders if they are sanctioned by the Emperor; Clause No 2 - Military Orders which must be publicly announced will be dated and countersigned by the responsible War or Navy Minister. They will be accompanied with an Imperial edict bearing the Imperial signature and seal; Clause No 3 - The Military Orders are published in the official gazette; and Clause No 4 - The Military Orders are immediately enforced if the date of enforcement is not stated.

Principles in Assignment of Military Officers as War Minister

There were two major measures for a system in assigning officers as War Minister. The War Minister acted as a member of the cabinet to carry out government policies and also assisted the Emperor on important matters concerning military affairs which were not involved in state affairs. He had to possess sufficient qualifications and experience to achieve his purpose. He was responsible for consolidating the civil and military affairs and achieving cooperation between the "Supreme Command" and State Affairs.

In order to concentrate its attention on its basic responsibilities, it was considered better if the Armed Forces were to remain out of politics, generally. If a civilian official were assigned as War Minister who had peace-time power to control Armed Forces personnel and civilian employees, the Armed Forces could be used as a tool for political issues. Too, Armed Forces personnel might enter political parties. This could cause poor relations between branches and reduce control and unity in the Army and Navy.

The system of assigning a military officer as War Minister and a naval officer as Navy Minister evolved from a custom calling for the War and Navy Ministers to be appointed from candidates submitted by the Army and Navy. Usually, the branches were requested to recommend a candidate for the position; however, this was not a regulation. The branches did not coerce the candidate to accept the position, but left it up to the Premier and the officer recommended.

Imperial General Headquarters and Government Liaison Conferences

In November 1937, Imperial General Headquarters was created to coordinate Army and Navy operations resulting from the China Incidents. Immediately after this, a Liaison Conference system between Imperial General Headquarters and the government was developed to coordinate matters of joint importance to the "Supreme Command" and domestic or foreign (civil) departments. Later, this conference had some modification in its formation and methods. Although it was called, variously, the Round Table Liaison Conference between the Imperial General Headquarters and the government, the Supreme War Direction Conference, etc, the conference principle was maintained continuously until the termination of the war with no changes in the fundamental objectives.

After the formation of the Konoye Cabinet II, 22 July 1940, national and foreign policy decisions became increasingly important during the war. The conference acted as the Supreme War Command and was of major governmental importance. Additional references to the conference liaison system in the text are referred to as the Conference.

Legislative Characteristics of the Conference

The Conference was established by mutual design and agreement between the government and the "Supreme Command". In contrast to this, the Cabinet Council was provided for legislatively in the Constitution. Where decisions of the Cabinet Council were authorized by regulations providing for cabinet organization[5] the Conference had no such authorization. Members of the Conference were jointly and individually responsible to see that decisions of the Conference were executed properly by the government and the "Supreme Command".

Decisions were formally executed through separate action by the "Supreme Command" and the government. The Premier would refer a matter to the cabinet council and the two Chiefs of Staff would carry out decisions of the Conference requiring action through Imperial General Headquarters. The relation between the two Chiefs of Staff and the War and Navy Ministers has been mentioned, previously.

---

[5] The cabinet organization Clause No 5 - The following subjects must be referred to the cabinet council:

Legislative bills, budgets, and statement of accounts; Foreign treaties and important international stipulations; Imperial ordinances concerning the enacting of government organizations, rules, and laws; supervision of disputes between the ministries; petitions granted by the Emperor or transferred from the Diet; extra expenditures; assignment and resignation of the prefectural governors and officials directly appointed by the Emperor; and, important administrative affairs in serious situations which are handled by the heads of each ministry must be approved by the cabinet council

Although the Conference had no legislative authority and its decisions were subject to mutual agreement, the matters which were decided upon received full respect from the "Supreme Command" and the Government. Consequently, the Conference had the highest authority to conduct war and played a significant role.

Relationship Between the Emperor and the Conference

The State Ministers had full responsibility for state affairs and for such items acted as adviser to the throne. The two Chiefs of Staff took full responsibility for "Supreme Command" matters and assisted the Emperor in their field. The Conference did not change this alignment of responsibilities. They were clearly separated into the individual fields of State Affairs and the "Supreme Command". They were entirely different from the State Minister's joint responsibilities on Concurrent Affairs decided upon at the cabinet council.

One of the matters decided upon by members of the Conference was to make a formal report of important matters to the throne for approval. This report was made over the joint signatures of the Premier and the two Chiefs of Staff (or all three of them reporting in person). However, the execution of matters decided remained as before with the State Affairs being handled by the Premier and "Supreme Command" affairs being handled by the two Chiefs of Staff. The idea for joint signatures was developed for liaison purposes in reporting to the throne.

Conference (Council) in the Imperial Presence

This type of meeting meant a conference in the presence of the Emperor and not one presided over by the Emperor. This council was a meeting for discussing important national policies so that the proceedings could be heard by the Emperor. The subjects decided upon at this council still had to be passed through the legislative procedure.

At the end of the war, this council in the Imperial presence remained unchanged in every respect.[6]

Conference (Council) Agenda Example[7]

Important subjects concerning the State Affairs and the Supreme Command were taken up in regular sequence as indicated by a typical agenda: important national policies such as the fundamental plan for conducting the war, etc; important diplomatic measures; regulations concerning military operations and national power; and, the administration of occupied territories, and the disposition of the territories.

The people present at council presentations included for the government:

> The Premier, Foreign Minister, War Minister, and Navy Minister; and, for the Supreme Command
> The Chief of Army General Staff and Chief of Naval General Staff

In addition, specified state ministers attended at certain times and other cabinet ministers were called as needed. The President of the Privy Council always attended this council if the Emperor were present.

---

[6] At the termination of the war, the Emperor was reported to have made a personal decision at the council. This was believed to be true by the general public. Actually, it was expressed as a desire (according to government tradition) and made an effective decision through Council and Cabinet action.

An effective decision for terminating the war was so extremely delicate that it may have caused anarchy in the nation. As a result, the Premier could not give a decision from the council. He solicited the Emperor to express his opinion. The Emperor's statement agreed with the Foreign Minister's opinion. After the council, this subject was presented and decided again at a cabinet council. It was solely because of the fact that the government and the Supreme Command could not decide the grave matters for terminating the war that the Premier solicited the Emperor for his opinion. The public also acknoledged this fact and agreed for the termination of the war. This decision was an exception which would have been entirely impossible without the Emperor's power.

[7] This Agenda for the Council was also the sequence used in order of business for the Conference.

CHAPTER II

General Situation Before the War

Military Preparations

Immediately after World War I, the Japanese Army was inferior to those of other world powers in size and quality. However, when the China Incident started following the Manchurian Incidents, Japan maintained a sizable number of troops. The object of such military preparation was to provide the necessary strength for conducting and quickly terminating the China Incident. At the same time, it was considered necessary to secure sufficient strength for defense against Russia.

From 1940 to the beginning of 1941, Japan anticipated successful diplomatic negotiations and did not undertake large-scale war preparation even though she faced international problems with Britain and America. Immediately after the outbreak of the Russo-German War in June 1941, Japan rapidly increased military preparations. This was done as a precaution against a possible Soviet attack resulting from the existence of the Tripartite Alliance. At the end of July 1941, America, Britain and the Netherlands broke off economic relations with Japan. In September 1941, only three months before the outbreak of war, Japan felt forced to start war preparations to meet any emergency in case war with America and Britain became inevitable. During this period, Japan was following a national policy of dual tactics (diplomatic negotiations and war preparations) and could not concentrate her entire effort to war preparation against these two powers. War preparations for the Pacific, particularly against America, Britain, and the Netherlands were minor. The initial military strength at the beginning of the war was gathered by transferring a part of the general National Defense Power to the South. Later, depending on the progress of war, the main strength could be gradually poured into the South. Faced with these

Regular Members of the Liaison Conference
July 1941 - August 1945

Position / Period	Premier	Foreign Minister	War Minister	Navy Minister	Chief of Army General Staff	Chief of Navy General Staff
18 Jul 41--18 Oct 41 (Third Konoye Cabinet)	Prince Konoye Ayamaro	Admiral Toyoda Teijiro	General Tojo Hideki	Admiral Oikawa Koshiro		
18 Oct 41--22 Jul 44 (Tojo Cabinet)	General Tojo Hideki	Togo Shigenori ----2 Sep 42---- Tani Masayuki ----20 Apr 43---- Shigemitsu Mamoru	General Tojo Hideki	Admiral Shimada Shigetaro	General Sugiyama Gen ----22 Feb 44---- General Tojo Hideki	Admiral Nagano Osami ----22 Feb 44---- Admiral Shimada Shigetaro ----2 Aug 44---- Admiral Oikawa Koshiro
22 Jul 44 -- 7 Apr 45 (Koiso Cabinet)	General Koiso Kuniaki		General Sugiyama Gen	Admiral Yonai Mitsumasa	General Umezu Yoshijiro	
7 Apr 45--17 Aug 45 (Suzuki Cabinet)	Admiral Baron Suzuki Kantaro	Togo Shigenori	General Anami Korechika			----29 May 45---- Admiral Toyoda Soemu

Remarks:
a. During the Tojo Cabinet, Finance Minister (Gaya Okinobu and, after 19 Feb 44, Ishiwata Sotaro) and the President of the Planning Board (Lt Gen Suzuki Teiichi) were authorized as regular members of the Liaison Conference.

b. When the Conference was held in the Presence of the Emperor, it was called a Council in the Imperial Presence and the President of the Privy Council attended. The Presidents were Hara Yoshimichi until 10 Aug 44, Adm Suzuki Kantaro from 10 Aug 44 until 7 Apr 45 and Baron Hiranuma Kiichiro from 7 Apr 45 until the end of war.

conditions, Japan had to rush into full mobilization to maintain her very existence.

In addition to armament, war preparations included industry, commerce, finance, monetary exchange, diplomacy, communication, and measures for maintaining public order, public opinion, etc. This report will describe the war preparations carried out by the Army. They were not originally planned for the Pacific Campaign but later were of value in that operation.

The results of the Sino-Japanese and Russo-Japanese Wars reduced the menace from China and Russia, and Japan established some rights in China. At the same time, Japan increased her rights on tha Asiatic Continent gradually through economic and political agreements.

Before the Manchurian Incident, Japan's military preparations were extremely inferior to other world powers. The peace-time strength was seventeen divisions while the war-time strength was established as thirty divisions. In case of an emergency, it was extremely doubtful whether Japan could wage war against a single power. Although, every effort was being made by the administration, it was not possible to create sufficient armament to assure adequate national defense.

In 1931, upon the outbreak of the Manchurian Incident, Japan was forced by circumstances to carry out the fight.

The great expansion of military preparations by Russia and her pressure against Manchuria forced Japan to increase her military strength for national defense. Studies regarding this situation were begun. The Army General Staff concluded that Japan required sixty divisions in peace time and ninety to a hundred divisions in war time, but the economy could not support such an increase. The government approved an army-sponsored bill seeking an increase of six divisions in 1936. During 1937 and 1938, the government approved an army plan to add 14 divisions by the end of 1943. Because of national conditions, especially financial, the government could not have approved the full needs as a continuing project. As a substitute the government was asked for the necessary expenditures each fiscal year. In this way, the above increases in strength were accomplished.

From 1938 to 1941, the combat zone in China gradually enlarged. Simultaneously, the necessity for defense against Russia was increasing. To meet these factors, the gradual build-up in forces was undertaken each year. The purpose was to achieve a rapid settlement of the China Incident and to develop security against Russia. The increased strength of the divisions, the Army Air Forces, and the mobilization of officers and enlisted men are shown in the following table Nos 1, 2 and 3.

(1) Table Showing the Number of Divisions
(From 1937 to 1941)

Year Disposition	1937	1938	1939	1940	1941
Homeland Korea	3	2	7	11	11
Manchuria	5	8	9	12	13
China	16	24	25	27	27
Total	24	34	41	50	51

Remarks:
1. From 1937 to 1940, the number of divisions is shown as of the end of each respective year, while in 1941, the total as of early November is shown.
2. In addition to these in this table, there was a Cavalry Group.
3. In 1937, there remained some margin for mobilization, but from 1938, and on, the number of divisions conformed to the capacity to equip and train them.

(2) Table of the Army Air Forces
(From 1937 to 1941)

Year Classification	1937	1938	1939	1940	1941
Fighters	21	24	28	36	56
Light Bombers	12	16	26	28	36
Heavy Bombers	9	17	19	22	27
Reconnaissance Planes	12	13	18	20	32
Total	54	70	91	106	151

Remarks: 1. The figures in this table present the number of squadrons at the end of March of each year. The figures of 1941, however, show the number of squadrons as of early November.

2. Although the number of squadrons increased, about a year was required before the newly organized unit could reach actual combat strength.

(3) Table Showing the Army Conscription
(From 1936 to 1941)

Year	1936	1937	1938	1939	1940	1941
Personnel (1,000)	170	170	320	340	320	330

Even with this increasing Army strength, it was impossible to give a decisive blow against the enemy in China. At the same time, the Army could maintain only one third the Soviet Army's fighting power along the Manchurian border. Thus, the anxiety over national defense could never be eliminated. This increase in the Army became a factor in the Pacific War preparation, but the main objectives were for the China Incident and Manchurian Defense.

With the outbreak of the war in 1941, a part of these forces was sacrificed by being transferred rapidly to the south to cope with the new situation.

In December 1941, the total strength of the Army consisted of 51 divisions (excluding one cavalry group), and 59 brigade size units of various types as the main land units, and approximately forty air-regiments. The disposition of troops and the operational supplies were as shown in Charts 2, 3 and 4.

Training Programs

The important manuals and regulations such as the "Military Training Regulations", "Field Operations Service Regulation", "Battle Principle", and others of the various branches which had been the training standards for a long time were taken from World War I references. A special training plan was established for the national forces which would develop the best potential of the soldiers. As part of this training program, attention was centered on: recommendation of mobile combat tactics; adoption of an encircling annihilating attack; substantial improvement of coordinated operations by all branches of service; the importance of close combat; the consistent encouragement of night attacks; training for self-decision by all officers and men; and, emphasis on training of the two-year soldier (two years being considered the time necessary to develop a qualified soldier).

Before the Manchurian Incident, there was no idea as to who the enemy might be and training was conducted strictly according to the manuals.

After the Manchurian Incident, the training emphasized possible tactics for use in Manchuria against Russia. Even after the China Incident in July 1937, the training emphasis remained unchanged. Field Operation Service Regulations prepared in 1939 were developed as the result of the possible operations against Russia.

The Disposition of the Army Land Units
(December 1941)

Classification Area	Name of Hq	Location	Divisions	No of Mixed Brig
Homeland Korea Formosa	Gen Defense Cmd	Tokyo	0 (a)	
	Eastern Dist Army Hq	Tokyo	52d	4
	Central Dist Army Hq	Osaka	53d, 54th	3
	Western Dist Army Hq	Fukuoka		3
	Northern Dist Army Hq	Sapporo	7th	1
	Korea Army Hq	Seoul	19th, 20th	
	Formosa Army Hq	Taihoku		
Manchuria	Kwantung Army Hq	Changchun	10th, 28th, 29th	1
	3d Army Hq	Mutanchiang	9th, 12th	4
	4th Army Hq	Peian	1st, 14th, 57th	5
	5th Army Hq	Tungan	11th, 24th	4
	6th Army Hq	Hailun	23d	1
	20th Army Hq	Chihsi	8th, 25th	4
	Kwantung Defense Cmd	Changchun		5
China	China Exped Army Gen Hq	Nanking		
	North China Area Army Hq	Peiping	27th, 35th, 110th	5
	1st Army Hq	Yangchu	36th, 37th, 41st	3
	12th Army Hq	Licheng	17th, 32d	3
	Mongolia Garrison Army Hq	Wanchuan	26th, Cav Gp	1
	11th Army Hq	Hankou	3d, 6th, 13th, 34th, 39th, 40th	2
	13th Army Hq	Shanghai	4th(c), 15th, 22d, 116th	5
	23d Army Hq	Canton	38th, 51st, 104th	1
The South	Southern Army Hq (Gen)	Saigon	21st(b)	2(d)
	14th Army Hq	Takao	16th, 48th	1
	15th Army Hq	French Indo-China	33d(b), 55th	
	16th Army Hq	Takao	2d	1
	25th Army Hq	Sanya	Guard, 5th, 18th, 56th(b)	

Remarks:
  a. In addition, 10 Depot divisions were in the Homeland.
  b. Actual dates for transfer of command were departure dates from previous stations: 21st from Chingtao (20 Jan 42); 33d from Nanking (13 Dec 41); and 56th from Homeland (16 Feb 42)
  c. Directly attached to the Imp Hqs, 4th Div (Shanghai).
  d. Directly attached to the Imp Hqs, South Sea Det (Bonin Is).

The Disposition of the Army Operataional Supplies

(December 1941)

Supplies	Unit Quantity	Total Quantity	Disposition of Dumps			
			Homeland	South	North	China
Ammunition	(quantity used by a division in Std Campaign)	105 (14)	10	17 (6)	48 (8)	30
Motor Car Fuel	1,000 cars per month	375 (10)	140	50 (10)	125	42
Aviation Fuel & Ammunition	One Air Brig per month	77 (Ammunition) 165 (Fuel)	5 88	12 20	45 50	15 7
Rations	One Div per month	370 (34)	86	98 (34)	103	83
Remark	The figures shown in parenthesis represent supplies produced during December, and are included in the figures without the parenthesis. This table includes the shift in supplies described in the next chart.					

Chart 3

The Disposition of the Army Air Units

(December 1941)

Classification Area	Unit	Location	Number of Air Regt (Indep Squadrons) Fighter	Lt Bmr	Hv Bmr	Reconnaissance	Direct Support	Total No of Regt (Indep Sq)	Total (Indep Sq)	Total No of Sq
Homeland	1st Air Gp	Kagamigahara	2			1		3	3	9
Manchuria	2d Air Gp / Air Corps Directly Attached Unit	Mutanchiang	5	4	1	(2)	(3)	10 (5)	17 (5)	56
		Changchun	3	1	3			7		
China	1st Air Brig	Nanking	1 (1)	1		(3)	1 (2)	3 (6)		16
	3d Air Gp	Phnompenh	5	4	4	1 (5)	(1)	14 (6)		
The South	5th Air Gp	Heito	2	2	1	(3)	(1)	5 (4)	19 (12)	70
	21st Indep Air Unit	Hanoi	(1)			(1)		(2)		
Grand Total			18 (2)	12	9	2 (14)	1 (7)	42 (23)		151

Remarks:
a. The figures in parentheses represent the number of independent air squadrons.
b. The location shows the location of the headquarters of each unit.
c. Besides the above there were some air regiments (for example 3d and 4th Air Regts) in the homeland. But they were charged with air training mainly; not suitable for operational strength.

In both incidents, the main force of the Japanese National Army engaged inferior enemies with poor equipment. Success caused relaxation of the training standards.

Following the Japanese Army experiences against Russia in the battles of the Changkufeng in 1938 and Nomonhan incidents in 1939, training emphasized systematic, scientific fighting techniques and realistic combat training. China Incidents continued and drastically increased the operational strength requirements of the Japanese National Forces. To meet this need, Japan mobilized the officers and soldiers of all ranks from the first and second reserves. With this expansion, training standards declined further and the valuable high standards of a picked-Army were a thing of the past.

Training the Army received before the Pacific War was inadequate. Most of Japan's new actions would require landing operations because of Japan's geographic location. However, the training was given only to specific divisions. Previously, the necessity for a blockade against China in 1940 and 1941 had spurred some training in landing operations.

In early 1941, the international situation was appraised by the Army General Staff and revisions were developed in battle training plans to include countermeasures not only against Russia, but against American and British fighting methods. A collection of data and investigation of fighting methods was made, but time prevented gaining the results desired. The enlarged tactical training program was started in June 1941 for specific units in Formosa, South China and French Indo-China. Some reference books such as the "Characteristics of the Operations in the Torrid Zones", "Common Sense of the American and British Forces", "Simplified Southern Operations", etc. were compiled to help in training orientations. However, the material was very poor and could not be used for training manuals. Because of the China Incident, it was difficult to provide this additional training for the troops located there.

Subsequent to the China Incident, field exercises such as the Grand Maneuver, General Officers' Maneuver, Staff Officer's Maneuvers, etc. had been suspended. The study and training of higher strategy and tactics were generally insufficient and the training to meet the American and British Forces was unsatisfactory.

For several years, there had been discussions and investigations concerning the type of air force tactics to be used. There was a method of annihilating attack (similar to US strategic tactics) by the concentrated use of the air force against major target or a method of directly supporting the land force. The former principle was decided upon in 1939 and 1940. Intense training was carried out resulting in great achievements during the initial operations of the Pacific War.

Expansion of National Defense Industries and War Materiel

Japanese armament before the Manchurian Incident was approximately twenty years behind those of other world powers. In 1936, ways were studied for modernizing Japan's military power. However, years of negligence in developing new weapons and armament greatly hampered an increase in munitions factories. The basic national defense production capacity was very weak having been based previously upon small industries.

The Army prepared a budget and established a Five Year Plan for the munitions industries in the spring of 1937. Need for expansion of the basic industrial facilities to support a munitions increase was apparent to the Army. However, the legislature did not develop a bill to answer requests for such legislation. As a result, the army drafted a recommended Five Year Plan for basic industries and submitted it for consideration. As such, it was not accepted. Points were included, however, in the National

Mobilization Laws of 1938. These projects received special emphasis due to the rapidly increasing powers of the adjacent countries. Demands of the China Incident in July-August 1937 suddenly changed the conditions, bringing the weakness of our national defense industries to light. A national mobilization of munitions industries was essential. They were placed under military control with the approval of the Diet on 5 September 1937.

From then on, the peace time production methods which were being used to carry out the Five Year Plan for the munitions industries were abandoned. With new war time methods and military control, production was to be accelerated.

The original mobilization program for the munitions industries was limited to six months. Because the China Incident persisted, it was renewed each fiscal year. With the enactment of the National Mobilization Laws, 24 March 1938, the necessary economic control regulations were gradually developed to provide authority to execute actions necessary to fulfill most objectives of the goals incorporated in the Army Five Year Plan draft.

The "Five Year Plan" for the basic industries was carried out immediately in Manchuria but the start of the plan in Japan was retarded by the China Incident which cut off some sources of natural resources. As a result, it became a Four Year Plan beginning in 1938 with the first year spent merely in planning. In addition, the quotas listed in the plan had to be reduced several times, thereby causing remarkable slow down in its overall results.

Aviation, munition and parts manufacturing industries were greatly expanded under this plan. The special steel manufacturing industry achieved a remarkable success. The machine tool industry surpassed it's goal. And, the light metal industry made rapid progress. However, every other basic industry was far from its goal. The synthetic oil industry and the development of hydro-electric power suffered particularly from the lack of materials. In order to fill the void caused by the synthetic oil industry being unproductive, an attempt was made to import synthetic oil production facilities from Germany through a trade agreement. The outbreak of war in Europe in September 1939 caused this to fail.

Efforts were made to stockpile oil through a trade agreement with the Netherland East Indies, but negotiations failed here, too, causing a critical point in the defense structure. The Second Konoye and Tojo Cabinets both tried in vain to overcome the weakness of Japan's oil industry but were unsuccessful due to lack of materials, experienced technicians and industrial power. This was also influenced by the heavy demands for the manufacture of munitions.

Finally, near the end of 1940, the munitions industries were capable of producing replacements for battle losses as well as the mobilization needs. Just before the Pacific War, the following production capacity was possible:

Yearly Production Capacity Schedule

Classification	1941 Fiscal Year	1942 Fiscal Year	1943 Fiscal Year
Army Planes (quantity)	Approx 3,500	Approx 5,300	Approx 10,000
Tanks (quantity)	Approx 1,200	Approx 1,500	Approx 1,800
Ground Ammunition (quantity used by a division in std campaign)	43 battles	50 battles	50 battles
Bombs (monthly need of one air brigade	22 months	80 months	80 months

The distributing of ammunition and aviation fuel, the percentage and the transfers made at the outbreak of war in 1941 were as follows:

Ammunition	Manchuria 19% ←27%	Homeland 52% 13%→	The South 0%
		China 29%	
Aerial Navigation Fuel	Manchuria 16% ←14%	Homeland 80% 12%→	The South 0%
		China 4%	
Note	←———	Transfers made in July 1941 to meet the requirements in Manchuria after the Russo-German War.	
	———→	Transfers made immediately before the War in 1941	

Reserve Army Supply Stockpile Preparations

The raw materials for weapons, ammunition, clothing, etc were accumulated satisfactorily but no attempt had been made to stockpile petroleum products before the China Incident. In 1936, when the military armament build-up was planned, only 200,000 Koku (less than 40,000 kiloliters) of aviation fuel was allocated for stockpile reserves during the next few years. Anticipating a sudden change in trade conditions after the China Incident due to possible complications in foreign relations, necessary crude oil for manufacturing approximately 150,000 kiloliters of aviation fuel was immediately imported from America in the fall of 1937 to carry out the Chinese Operation for a period of one year. This was the turning point of our Army policy for mobilization of supply reserves.

This procedure was repeated several times. The last such shipment was in the spring of 1941. Similar measures were taken to replenish other important supply reserves (tool machines, tungsten, nickel, etc) which had become depleted. Faced with threatening world conditions in 1940, the Army demanded from each government department strict maintenance of necessary supplies. Approximately a three-year supply, or a two-year supply at least, for national consumption had to be imported. Munitions held a high priority because of the unreliable foreign trade conditions. The necessary imports were arranged as a method to meet the crisis of a national shortage. This was called the mobilization of emergency supplies. The oil stock as of the end of March 1941 was as follows:

Estimated amount including the Army and Navy

    Approx 1,170,000 kiloliters Aviation gasoline
      "   830,000   "   Ordinary gasoline
      "   320,000   "   Kerosene
      "   320,000   "   Light Oil
      "   4,430,000   "   Heavy (crude) oil
      "   360,000   "   Machine Oil

The Army and Navy oil requirements for the fiscal year of 1941, mainly for the China Incident were as follows:

    Approx   150,000 kiloliters Aviation gasoline
      "   80,000   "   Ordinary gasoline
      "   10,000   "   Kerosene
      "   4,000   "   Light Oil
      "   1,030,000   "   Crude Oil
      "   150,000   "   Machine Oil

At the time (end of July 1941) of the American, British, and Dutch embargo on oil, it was estimated that a stock of approximately 850,000 kiloliters of aviation gasoline and approximately 2,350,000 kiloliters of crude oil would be available for uses other than filling requirements of an additional two years involving operations for the China Incident. This amount of oil stock would not allow the Army and Navy air forces to operate with their full strength for over twelve months. The Navy surface forces would be able to handle a delaying operation for one year, but in case of continuous decisive battles, only six months at most.

CHAPTER III

Pacific War Operational Preparations

The China Incident became more involved during 1938 and 1939 and Japan could not attempt a short decisive action because of the personnel required and shortage of equipment. Instead, Japan was forced into unending battles. Twenty-five divisions were used for combat, occupation of major cities, and protection of supply lines.

In eastern Russia, around the outer border of Manchuria, the Soviet Army had 20 sniper divisions and not less than 1,000 planes. In contrast, the Japanese Kwantung Army had a defense of only six to eight divisions, approximately 300-400 planes and 300 tanks.

With the limited arms and materials available Japan was not capable of any sustained engagement against a third power. In spite of this, from 1940 on, the constantly changing world conditions forced Japan to prepare for such a possibility.

In the summer of 1941 plans being carried out were concerned mainly with the Russo-German War. Secondly, they concerned the American, British and the Netherlands' economic blockade against Japan in the summer and autumn of the same year.

Preparations Related to Outbreak of Russo-German War

The European War which broke out between Russia and Germany on 22 June 1941, was an important factor as a cause of World War II. The difficulties of international diplomacy caused by conflicting relationships held by Japan with both the Soviets and Germany and Italy indicated a potential critical emergency. The Army General Staff evaluated the development from every angle, especially a possible Russian invasion of Manchuria. In order to prepare for defense of Manchuria in case of Soviet invasion, troops there were reinforced immediately.

As of June 1941, the Kwantung Army was composed of the 1st Division, the 8th through 12th Divisions, the 14th Division, the 23d through 25th Divisions, the 28th Division and the 29th Division. There was a total of twelve divisions plus the 1st and 2d Tank Brigades and 2d and 5th Air Groups. Most of the ground units were incorporated into the 3d through 6th Armies and the air groups into an Air Corps with both being placed under the command of the Kwantung Army commander. The 10th, 28th and 29th Divisions were assigned directly to the Kwantung Army. Its commander was held responsible for the defense of Manchuria.

In the beginning of July, the Army General Staff decided to increase the strength of the Kwantung Army by fall the same year. The Army General Staff called this reinforcement the "100th Preparation" while the Kwantung Army called it the "Special Maneuver of the Kwantung Army".

The Kwantung Defense command was established with five independent garrisons as organic units. Each division would be reinforced to be overstrength. The 51st and 57th Divisions would be added (these were previously Depot Divisions under the mobilization). Air strength would be increased. All line outfits attached directly to the army such as the field heavy artillery regiments and battalions, antiaircraft battalions and companies, independent antitank battalion, automatic cannon companies, independent engineer regiments, signal units, railway units, etc would be increased. Support organizations such as the motor transport units, transport companies (draft and pack horse), service units, and the medical and veterinary units would be reinforced.

As a result, the strength of the Kwantung Army would be fourteen divisions plus units directly assigned to the Army. They totalled approximately 700,000 men, 140,000 horses and 600 planes. However, in comparison with the Far Eastern Soviet Army of about twenty divisions, 1,300 tanks and 1,500 planes our defense force was still inadequate. In September, some strength was taken from the Kwantung Army as the war situation in the South Pacific began developing.

At the same time, the army in Korea was enlarged by over-strength personnel assignments to the 19th Division and some auxiliary units. Some defensive and signal units of the Northern Army were strengthened, too.

Preparations Related to Economic Blockade by US, Great Britain and the Netherlands

The Russo-German War and the movement of our troops on 28 July 1941 into French Indo-China caused a break, temporarily, in the American-Japanese negotiations. On 26 July, America and Britain, and on 28 July, the Netherlands froze all Japanese funds in their countries to retaliate against the Japanese invasion of French Indo-China. This stopped all trade relations with these countries and had a serious effect on Japan's existence. In the beginning of September, the government and the Imperial Headquarters had a solemn discussion on national policy at a Liaison Conference. They decided upon a policy of carrying on diplomatic negotiations with America and Britain so as to improve the situation. At the same time economic self-sufficiency and defense would be boosted. It was also decided to complete military preparations by the end of October under resolution not to refrain from war with the United States, Britain and the Netherlands, in case the planned negotiations failed. The prospect of war was not to be avoided if it were necessary to accomplish the self-existence and self-defense of Japan. The defensive preparations made immediately after the outbreak of the Russo-German War were centered in Manchuria but were gradually shifted to the South. The military preparations were performed concurrently with the diplomatic negotiation. In case the negotiation succeeded, the military preparation was to have been declared a maneuver. It was hoped the preparations would end as a maneuver.

Pre-War Estimate of Enemy Situation

In September 1941, Imperial General Headquarters made an estimate of the strength and location of American, British, and Netherland Armies in the Southern Territories as shown on Charts 5, 6 and 7. The total Army strength of the enemy in the South was approximately 380,000 troops and 700 planes. This was rapidly increased by the end of the year.

Since the Southern Operational area was under colonial control of America, Britain and the Netherlands, it was estimated to have been undesirable for them to create consolidated fighting power and spiritual coordination between the white people and the natives.

Although the enemy air forces in Siam and Burma were inferior in strength, the enemy was believed to be capable of attacking our landings with bombers and torpedo bombers from Malay under cover of the newly arrived "Spitfires". The Netherland Air Forces might support the British Air Forces from Sumatra and Borneo. The enemy air force in the Philippines was considered inferior having many obsolete planes except a few bombers.

Because of the threatening situation on the European Front, it was believed that the Far Eastern Soviet Army was transferring some of her strength there. Her strength in the Far Eastern Territory, estimated at approximately twenty divisions, 1,300 tanks and 1,500 planes, was declining. If the Southern Operation were carried out, united action by America, Britain and Russia was considered certain. It was also anticipated that with the progress of the European War, Russia might begin offensive action against Japan, or America might advance her Army (especially her Air Force) to the Far Eastern Soviet Territory.

Estimated Army Strength of the Enemy in the South
(September 1941)

Classification / Territories		Unit	Quantities	Number of Units	Personnel	Total Personnel
Malay	Regular Army	British troops	British	7 inf bns as the nucleus	11,000	60,000 to 70,000
		Indian troops	Partly British Majority Indians		30,000 to 35,000	
		Australian troops	Australians	One div as the nucleus	20,000 to 25,000	
		Malayan troops	Partly British Majority Malayans			
	Volunteers		Insufficiently trained and equipped		20,000	20,000
Burma	British troops		British		2,000	35,000 plus Chinese troops
	Indian troops		The main staff are British	1 inf brig as the nucleus	7,000	
	Burma native troops		Poor quality	26 inf bns as the nucleus	26,000	
	Chinese troops				?	
British-Borneo	Regular army		Mainly consist of Indian troops		1,000	3,500
	Volunteers				2,500	
Hongkong	Regular army				13,500	19,000
	Volunteers				5,500	
Philippines	Regular army		Half Americans Half Nationals		42,000	162,000
	Marines		Americans		900	
	National defense army		Nationals		120,000	
Guam	Marines				300	1,800
	Native troops				1,500	
Netherland Indies	Inner Territory troops		Partly European	2 divs as the nucleus	50,000	70,000
	Outer Territory troops		Partly European	15 inf bns	20,000	
Total	Regular army					223,000 to 233,000
	Total Strength					272,000 to 382,000

Remarks:
1. In addition, there were approximately 500,000 troops in India, 350,000 in Australia, and 100,000 in New Zealand.
2. In addition the Regulars of Siam were believed to total about 30,000.
3. The total personnel of the Regular Army included the following troops: Regular Armies in Malay, British Borneo, Hongkong and the Philippines; all of the troops in Burma and the Netherland-Indies, Marines in Guam and the Philippines.

Chart 5

Estimated Enemy Air Forces in the South

(September 1941)

Classification Territories	Airplanes		Number of Squadrons	Number of Planes	Total Planes
Malay	Bombers		4	48	Over 200
	Fighters		4	48	
	Reconnaissance Planes		4	48	
	Seaplanes		3	18	
	Torpedo Bombers		2	24	
Burma	Bombers		1		Approx 50
	Fighters and Bombers		1		
	Pursuit planes		2		
	Volunteer army		1		
Hongkong	Training planes				Approx 10
Philippines	Bombers		1	13	Over 160
	Pursuit planes		3	75	
	Reconnaissance planes		1	18	
	Sea planes	Patrol Bombers	2	30	
		Carrier planes		30	
Netherland Indies	Army Planes	Bombers	6	30	Approx 300
		Fighters	7	130	
		Reconnaissance planes	6	36	
	Sea planes			120	
Total					Approx 720
Remarks	1. In addition to this chart, there were believed to be approx 200 planes in India, 250 in Australia, and 100 in New Zealand. 2. In addition, approx 180 planes were believed to be in Siam.				

Estimated Enemy Naval Forces Operating to the South
(September 1941)

Country	Location	Battle ships	Aircraft carriers	Cruisers	Destroyers	Submarines	Other
Britain	China & Philippines area			1			2
	Hongkong				3		53
	Singapore	2		4	56		24
	Colombo area			9	2		13
	Bombay Area				2		9
	Eastern Africa	1	1	5			
	Aden & Red Sea Area			2	3		1
	Australia area			5			19
	New Zealand area						11
	East Of Hawaii	1		1			
	Mediterranean Sea	5	4	15	55	20	2
America	China & Philippines area		4	2	14	17	26
	Hawaii area	7	7	18	46	28	43
Netherland	Netherland Indies			5	8	19	56

Chart 7

On the day the Tojo Cabinet came into power, studies were inaugurated in the Liaison Conference regarding international conditions and in particular regarding objectives, methods and possibilities of success in waging war against the United States, Great Britain, Holland, and China, simultaneously.

As the result of the above study, on 15 November 1941, a decision was made regarding the objectives and principles to follow in bringing such a possible war plan to successful conclusion. This decision was entitled, "Plan for Expediting the Termination of War against the United States, Great Britain, Holland and the Chiang Kai-shek Regime". Its main points were as follows:

1. By carrying out a speedy armed offensive, Japan will capture American, British and Dutch bases in East Asia and the Southwest Pacific area and establish a strategically superior position.

2. By firmly securing the southern vital resources areas and the main lines of communications, Japan will establish a structure that will be self-sufficient for an extended period of time.

3. Every effort will be made to draw out the main strength of the American Navy at an appropriate time, seek a decisive battle, and destroy it.

4. Japan, Germany and Italy will cooperate and make effort to subjugate England first. For this purpose, Japan will endeavor to sever lines of communications between England, Australia, and India by employing political strategy and destroying commerce, and cause the latter two countries to revolt against the former. At the same time, Japan will promote the independence of Burma and by utilizing this result, instigate an independence movement in India. For the subjugation of Great Britain, Germany and Italy, in particular, will be counted on to counter-blockade England; to intensify their

operations in the Near East, North Africa and Suez areas; and if possible, to execute a landing on the British homeland.

5. Japan will further intensify her military and political strategy to subjugate the Chiang Kai-shek Regime in China by exploiting the results of the operations against the United States, Great Britain and the Netherlands to halt the flow of aid to Chiang Kai-shek and to destroy China's fighting power; by getting full control of the foreign concessions in China; by guiding and utilizing the Chinese residents in the South Seas; and by intensifying operations against China.

6. Every effort will be made to prevent the outbreak of a war with the Soviet Union during the operations in the Southern areas.

7. An agreement not to initiate separate peace with the United States and Great Britain will be made with Germany and Italy. Also, plans will be made to avoid making peace with Great Britain immediately in the event of her surrender, and to make her induce the United States to make peace, thus ending the war at once.

8. The development of the war, trends of the international situation, etc, will be carefully studied at all times, and every effort will be made to grasp the following opportunities to terminate the war:

    a. Opportunity to complete the principle phases of the operations against China, especially the surrender of the Chiang Kai-shek regime.

    b. Opportunity to complete the principle phases of the operations against the Southern areas.

    c. Opportunities which may be afforded by important changes in the European situation, especially the downfall of the English homeland and the termination to the Russo-German war.

Note: There is some evidence to support the fact there was early reasoning by Japanese military and political circles regarding a favorable opportunity for gaining dominant diplomatic control of the Southern area and its natural resources as the result of the European war. This view was most strongly supported in 1940 when Germany overran Holland. The Japanese Foreign Minister, in April 1940, declared Japan's serious concern regarding any change in the status quo of the Netherlands East Indies. Immediately after the invasion of Holland by Germany, he reaffirmed his previous statement in an attempt to prevent any invasion of the Netherlands East Indies by Germany, Great Britain and the United States. He obtained a verbal understanding from Germany which provided that Germany would have no interest in the Netherlands East Indies. Even following the start of the Russo-German war, it was felt this understanding was secure since it was believed Germany would be successful in its military actions. Throughout 1941, Japan continued to have hopes that German and Italy, if possible, would make a landing on England. Chances of this happening decreased following the outbreak of the Russo-German war. In any event, it was considered there was a good possibility of England having to capitulate because of her military and economic weaknesses due to geographic dispositions of the Empire. England's capitulation was considered to be a valuable aid in developing Japan's dominance in the Southern area.

Development of Southern Operation Plan

To meet the situation in the South, strength would be taken from Manchuria, Korea, or organized in the Homeland to obtain the necessary operational force. The units would be gradually transferred to Central and Southern China, Formosa and French Indo-China. A troop movement plan was established.

Units to be sent to the Southern China area included: the 51st Division (from Manchuria); air service units (main force from Manchuria); one tank regiment, six independent anti-tank companies (from the Homeland); and, some of the signal units and line of communication units (from the Homeland and Manchuria).

Units to be sent to Formosa included: the 3d Tank Brigade which would include two tank regiments (one from Manchuria and the other plus headquarters personnel from the Homeland); four independent anti-tank companies (from the Homeland); air units (main forces from Manchuria); and some artillery, signal, and line of communication units (from the Homeland and Manchuria).

Units to be sent to the Northern French Indo-China area included the 4th Independent Mixed Regiment (from the Homeland); air service units (main force from Manchuria); and some line of communication units, etc (from the Homeland and Manchuria).

Reinforcement and establishment of air and sea navigation installations would be made in Formosa, Palau, French Indo-China, Southern China, etc.

Establishments for line of communication bases and the stockpiling of operational supplies and munitions in Southern China, Formosa and French Indo-China would be speeded up. Fittings and armament for requisitioned ships would be prepared. The Homeland Land Defense areas and the national air defense would be strengthened.

These measures were activated immediately and being carried out as scheduled by the end of October. In the beginning of November, the Tojo cabinet decided to exert further efforts for the negotiations to come to a compromise with the United States. The Army and Navy would complete their war preparations by the beginning of December. Following the above decision on 6 November, the Army General Staff issued the following order of battle and the preliminary orders for the Southern Army and others.

Southern Army Order of Battle Outline

Southern Army Commander: Count, General Hisaichi Terauchi

General Headquarters Southern Army (21st Division, and 21st Independent Mixed Brigade). 14th Army (16th and 48th Divisions and 65th Brigade). 15th Army (33d and 55th Divisions, some units of latter were excluded). 16th Army (composed of the 2d Division and the 56th Mixed Infantry Group). 25th Army (composed of a Guard Division, 5th, 18th and 56th Divisions, some units of the latter were excluded). 3d Air Group (composed of five fighter regiments, four light bomber regiments, four heavy bomber regiments, and one air reconnaissance regiment). 5th Air Group (two fighter regiments, two light bomber regiments and one heavy bomber regiment). 21st Independent Air Unit.

> Note: On 27 November 1941, the 56th Division was transferred from the Western District Army to the Twenty-fifth Army. On 4 January 1942, the 38th Division was withdrawn from the Twenty-third Army, and the 48th Division was withdrawn from the Fourteenth Army to be attached to the Sixteenth Army. The South Seas Detachment organized from elements of the 55th Division operated in the Southern area but was under control of the Army General Staff.

Army General Staff Assignment of Objectives and Missions in Southern Operation

The Army General Staff will prepare plans for the attacks against strategic areas in the South. In cooperation with the Navy, the Commander of the Southern Army will concentrate its main force in French Indo-China, Formosa, Southern China and Nansei Islands and Palau Islands areas to prepare for an attack against strategic territories in the South. Order for the attack will be issued later. In case of attack by one or more forces of the US, Britain and the Netherlands, the Commander of the Southern Army will be able to counterattack with the troops stationed in the respective areas. In dealing with the above situation, every effort will be made to settle the situation, locally.

For the China Expeditionary Army commander

In cooperation with the Navy, the China Expeditionary Army commander will prepare to attack Hongkong with a force consisting mainly of the 38th Division, commanded by the 23d Army commander.

For the South Sea Detachment commander

In cooperation with the Navy, the South Sea Detachment commander will advance his force to the Bonin Islands and prepare an attack against Guam.

On 15 November 1941, the Army General Staff issued preliminary orders to the Southern Army commander to execute the following general operational preparation: In cooperation with the Navy, he would be prepared to quickly attack the strategic territories in the Southern area. The orders for attack were to be issued later. The strategic territories to be occupied were the Philippines, British-Malay, every strategic point in the Netherland Indies, a part of Southern Burma, etc. In carrying out the operation, the stability of Thailand and French Indo-China was to be maintained to the fullest extent. At the same time, the blockade of China would be directed from this area. In occupied territories, military administrations were to be established for public security, and to obtain important resources for national defense and self-subsistence.

The respective army and navy units coordinated plans and preparations according to this outline. Imperial General Headquarters waited for results from the American-Japanese negotiations, with-holding only the time for attack.

The purpose of the Southern Operation was to destroy, occupy and maintain important American, British and Netherland bases in Eastern Asia. The territories planned for occupation were the Philippines, Guam, Hongkong, British-Malay, Burma, Java, Sumatra, Borneo, Celebes, Bismarck Archipelago, Netherland Timor, etc.

In close coordination between the Army and Navy, operations would begin simultaneously against the Philippines and British-Malay to complete the mission in the shortest possible time.

Operations were to be launched with a landing on Malay by the advanced units and air attacks on the Philippines. The main force was to land first in the Philippines, taking advantage of the air attacks, and then in Malay to rapidly occupy these areas. In addition, strategic territories of Guam, Hongkong and British-Borneo would be occupied during the initial stage of the operation. During this First Phase, the strategic territories of the Bismarck Archipelago and Netherland-Borneo would be occupied as soon as possible. Strategic points in southern Sumatra were to be captured during the Malay Operation in preparation for an operation against Java. The important resources in these areas would be protected. Also, strategic territories of the Moluccas Islands and Timor would be occupied.

Upon establishing air bases for use against Java and gaining air superiority, that island would be occupied. After occupying Singapore, the strategic areas in northern Sumatra would be taken at the proper time.

Although our Combined Fleet might have to take counter offensive measures to meet the main American Fleet and though Russia might enter the war, the Philippines and Malay Operations were to be carried out notwithstanding.

During these operations, air bases, etc in southern Burma would be captured at the first opportunity. If a lull developed and circumstances permit, an operation for control of Burma would be executed.

The strength to be used in this operation consisted of eleven divisions, nine tank regiments, two air groups, and other units directly assigned to the Southern Army. The outline for the tactical grouping of the Army and the assigned operational areas was as follows:

Southern Army (a group consisting of a division, and a mixed brigade for the French Indo-China area)

    14th Army – Two Divisions for the Philippines area. Air Support to be provided by 5th Air Group.

    15th Army – Two Divisions for the Siam and Burma areas.

    16th Army – One Division (two more divisions would be assigned after completion of other operations to operate with 16th Army) for the Netherland Indies Area.

    25th Army – Four Divisions for the Malay area. Air Support to be provided by 3d Air Group.

Other Forces

    23d Army – From the Chinese Expeditionary Army, One Division for the Hongkong area.

    South Sea Detachment (directly assigned to the Imperial Headquarters). Three infantry battalions for Guam, Bismarck Archipelago, etc.

Action date was to be ordered later. If the American-Japanese negotiations were successful, the plans were to be suspended.

Hongkong, Guam and Bismarck Archipelago Assignments and Strategy

After confirming the beginning of landings by the advance units on Malay, a group of the 23d Army would start the Hongkong operations in cooperation with the 2d China Expeditionary Fleet. The enemy fleet would be destroyed first and after crushing the enemy positions in the Kowloon (on Chiulung) Peninsula, Hongkong would be occupied. Army General Staff assignments and strategic plans for the Guam and Bismarck Archipelago included: The South Sea Detachment would occupy Guam Island in cooperation with the 4th Fleet and later was to capture the air bases in the Bismarck Archipelago to eliminate a potential enemy menace against the South Pacific

Islands. When the South Sea Detachment would occupy Guam Island in cooperation with the 4th Fleet and later was to capture the air bases in the Bismarck Archipelago to eliminate a potential enemy menace against the South Pacific Islands. When the South Sea Detachment had occupied Guam, a naval land combat unit was to take over the defense by relieving the detachment. Then, the Army cooperating with the Navy would occupy Rabaul at the first opportunity and establish air bases. Defense of that territory would be turned over to a naval land combat unit and the South Sea Detachment would return toward Palau.

Air Force Operational Assignments

In cooperation with the Navy Air Forces, the Army Air Force was to attack enemy air bases at the outbreak of war. They were to capture air superiority as an aid to Army landing operations and to support later land actions. The main objective of the army air unit would be the Malay area. At the outbreak of the war, air bases would be established in Southern Formosa for the Philippines campaign and in Southern French Indo-China for the Malay campaign. Air attacks were to start on the date of the Malay landing. The Army Air Force was to be responsible for the aerial cover of the convoy's landing force. Air attacks would be carried out at dawn with an objective of destroying the main enemy bases in a single attack. This was to be done to make the movement of the landing force easier. After the landing, the air base would be moved quickly forward for close support of land operations.

Line of Communications (Logistical Support)

Southern French Indo-China would be the main advance base (depot) for the general Southern Operations; Formosa would be the relay supply base; and the Canton Sector would be the auxiliary relay supply base. Initial supplies for one full operation would be sent with the landing operation supplies from the Homeland and Manchuria. The greatest portion of combat supplies possible would be sent to the South, with the Homeland, Manchuria and China as the source of supply. In China, self-subsistence would be emphasized and strengthened. The relation of the China Operation with the Southern Operation provided for cooperation between the Army and Navy in maintaining the present strategic situations. After taking care of American, British and other enemy powers in China, efforts would be turned toward the subjugation of Chiang Kai-shek's power. In case a Russian invasion were indicated after the beginning of the Southern Operation, necessary strength would be transferred to the Manchurian area as needed. At the same time, occupied territories in China would be readjusted and important areas maintained to check any rise of enemy power.

If America should cooperate with Russia in the North or if the Russian Army should challenge us by herself, the necessary units transferred from the Homeland or China were to destroy the Russian Air Forces in the Far Eastern Territories.

Proposed Southern Operation Military Administration

As soon as the Southern operation was begun, a military administration would be enforced in occupied territories with the responsibility resting on the Army in the specific area of operation. This policy was established by the Conference. Methods and policies of the military administration were developed for the purpose of restoring public security, rapid control of important resources for national defense, and protecting self-subsistence for the Army engaged in the operation. As an aid to enforcing the military administration, the existing government organization and public customs would be utilized and respect as much as possible. The Army of Occupation would secure and develop important resources for our mobilization program if it did not interfere with the operation. In securing resources, and maintaining self-subsistence for the Army of Occupation, full consideration was to be paid not to disturb public welfare and not to jeopardize the pacification service. The nationals of America, Britain and the Netherlands would be directed to cooperate with the military administration. Those who did not comply would be asked to leave or other measures would be taken. Current privileges for the citizens of the Axis Powers would be respected but any increase in their number would be restricted. Chinese merchants residing in occupied territories would be required to comply with Japanese policies and to break their ties with the Chiang Kai-Shek Government. The native national of any country would be taught to rely upon the Japanese Army. Japanese people who might desire to move to occupied territories after the operations begin must be highly qualified. Those who had previously lived in such territories would be given preference.

Division of duties between the Army and Navy in military administration of the occupied area was decided by the respective departments in Imperial General Headquarters. The main responsible territories of the Army (the sub-responsible territories of the Navy) would be Hongkong, Philippines, British-Malay, Sumatra, Java, British-Borneo and Burma. The main responsible territories of the Navy (the sub-responsible territories of the Army) would be Netherland-Borneo, Calebes, Moluccas Island, Lesser Sunda Isles, New Guinea, Bismarck Isles, and Guam.

CHAPTER IV

First Phase of the War

PART I First Stage (December 1941 - June 1942)

Decision as to Time and Date for Beginning War

On 1 December 1941, the Conference decided on war. The Imperial General Headquarters then set 8 December 1941 as the date for its beginning, reasons being:

1. From the Naval Operational point of view, Japan had little hope for success after March 1942 because of the difference in Naval strength between Japan and the United States.

2. Any delay in the beginning of hostilities would mean a wasteful use of liquid fuel depleting critical fuel stockpiles which could not be replaced unless the operations plan for procurement from the South were started. It was estimated that if the beginning of hostilities were delayed until after March 1942 even the fuel demands for the first phase military operations could not be met.

3. It would be disadvantageous for Japan to delay beginning war if she expected to complete the first main step of the operation (expected to take at least five months) prior to the spring of 1942. That would be the most suitable time for the Manchurian Operation considering the possibility the USSR might join the war in the North.

4. It would be disadvantageous for Japanese forces if they delayed operations since the enemy would have an opportunity to accomplish full preparations for war in each southern district.

5. January and February were not satisfactory months for landing operations because of seasonal weather conditions in Malay.
6. 8 December seemed to be the most appropriate time because of the favorable tide and moon.

Because of these reasons, 8 December appeared to be the last favorable opportunity for Japan to launch military operations. A critical decision had to be made concerning the Japanese-American negotiations then in progress. The Conference made its decision to start war since there was little hope that the negotiations would be completed successfully.

Following this decision, the Army General Staff issued the following orders on 1 December (the same day) regarding the beginning of War.

Summary of Orders Issued to Southern Army Commander

Japan has decided to begin war against the United States, Great Britain, and the Netherlands.

The Southern Army commander will begin attack operations on 8 December. If negotiations between the United States and Japan are successful, operations will be ceased at once.

Before 8 December, the Southern Army commander will carry out the following orders:

(1) If we are attacked by the enemy, we will begin operations at a suitable time in cooperation with the Navy.

(2) If Great Britain invades Thailand, we will also enter Thailand at a suitable time, in cooperation with the Navy.

(3) If enemy planes repeatedly reconnoiter our important positions and convoys, action will be

taken against them.

Summary of Orders Issued to China Expeditionary Army Commander

The China Expeditionary Army commander will attack Hongkong with a unit consisting chiefly of the 38th Division under the Command of the 23d Army Commander in cooperation with the Navy.

Operations will begin immediately after receiving confirmation on the beginning of the landing and the air raids against Malay by the Southern Army.

After attacking and securing Hongkong, a military administration will be established.

Prior to 8 December, the China Expeditionary Army Commander will carry out the following orders:

    (1) If the enemy attacks before the beginning of war, they will be intercepted at an appropriate time.

    (2) If enemy planes repeatedly reconnoiter our military movements, immediate action will be taken against them.

The China Expeditionary Army commander will eliminate the Tenshin-British Concession, the Shanghai Joint Concessions, and other properties of the enemy nations in China. If it becomes necessary, military authority may be used.

The South Sea Detachment commander was ordered by the Army General Staff to attack Guam Island immediately after 8 December in cooperation with the Navy. After the capture of this island, the strength was to be assembled on Palau Island to prepare for the coming operation against Rabaul.

Alternate Plans for the Malay Attack

Plan A: If the enemy air force were not as large as anticipated, it would be possible to carry out the aerial annihilating attack simultaneously with the landing operations of the Advance Army Group.

Plan B: Since the landing operation against the northeastern coast of Malay would be under the protection of a land-based air force whose base was located deep within south French Indo-China and the enemy might increase their air strength in the Malay areas, it was necessary to check the enemy by first carrying out an aerial annihilating attack. After completion of this operation, a landing was to be carried out by the Advance Army Group.

Decision: It had been decided by the Army General Staff that the plan for conducting the operation would be decided according to the war situation just before the beginning of war. On 3 December, the Army General Staff ordered the Southern Army to use Plan "A".

Orders for the Kwantung Army and the China Expeditionary Army Related to China Incidents

On 3 December, the Army General Staff issued orders to the Kwantung Army and China Expeditionary Army commanders related to China Incidents. The Kwantung Army was to avoid border incidents and if any did occur to settle them locally because the Imperial Headquarters was attempting to prevent war with Russia.

The China Expeditionary Army commander would tighten the present anti-enemy blockade and destroy the enemy will to fight a prolonged war. This plan sought an early settlement of the China Incident.

Summary of Operational Progress During First Stage Period

When war began on 8 December 1941, the 15th Army marched into Thailand on the basis of the Japan-Thailand negotiations which were begun on the evening of 7 December 1941, and reached the advanced objective at Bangkok on 9 December. Success of the negotiations had been assured by the Japanese Military Attache. Agreement to access and movement of troops was acknowledged by the Premier of Thailand on 8 December. Discussions covering an offensive and defensive alliance were concluded on 21 December.

In Malay, the 25th Army landed on Songkhla and Kotabharu on 8 December opening up the Southern Route. In the Malay Naval Battle of 10 December heavy losses were inflicted upon the British Fleet and by the end of December, Ipoh and Kuantan were occupied. On 14 and 15 January 1942, Japanese troops broke into Johore and occupied Malacca. Continuing onward, they landed and occupied Singapore on 9 February and 15 February respectively. In the meantime, the 15th Army occupied Moulmein on 31 January 1942.

The 32d Army occupied Kowloon City on 12 December and started a general attack against Hongkong on 14 December. By 25 December, Hongkong was occupied.

In the Pacific area, Guam was occupied by the South Seas Detachment on 10 December and the occupation of Wake Island came on 23 December. On 23 January, Rabaul was captured by the detachment.

During the first part of February, the Army General Staff issued orders to the South Sea Detachment commander directing him to cooperate with the Navy and occupy strategic positions in British-New Guinea and Bismarck areas. Main positions of Andaman Island were to be occupied and also consolidation of positions in Portugal Timore was to be executed by the Southern Army commander.

In the Philippine area, our navy and army units were successful in their aerial annihilation battle of 8 December. Two advance forces of the 14th Army landed in Northern Luzon on 10 December 41. On 20 December, an element of the 14th Army landed on Lingayen and Lamon on 22 December. On 2 January 1942, the City of Manila was captured.

Following the occupation of Manila, the enemy forces on Luzon island fortified and isolated themselves at established positions on Bataan Peninsula and Corregidor and fought back stubbornly.

In an attempt to drive the enemy out of Bataan and Corregidor, the 14th Army made a fierce attack with the 16th Division and the 65th Brigade. However, we were unable to force the enemy to surrender due to their skillfully constructed jungle positions in depth. Also they were fighting a bitter defensive battle.

Considering the enemy strength and terrain, the Army General Staff realized that the present commitment of the 14th Army was inadequate to accomplish a rapid occupation. It was decided to have the Southern Army carry out a mopping up campaign against the other islands in the Philippines and at the same time prepare to assault Bataan with superior strength. To strengthen the Army in the Philippines, the 4th Division was sent from Shanghai in February and March and an infantry regiment and a mountain artillery battalion from the 21st Division in Northern China was sent the latter part of February. Both units were placed under command of the 14th Army Commander.

In addition, heavy siege guns and other artillery units were resupplied and reinforced with ammunition and operational materials to combat the enemy positions near Bataan and Corregidor. The general attack upon Bataan was begun on 3 April and by 9 April the entire Peninsula was occupied.

Then, the 14th Army prepared an attack on Corregidor while continuing its mopping-up campaign over a wide area. With the fall of Corregidor on 7 May, the entire American-Philippine Army on the Philippine Islands surrendered.

Java Operations Planning

During the last part of December, Imperial General Headquarters received a joint recommendation from the Southern Army and 2d Fleet commanders that operations against Sumatra and Borneo be speeded up so the Java Operation could be moved up about one month ahead of the prearranged plan.

It was decided that, since Japan was now in a position to carry out its major operations in the Southwest Pacific, occupation in those areas should be rushed before the enemy had sufficient time to recover its losses and reorganize. This would also improve the over-all military situation for Japan. If Japan could complete the above-mentioned movement, she could deal with the movements of the Soviet Army near Manchuria, which was regarded as a potential active front in the spring.

Taking all this into consideration, Imperial General Headquarters accepted the recommendations of the commanders and made plans to take the next step. On 4 January 1942, shortly after its occupation of Hongkong, the 38th Division was assigned to the 16th Army. After being reorganized and resupplied its main force was brought up to Banka and Palembang. Its Eastern Detachment (Ito Det) was dispatched toward Amboina and Kupang.

The 48th Division, which had been participating in the Philippines Operations, was transferred to the 16th Army and reorganized on 14 January although their Philippines' operations were not yet completed. The 16th Army commander and the 2d Division which had been in the Japanese Homeland preparing for action started to move out about the middle and latter part of January. Special efforts were made to speed up Air Force organization to protect convoys. Also, plans for strengthening lines of communications were given top consideration.

In the Borneo area, the Kawaguchi Detachment made a successful landing on British-Borneo on 16 December. The Sakaguchi Detachment of the 16th Army occupied Tarakan Island on 11 January and Balikpapan on 24 January. The Eastern Detachment (Ito Detachment) which had been formed from elements of the 38th Division occupied Amboina on 31 January and Kupang on Timor Island on 20 February. Makassar (captured by Navy forces) and Bandjermasin (captured by the Sakaguchi Detachment) came under our control on 9 or 10 February.

During the Java Naval Sea Battle on 4 February, in the Java and Sumatra area, additional heavy damage was inflicted on the British Netherlands Fleet. The 38th Division coordinated its attack with the descent of the Airborne Raiding Force (from 1st Air Raiding Group of the 3d Air Group) on 14 February and occupied Palembang on 17 February. During the last part of February, the enemy fleet was defeated again in the Soerabaja Naval Sea Battle. At this time, Japanese Forces were moving to attack Java.

On 1 March, the remaining enemy fleet in the Java-Sumatra area was defeated in the Batavia Sea. On that same day, the 16th Army succeeded in making a landing on Java. After the surrender of the Netherlands Army on 9 March, operations in the area were completed.

Burma Operations Planning

Ever since the Burma Operation began, the Army General Staff had been anxious to complete its conquest quickly because of the strategical value Burma held as key point in the northern flank of the Southern area. Burma was invaluable for the blockade against China. However, the overall strength would not permit a full-scale Burma Operation at the same time as other Southern Operations. About the middle of January, war operations were progressing so well this viewpoint was reversed. On 22 January, the Southern Army commander was ordered to proceed without waiting for completion of operations in other areas. Thus, action to occupy major points in Burma was started much earlier than scheduled.

Before the war, the main enemy strength in Burma was estimated at 35,000 men for the Army and 70 planes for the Air Force. However, indications were that the enemy had increased its strength since then. At the time of operations, there were approximately 10 Chinese Divisions along the Burma-China and the southern Burma Border. The unit used by the Japanese in the Burma Operation was the 15th Army (33d and 55th Divisions as a nucleus supplemented by service units plus necessary air force strength). The 56th Division was also scheduled to be used in north Burma because of Chinese Army strength and its reinforcements.

Reduced to a basic outline, orders for the Burma Operation issued to the Southern Army by the Army General Staff covered two points:

1. The object of the Burma Operation is to defeat the British Army in Burma and to secure and occupy the main points in Burma, while at the same time strengthening the anti-China Blockade.

2. The 15th Army will advance along the line of the Salween River in the vicinity of Moulmein and after making operational preparations will take the main elements from the area along the Moulmein-Pegu Road and occupy important positions in Central Burma.

In the Burma Theater of operation, the 15th Army occupied Rangoon on 8 March and went ahead with operations against Central Burma. On 29 April, Lashio and the China-Burma border were occupied and on 1 May, the strategic points of Mandalay were occupied. During the first part of May, Bhamo, Lungling in Yunnan Province, and the Akyab Airdrome had been occupied.

The Navy carried out attacks on Colombo and air raids on Ceylon during the first part of April. They also gained the upper hand on the Indian Ocean. On 7 May, a naval battle took place on the Coral Sea. As a result of this battle, the Japanese plan to attack Port Moresby by sea was abandoned.

Situation Review and Tentative Plans

By mid-March the First Stage of the Southern Operations had progressed quite successfully and occupation of the desired areas was in sight. However, we anticipated that following our offensive operation American-British forces would counterattack from both the East and West. Imperial General Headquarters made a study of the expected operations and prepared a tentative plan of operational conduct. The Southern Operation was to be completed first, and then consolidation and regrouping would be accomplished. At the same time, a military administration would be established to promote peaceful relations in occupied areas and establish friendly operating conditions. It was to be maintained firmly for a long period.

Efforts would be made to occupy the main areas of Central Burma and destroy the enemy, especially the Chungking Army, during this period.

We would consolidate our gains achieved during the first phase operations with the objective of holding the advantage forever. At the same time, the US and British Forces would be kept on the defensive by our diversionary operations around the perimeter of the main occupied area.

Our national defense program would be enlarged and additional units needed would be organized. At the same time, the Southern area would be reorganized and forces reduced within limits allowing above operations. Objective of this was to develop much larger reserve forces of the Army.

The good results obtained in the Southern Operation were to be exploited and an attempt made to settle the China Incident rapidly through political and strategic methods.

Attempts would be made to maintain the current state of relations with Russia. At the same time, as a precaution against any change, defense plans would continue to be strengthened.

The most important problem in the future political and strategic conduct was how to organize and maintain reserve forces which would be available for any emergency. Another problem was the question of where our diversionary operations outside the defense perimeter should be directed.

This tentative plan, prepared in mid-March, was a guide throughout the following months and energetic efforts were made by the Southern Army to achieve its objectives. In late May, restoration of peace and order in the occupied areas and the establishment of the military administration were progressing smoothly.

The primary objective of the Army General Staff then turned to establishment of a stable defensive situation and securing self-sufficiency for the Army in the Southern District. Continued efforts were made to strengthen the National Defense power in depth. This was to be done by training, reorganization of units and by securing important defense resources from the South.

First of all, by accomplishing the defeat of China and Britain it was considered any major war effort by the United States might be discouraged. Also, planning of possible countermeasures against a potential attack by Russia was necessary. The plans, especially those concerning the operational order, time, method, etc, would have to be decided after a careful study of our National Economic Capacity and related elements. Imperial Headquarters had to consider many factors at this critical time including the movement of forces in consolidation of gains made as well as immediate and long-range operational planning along with their production and operational requirements. Flexibility of plans was essential to meet all situations.

After determining the number of troops to be stationed in the Southern District and perimeter territories, the main body of other units would be returned or transferred to the Homeland. Others were to be transferred to Manchuria and China. Divisions which could possibly be taken off the line included the Guard Division, the 2d, 4th and 5th Divisions which were to be transferred to the Homeland. The 33d Division was to be sent to China. The 16th Division was to proceed to Manchuria.

> Note: After this had been scheduled, due to increased enemy activity during the next few months, the only units actually transferred were the 4th Division and a few units under the direct control of the Army.

The 14th Army was placed under the direct control of the Army General Staff. These changes were established to relieve the Southern Army of some of its heavy responsibility and aided in the effectiveness of the military administration in the Philippines.

The Kwantung Army was to demobilize part of its strength, especially the older soldiers within limits assuring effective defensive and operational preparations in Manchuria. At this same time, the China Expeditionary Army was directed to organize the 3d Tank Division. The Kwantung Army was to organize the 1st and 2d Tank Divisions. This was part of a plan to enlarge the Japanese armored strength. 1st & 2d Area Army headquarters, Armored Army headquarters, and 2d Army headquarters were to be established to strengthen the command system in the Kwantung Army.

The 52d Division was to be demobilized in the Homeland (Note: due to the increase in enemy activity starting in May & June this was not carried out.

The 3d Air Army headquarters was to be established in the Southern area. Its nucleus would consist of approximately five Air Brigades. Its responsibilities were to be the offensive air operations in India and China and air defense of important points in Sumatra and Java.

One Air Division headquarters and the necessary units for it was to be transferred to the China area from the South after the Air Army headquarters had been established.

Two Air Divisions were to be placed under the command of the 2d Air Army commander in order to aid and strengthen northern area aerial and military preparations. Some of the Southern Area Air Units were to be transferred to Manchuria with this change in the organization.

After the occupation of areas which had been planned and after the First Phase of the operation, we would either proceed to occupy strategic points on the perimeter or adopt a passive role. If necessary, we would make them advanced outposts in our defense zone. At the same time, we would endeavor to disrupt enemy efforts to construct key points for their expected counterattacks. Their supply lines in the perimeter would be upset through harassing raids.

After studying this proposed operation, the perimeter locations where the operation would be carried out were set as follows: Aleutians, Fiji, Samoa, New Caledonia, Eastern New Guinea, Cocos, eastern India, Colombo and Ceylon (Colombo and Ceylon were to be neutralized). Actions resulting from this tentative plan are described in the following sections.

Imperial General Headquarters prepared an estimate on current and potential enemy strength throughout the world in May. See Charts 8 and 9.

Estimate of the Enemy Strength, May 1942

Area \ Distribution	Ground Strength	Air Strength	Remarks
United States	1,800,000 men (43 divisions completed)	3,500 active Front Line Planes	Expected increase for year 2,000,000 men; and about 6,000 front line planes.
Panama area	Army 45,000 men	450 planes	
Alaska & the Aleutians	Army & Navy 8,000 men	150 planes	
Hawaiian Is	Army 35,000 men	400 planes	
Midway	Army & Navy 1,700 men	50 planes	
Samoa	US Navy 750 men	20 planes	
Fiji	US & British 7,000 men	20 planes	
New Caledonia	US & Free French Govt 3,000 men	10 planes	
Australia	350,000 men (10 divisions)	500 planes	Number of US men having arrived in Australia and New Zealand, approx 2-5 divisions. Powerful units added in Southwest New Guinea & Northern Australia.
New Zealand	70,000 men (3 divisions)	250 planes	
Iceland & Northern Ireland	US Troops (1-2 divisions)		
Great Britain	2,000,000 men (approximately 45 divisions completed)	5,000 Front Line planes	Number of divisions to be added, 7-8; and, number of planes to be added, 2,000-2,500 during year.
Near East	150,000 men (10 divisions)	300 planes	
Northern Africa	300,000 men (16 divisions)	700 planes	
Western Africa	Some US Troops indicated		
Southern Africa	80,000 men (5 divisions)	200 planes	
Madagascar	British 1 division		
India	500,000 men (British Army, 7 divisions; & India Army, 23 divisions)	350 planes	
Ceylon	(1-2 divisions)		
Canada	130,000 men (5 divisions)	250 planes	

Chart 8

Preliminary Planning for a Chungking Operation

During the first part of April, the China Expeditionary Army commander was expected to make careful analysis and recommendations regarding a proposed China operation plan of the Army General Staff. The tentative plan was drawn up as a preliminary to major offensive operation in Chungking when the best opportunity was available.

General objectives of the tentative Army General Staff plan were developed to take advantage of our successful results in the Pacific War operations. Special attention was to be given operations for the China Incident. Efforts were to be made to develop a large-scale plan to solve this matter if conditions permitted. Russian activity would have an important bearing on our decision. If the situation made it impossible to carry out a large-scale Chungking operation, previous strategy would be maintained. At the same time, increased effectiveness for the economic blockade of the Chungking government would be developed by cutting off the Burma Road.

Confidence of the people in occupied zones was to be developed by endeavoring to enforce a satisfactory public peace, conducting political adjustments and supplying economic pressure. Also, political and economic pressure were to be directed against people in unoccupied areas. After cutting off the Burma Road, smashing blows were to be thrown against the remaining enemy forces.

For this proposed Chungking operation several divisions were to be transferred from another area to China. Objective was to destroy the fighting power of the Central Army which was the nucleus of enemy resistance.

It was considered that the best time to start such a plan would be following the cut-off of the Burma Road and when China began feeling the economic pinch resulting from our successes in the Southern area. Also, following conclusion of the Southern opera-

Estimate of Possible Increases in Fighting
Power of US-British Forces (May 1942)

	Present	Future	Remarks
US	Monthly output of approx 2,700 planes and 500 tanks.	By middle of 1943 the monthly output will be approx 3,200 planes. By 1943 - 3,000 tanks monthly.	Due to the resources in manpower and material, the fighting strength will be greatly increased.
British	Monthly output of 1,300 planes.		The fighting power may be increased gradually, but from the standpoint of manpower, it is quite a difficult task to increase the number, all at once.
India	One division can be organized monthly. However, on the aircraft production side there are only assembly plants.		
Canada	Monthly output of aircraft approx 500.		
Australia	Monthly output of aircraft approx 60.		

Chart 9

tions, we would have a large force available which would make the Northern situation far more secure. The earliest possible time for this operation would be toward the end of fall.

Aleutians, Midway and Southeast Area Operations Plans

The Navy Section of Imperial Headquarters advocated the idea that we must occupy Australia because since the beginning of 1942 American air and sea communications with Australia and New Zealand had been extremely active. This posed a threat since it was apparent United States Forces probably would use Australia as the jumping off point for any future counteroffensive.

The Army General Staff of Imperial Headquarters thought differently. Considering our available fighting strength, occupation of Australia was clearly beyond our offensive capacity. Furthermore, it was argued if this ridiculous operation were to be attempted it would surely fail because military supplies necessary for such an operation could not be maintained due to the shortage of shipping. Lastly, it was out of the question to provide the ten or more divisions which were estimated as necessary to carry out such an operation.

Because of these conflicting opinions the operation was not carried out. The Naval and Army Sections agreed without any great controversy on an alternative plan. This called for occupation of possible American jumping-off points for operations against our Homeland. The enemy was to be stopped as far east in the Aleutians as possible. Australia was to be isolated by severing the line of communications between it and the United States. This was to be done by seizing Fiji, Samoa and New Caledonia. The enemy counterattack potential was to be gradually eliminated by hitting the enemy bases from the air and sea and by strengthening the situation in Eastern New Guinea area through the occupation of Port Moresby. This method of operation would not require a large number of forces.

Plans were developed to seize Port Moresby and the vicinity before the enemy had an opportunity to increase its strength. However, our transport convoy encountered the US Fleet in the Coral Sea and a battle was fought between 7 and 8 May. Though our fleet losses were less than the enemy, we lost more than half of our carrier planes which were essential in the planned amphibious attack. The Port Moresby invasion by sea was postponed as a result.

Next step was to have been the Fiji, Samoa and New Caledonia area operation. However, the Navy suddenly demanded that the plan be changed because the Commander in Chief of the Combined Fleet had insisted that an occupation of Midway should be carried out before the operation against the previously mentioned three islands. The Navy stated it would need only an infantry regiment to carry out this task.

The Army disagreed with such a change in the operational plan. Following negotiation, however, the Army General Staff acceded to the Navy demand.

The revised plan of operations was in two phases.

> First Phase of the Operation was to be in the direction of the Aleutians and Midway.
>
> Second Phase would be in the direction of Samoa, Fiji, and New Caledonia.

The Army decided to employ the North Sea Detachment (one infantry battalion, one engineer company, both under Major Hozumi) for the Aleutain Operation. The Ichiki Detachment (one infantry regiment, one engineer company, and one AT company, all under Colonel Ichiki) was to be used in the Midway Operations. Both of these units were to operate under Naval Command. The Navy had already decided to carry out this operation using the main body of its Combined Fleet.

Principle Orders Issued to the North Sea Detachment commander:

1. Imperial General Headquarters has planned to occupy the Western Aleutian Islands.
2. North Sea Detachment commander will cooperate with the Navy and be responsible for the attack and occupation of Adak, Kiska and Attu.
3. After the North Sea Detachment reaches the assembly point, the detachment will be under the Commander in Chief of the 5th Fleet.

Principle Orders Issued to the Ichiki Detachment:

1. Imperial General Headquarters has planned to occupy Midway Island.
2. The Ichiki Detachment will cooperate with the Navy and be responsible for the attack and the occupation of Midway Island.
3. After the Ichiki Detachment reaches the assembly point, the detachment will be under the command of the Commander in Chief of the 2d Fleet.

Our Combined Fleet moved into the Midway area with its main body and into the Aleutians with smaller units during the first few days of June to carry out the occupational operation.

On 5 June, our Fleet in the Midway area was defeated and landing operations were stopped.

Immediately, the convoy to the Aleutians was given an order to return. This return order was rescinded and the original landing plan for the Aleutians was modified with Adak Island being dropped as an objective. In view of the Midway defeat, it was considered too risky for our remaining naval units to cover a landing attempt at Adak. The landings on Kiska and Attu were completed successfully on 7 June and 8 June, respectively.

As a result of the Midway Sea Battle, our Fleet lost the majority of its aircraft carriers. This was our first major naval defeat since the beginning of the war throughout the Pacific and Indian Ocean. The loss of our sea force put a heavy handicap on our tactical operations causing us to avoid any positive offensive movements. In view of our National Economic Capacity we could not hope to regain our sea power during this long term operation.

The Ichiki Detachment was returned to direct control of the Army General Staff after reaching Omiya Island by orders issued on 12 June. The North Sea Detachment was placed again under direct control of the Army General Staff after 25 June by orders issued on 23 June. They were relieved, officially, of their duty to occupy Adak and were ordered to aid in security operations on Attu.

New Caledonia, Fiji, Samoa Islands and Port Moresby Operations Plans

While the Midway and Aleutian campaigns were being carried out preparations for the Fiji and Samoa Island Operations were being made. The battle orders were issued on 18 May for the 17th Army and included the following points:

1. Imperial General Headquarters has planned to occupy the important points of New Caledonia, Fiji, Samoa and to occupy Port Moresby.
2. The 17th Army commander will cooperate with the Navy and accomplish the above-mentioned missions.

Objective of the New Caledonia, Fiji and Samoa Islands operation was to interrupt supply lines between the United States and Australia by occupying and repulsing any enemy counterattacks from that direction. The Army employed the main body of the 17th Army for this operation. The 41st Infantry Regiment (5th Division), the Kawaguchi Detachment (three infantry battalions of the 18th Division), and the South Seas Detachment (three infantry battalions of the 55th Division) made up the main army force. The Navy employed the 2d Fleet and the 1st Air Fleet.

Staging area for the New Caledonia attack force was Rabaul where the force was to assemble during the last part of June. Units for the Fiji and Samoa campaigns were to gather at Truk Island during the first part of July. Support operations by the Combined Fleet were to begin around the first part of July depending upon the operational situation of the fleet.

Objective of the postponed Port Moresby operation was occupation of that area. This was planned to control the Coral Sea and to cut off the key enemy offensive position which might be used against the Eastern New Guinea area. For this operation, the Army employed other elements of the 17th Army. The Aoba Detachment (three Infantry Battalions from the 2d Division) was the nucleus. The Navy used part of its 11th Air Fleet and the 4th Fleet. The attack force was to be staged at Palau during the middle part of June. The Port Moresby operations were to start after the New Caledonia Operation and before the Fiji and Samoa Operations.

Preparations progressed satisfactorily for the Army, but due to the Navy defeat in the Midway Operations, Imperial General Headquarters was compelled to postpone the Fiji, Samoa, and New Caledonia Operations for approximately two months. Some of the scheduled attack units were delayed and sent to the Bismarck Archipelago area while the main body was sent to Mindanao and Pauau to await further orders. The units were to proceed with operational preparations and training at these places.

Operational Conduct for Southern Army Following Completion of First Stage in Occupational Operations

Objectives in the first stage of the first phase of Southern Army operations were completed in June. The Army General Staff issued new orders according to the previously discussed tentative plan on the coming duties for the Southern Army. This was done during the latter part of June. The orders were designed to be adaptable in meeting any kind of situation which might arise.

Following the surrender of the Philippines, the 14th Army was withdrawn from the Southern Army and placed under direct control of the Army General Staff on 27 June. On 29 June, the following principle orders were issued.

Principle Orders for the Southern Army commander.

1. In order to accomplish what was considered to be the final step of the war, the Army General Staff intended to establish self-support and firm control throughout the occupied area. Gains were to be consolidated and preparations made to defeat any attempts to upset our control of the important Southern areas.

2. The Southern Army was to cooperate with the Navy and be responsible for securing the important areas in the South. Necessary operational preparations for subjugation campaigns were to be made for use against important positions on the outskirts of this area.

    a. Defense plans would be completed in Burma, Malay, Sumatra, Java and British-Borneo, including military administrations.

    b. According to the Mutual Defense Alliances, cooperation would be given in the defense of Thailand and Indo-China.

    c. Pressure against Chungking through the blockade would be continued from Burma, French Indo-China and Thailand.

  d. Offensive air operations would be concentrated against India and China. Operations on the ground would be concentrated against the inland areas of India and China. No ground operations were to be started unless covered by specific orders.

  e. If necessary, cooperation would be given in the defense of areas under Naval administration.

Principle Orders for the 14th Army Commander

The 14th Army Commander was to cooperate with the Navy in establishing order in the Philippines. Plans were to be made to speed up introduction of the military administration upon the natives.

Due to the increase in size of the occupied area, an agreement had been drawn up on 2 June covering area administrative responsibilities. These conformed, generally, to the defensive areas of responsibility.

Army-Navy Central Agreement Regarding Southern Area Defense Responsibilities

Establishment by Imperial General Headquarters of a defense plan for the Southern area clarified the cooperative procedure between the Army and Navy. This was decided in the form of an Army-Navy Central Agreement on 29 June covering defense of the occupied area. The important Southern area sections concerned were those occupied Southern Districts west of Dutch New Guinea.

As a defensive objective, the Army and Navy would cooperate by launching attack operations of planes and ships to smash any potential enemy counterattack plan. The remaining enemy in occupied areas would be mopped up quickly and subjugation campaigns would be initiated against important positions on the outskirts of the defense perimeter. With close cooperation between Army and Navy, each important occupied area would be strengthened and any counterattacking enemies were to be annihilated. Necessary naval safe-guards would be established for sea communication in the South and between the South and the Homeland.

The Navy would be responsible for controlling and keeping the sea lanes clear all along the occupied areas. The Navy would carry out aerial attacks and submarine operations in the Australia and the Indian Ocean areas. Sea manuevers would be planned for surface forces to encounter and destroy enemy warships as the enemy situation allowed.

The Army would be responsible for destruction of enemy air power and important military installations mainly in the vicinity of Southwest China and Northeast India. The Army would cooperate with the Navy in checking and destroying enemy shipping where necessary.

Allocation of defensive responsibilities provided that the Navy would be directly responsible for all sea defense, exclusively, and for the ground defense of Andaman Island, Nicobar Island, Christmas Island, Lesser Sunda Islands, Netherlands East Indies (excluding Java and Sumatra), and Dutch Borneo. Other areas were to be the Army's responsibility. If an operational situation required it, the Army and Navy would cooperate in carrying out the responsibilities assigned individually. For example, if the enemy counterattacked areas mentioned as being defense responsibilities of the Navy, the Army would provide necessary forces as quickly as possible to help the Navy repulse any such enemy operation. In such case, the Army would be responsible for all ground operations excepting aerial defense. The Navy was to establish blockades and take action to prevent enemy passage through such places as channels, etc. This had as its objective the prevention of submarines from operating in occupied areas. If such blockades were to be established in areas under Army control, conferences were to be held with the local commander concerned.

The Navy was to be responsible for the sea defense of the main harbors (Singapore, Manila, Soerabaja, Batavia, Davao, Rangoon and Penang) in the important Southern District.

For its sea blockade and harbor defense operations, the Navy was authorized to establish ground defensive installations at necessary points in the responsible areas of the Army after conferring with the local commander concerned. Also, the Navy was authorized to place necessary Naval personnel in such areas.

The escort of vessels under Army responsibility was to be decided between the Army and Navy Commanders concerned.

Army forces were to be used in cooperation with the Navy for the defense of Timor. By the middle of August, the entire island (except air defense) was to be the Army's responsibility using its current strength. An element consisting of an Infantry Battalion as its nucleus would help in the defense after the middle of August. The entire force of the Army on Timor was to be withdrawn by the end of the year unless a great change developed.

Establishment of Air Bases in Important Southern Zones

Air bases were necessary in the coming operations and for protection of the important Southern areas. From June on, air bases were being set up in such places as Singapore (key base), French Indo-China, Thailand, Burma, Malay, Sumatra, Java and the Philippines. Planes were to be repaired and supplied at these local bases. It was necessary to increase the local supply capacities to satisfy requirements of these bases.

Air lines were to be established with special attention paid to security for the main lines which would provide liaison between the military air bases and routes of communication within the Southern Co-prosperity Sphere. These air lines were to be:

1. Formosa--Philippines--Eastern Borneo--Java Line
2. Formosa--Philippines--Western Borneo--Singapore Line
3. Hongkong--Southern French Indo-China--Eastern Malay--Sumatra--Java Line
4. Hongkong--Northern French Indo-China--Thailand--Western Malay--Sumatra Line
5. Philippines--Southern French Indo-China--Thailand--Burma Line

Line of Communication (Logistical Support)

The Army General Staff acted upon the following principles regarding the Line of Communication and traffic during the latter part of June in reorganizing the Southern Army.

The Southern Army commander was to strengthen his local self-support to cut down on his need for supplies from the Homeland. This was to ease the load on the Lines of Communication. Saigon and Singapore were designated to be the normal supply bases for the Southern Army.

The Southern Army commander would control the railway system in the occupied area. After the completion of the transportation network it was expected that the demands for military transportation, resources (raw materials) transportation, and essential public transportation could be met. Except for remote areas, the railway system was to be the principle method of land transportation.

Because of critical shipping shortages, it became necessary for Imperail General Headquarters to exercise extremely close control of ships operating to and from the Southern area (excepting Saigon and Singapore) carrying operational cargo to fulfill requirements as ordered by Imperial Headquarters. Though ships used were designated and handled in operations by the Shipping Transportation command, they were dispatched as being under direct control of Imperial General Headquarters. This was to prevent area commanders from taking control of them while they were operating in their territories. The shortage of transports was an operational problem in the consolidation of occupied areas.

The Southern Army commander was responsible for the inter-area transportation in the South which included transportation to the Naval Administration area and the Philippines except for areas specified later. In addition, he was responsible for intra-area transportation (except the Philippines). For this purpose, he was authorized to use the local agencies of the Shipping Transportation command stationed in the Southern area.

The Southern Army commander had supreme jurisdiction over non-military communications (signal) in the occupied areas. Each subordinate commander was responsible for handling these communications in his area. Steps were to be taken by the Southern Army commander to reorganize the non-military communications (signal) to relieve the Army Signal Unit's responsibilities.

The Chekiang-Kiangsi Operation

During this same period, US Army planes took off from aircraft carriers on the Pacific Ocean and attacked the Homeland on 18 April while enroute to bases in China. Imperial Headquarters decided to prevent such enemy activities by occupying enemy airfields in Central China at Lishui, Kanhsien, and Yushan.

The China Expeditionary Army commander was given orders during the latter part of April to begin operations which would destroy these main bases, especially in the direction of Chekiang.

The Chekiang-Kiangsi Operations were begun on 10 June and completed by early July.

International agreements concluded during this period included: the Japan-French Indo China Pact, 8 December; Japan-Germany-Italy Non-Separate-Peace Pact, 11 December; and, Japan-Thailand Offensive and Defensive Allaince, 21 December.

PART II Second Stage (July - December 1942)

Suspension of the Fiji, Samoa and New Caledonia Operations

The situation was quiet in the Southwest area during the last half of 1942. However, enemy counterattacks became more and more intense in the Southeast. A major development broke when a strong enemy force assaulted and occupied Guadalcanal and Tulagi Island on 7 August.

Because of the heavy losses sustained in the Midway Sea Battle, our remaining Combined Fleet found it disadvantageous to attack enemy land bases after July. This put Japan in a bad operational position. A plan to reduce this disadvantage was developed. Cooperation was to be undertaken with Germany and Italy in connection with their operations in Northern Africa and possible Near East operations. This plan, which was believed more favorable for our surface forces, called for our destroying enemy ships and interrupting enemy reinforcement efforts throughout the Western Indian Ocean area.

In July, Imperial General Headquarters, after considering the above factors, decided to suspend the second operations against New Caledonia, Fiji, Samoa and Midway. On 11 July, the 17th Army was relieved from its assignment to occupy New Caledonia, Fiji and Samoa. New orders were issued for it to occupy and secure Port Moresby in a coordinated land and sea operation with the Navy and carry on with its campaign toward Eastern New Guinea. Changes in the 17th Army's Operational Outline included:

1. The Objective was to be occupation of such strategic positions as Port Moresby and such mopping-up operations as were necessary to be carried out against enemy forces in eastern New Guinea. Control of the Coral Sea was to be directed from these areas plus the Solomons.

2. Strength to be used consisted of the main body of the 17th Army (approximately six infantry battalions as the nucleus); a unit centered on the 8th Naval Fleet; and, a unit centered on the 25th Air Flotilla.

3. The general strategy to be used called for the main body of the Army to capture Port Moresby and airfields in the vicinity from the direction of the Buna-Kokoda Road area. Part of the Army unit was to land, if necessary, in the vicinity of Port Moresby to help the ground advance during its final stages. The Navy was to destroy enemy air power in the Port Moresby area, check enemy ships in the North Coral Sea, and protect our transport units. It was to cooperate closely in support of ground movements. During or after the Port Moresby offensive operation, Eastern New Guinea and other strategic points were to be secured and occupied at appropriate times. Among these, Navy units, composed chiefly of the Navy Land Force and others, were to occupy outlying islands and strategic points along the North coast.

On 21 July the South Sea Detachment began landing on Buna and started the Eastern New Guinea Operation.

Conduct of Guadalcanal Operation

The Army General Staff of Imperial General Headquarters had never been informed by the Navy Section regarding a Naval Force stationed in Guadalcanal, Tulagi, etc. of the Southern Solomon area. This information was first received from the Navy Section when reports were received revealing an enemy counterattack in those areas on 7 August.

Approximately 30 enemy transports escorted by 2 aircraft

carriers, 1 battleship, 10 or more cruisers, and a large number of destroyers started landing operations on Tulagi and Guadalcanal on 7 August. After pushing back our units consisting of several hundred soldiers in Tulagi and 300 soldiers plus 2,000 airfield laborers in Guadalcanal, the enemy occupied Tulagi Harbor, and the Naval Airfield on Guadalcanal.

After the Army General Staff received this report, the Ichiki Detachment (in reserve on Guam Island) was ordered on 10 August to proceed to Truk and become a part of the 17th Army command. The Aoba Detachment which had been transferred to the 14th Army on 20 July was ordered returned to the command of the 17th Army. On 13 August, the 17th Army commander was given orders to continue operations in Eastern New Guinea and, simultaneously, recapture important Solomon Islands areas.

The 17th Army was to execute offensive operations against Port Moresby according to plan, as quickly as possible. It was to recapture important areas in the Solomons, in cooperation with the Navy. This was planned to take advantage of the successful results obtained in the First Solomon Sea Battle (Battel of Savo Island). In that battle, our 8th Fleet claimed sinking of 8 enemy cruisers and 6 destroyers.

The strength to be used for these operations included the 17th Army (composed of approximately 13 Infantry Battalions), and a unit composed mainly of the 8th Fleet and the 11th Air Fleet plus main strength of the 2d and 3d Fleets.

Part of the present 17th Army was to depart at once and attack the enemy on Guadalcanal in cooperation with the Navy. Strategic points on the island, especially the airfield, were to be recaptured. Efforts were to be made for an attack to quickly recapture Tulagi. The Port Moresby Offensive Operation was to be carried out as planned and the campaign against Eastern New Guinea was to be continued at the same time.

The first echelon of the Ichiki Detachment was transferred by destroyers and landed on Guadalcanal 18 August. An attack was launched on 20 August against the enemy but was ineffective. On this same date, approximately 30 enemy planes started operations from the Naval airfield which they had captured.

The second echelon of the Ichiki Detachment and a part of the Kawaguchi Detachment were to land on Guadalcanal on 28 August. The detachments being transported were assaulted on the same day by planes and suffered heavy damages. This interruption caused a one day delay in the landing operations. These two detachments had inadequate signal facilities and contact with Army Headquarters in Rabaul had to be channeled through Navy outlets causing delays and confusion in operations control.

The Army General Staff issued orders on 29 August placing the 2d Division in the Order of Battle for the 17th Army. It was formerly stationed in Java under command of the 16th Army.

The same day the Army General Staff revised the operational outline of the 17th Army for the recapture operation of the Solomon area and the campaign against Port Moresby by increasing the number of infantry battalions to be used by 5, making a total of 18 as the nucleus. There were to be no changes in Navy strength. Priority was given the recapture of Guadalcanal. Next in importance was Talagi. This was a shift away from the previous plan which called for concurrent execution of the Solomons and New Guinea operations.

Rabi Airfield in the Miline Bay area was to be secured during this revised operation. According to plan after the recapture of the Solomons, the Navy strength was to be diverted to New Guinea and our air forces were to attack enemy air forces there.

Ground forces were to advance southward from Kokoda. They were to occupy the Port Moresby Airfields Group in a joint operation with the Task Force which was to be landed at Port Moresby through cooperation of Army and Navy Units.

The Kawaguchi Detachment reinforced with three Infantry Battalions from the 2d Division (Aoba Detachment) on 12 September began an attempt to take the airfield but were thrown back without attaining their objective and received heavy losses. The enemy force was estimated to be a US Marine Division with a strength of approximately 10,000 men and this number seemed to be increasing.

During the middle part of September, the South Sea Detachment in Eastern New Guinea routed two enemy battalions. After crossing the steep Stanley Mountain Ranges, the Detachment prepared for the next step in its operations.

On 18 September, the Army General Staff made another change in the operational outline for conducting operations in the Southeast area.

Following an increase in Army strength and materiel, combined Army and Navy forces were to capture Guadalcanal Airfield. While waiting for reinforcements, the Navy was to prevent enemy personnel and supplies from being brought into the Solomons.

Before the beginning of the Port Moresby Operation, Rabi Airfield was to be taken by joint action of the Army and Navy.

The Navy was to strengthen and complete airfields in the Solomons and Eastern New Guinea.

After recapture of important areas in the Solomons and Eastern New Guinea, the following outlying points were to be secured.

- Solomon Islands (Includes San Critobal and Rennel Island)
- Louisiade Archipelago
- Rabi, Samarai Vicinity
- Port Moresby Vicinity (including KID Airfield)
- The coastal area of Papua Gulf was to be secured if the situation permitted.

After attack preparations for Guadalcanal had been made, the 17th Army (with the 2d Division as the nucleus) started an attack on 24 October. Due to enemy air superiority, the attack was a failure.

In Eastern New Guinea, the South Sea Detachment encountered supply trouble on the Stanley Mountain Ranges. Causes were given as enemy air superiority and rugged, mountainous terrain. The operation was a failure and the detachment was finally ordered to withdraw back to the right bank of the Kumusi River.

Situation Review and Plans (October 1942)

The Army General Staff studied the situation and concluded that China, the Indian Ocean, the Southwestern and Southeastern Pacific Ocean, or the Northeast area would be the enemy counterattack area. Necessary countermeasures were essential to meet the threat of enemy counterattacks apparent in each area. However, it was estimated that the enemy would not attempt a large scale air raid operation from the China bases as yet. This view was based on the enemy's difficulty in building up the necessary number of planes and amounts of fuel. Also, it was considered the development stage of enemy air bases had not advanced far enough.

Weather conditions in the Aleutian Islands probably would prevent the enemy from opening up large scale counterattack operations except during March, April, May, September, or October.

The Southeast Pacific appeared to be the most likely position from which the enemy might launch a counterattack. Reason for this was that Australia and its surrounding islands were connected to the US by a chain of islands and made the Southeast Pacific a very formidable position. Throughout this area, the enemy was able to deploy large air, ground and naval forces. This allowed them to threaten our command of the sea in the West Pacific, recapture our Southern Occupational area, and occupy our South Sea Islands. Air raids could be carried out easily against our important resources areas.

After a thorough study of the situation, we decided that the enemy probably would attack this Southeast Pacific area and would start a regular counterattack after deploying strength. This was considered to be a potentially decisive battle between Japan and US forces in this strategic area.

Taking the above factors into consideration, the Army General Staff planned to set up a command system to strengthen the fighting power for the Southeast Pacific area and especially for operations against the Solomon Islands. The 8th Area Army was to take charge of the Southeast Pacific Area Army operations in general. The 17th Army, under the command of the 8th Area Army, was assigned the Solomon Area Operations. The newly established 18th Army, also under the 8th Area Army, was assigned the New Guinea Area Operations. The 51st Division and necessary units under direct Army control were to be reinforced for another attack against Guadalcanal. Also, necessary Army Air Force Units were to be assigned.

It was believed that several more division would be necessary to carry out the operations in the Southeast area, including New Guinea. However, the choice of divisions and areas from which they would be taken were to be decided only after careful overall study of the operational situation for the coming year.

Southeast Area Operations (November - December 1942)

About the middle of November, in an effort to rebuild the strength of the 17th Army whose offensive on 24 October had failed, the Army General Staff tried sending by convoy approximately ten fast transports with reinforcements and supplies. However, the ships were sunk on 14 November. Neither supply or personnel transports got through because of the heavy enemy air bombardment. Attempts to use small craft also failed, making supply for Guadalcanal almost impossible. It was decided that the 17th Army should maintain its present positions until the 8th Area Army had an opportunity to prepare for a large-scale operation. During this time effective air operations preparations were vital to secure important positions in both the Solomons and New Guinea. Important in the preliminary plans for the coming operation was the fact that major points near our present positions on Guadalcanal should be secured. Strategic positions at Lae, Salamaua, and Buna were to be secured in New Guinea. Air Bases were to be constructed on the Solomons regardless of cost.

On 16 November, the Army General Staff issued the Order of Battle for the 8th Area Army, consisting of the 17th Army (2d, 38th and 51st Divisions as its main strength) and the 18th Army (South Sea Detachment and 41st Infantry Regiment as its main strength.)

The 8th Area Army commander was ordered to cooperate with the Navy in the occupation of the Solomons. At the same time, he was to secure selected positions in New Guinea and prepare for the coming operation. Meanwhile, the Navy had decided to employ a large part of its Combined Fleet in the coming operation.

In the overall operation, the Army and Navy were to cooperate first in stopping enemy air power in the Solomon area. At the same time, operational preparations for the Guadalcanal area were to be completed. The enemy was to be annihilated and Guadalcanal

Airfield to be recaptured. Also, Tulagi and other strategic parts of the Solomons were to be attacked and captured.

Another phase of the above operation called for important points of New Guinea to be secured by a joint Army and Navy effort. Preparations were to be made for the next operation in that area.

To gain our objectives it was necessary to strengthen our fighting power and secure the key offensive points on Guadalcanal. Simultaneously with the Army-Navy effort to stop enemy air activities, each important occupied position's defensive ability had to be strengthened, especially against air attack. Construction of necessary airfields by the middle part of December was established as an objective, too. As these airfields were completed, we were to eliminate the enemy's air superiority over Guadalcanal.

Taking advantage of the above operation, the transportation of munitions and reinforcement were to be started and plans made to complete operational preparations by the middle part of January. Then, enemy airfields and areas west of the airfields would be attacked and occupied by using all the strength necessary. After this, Tulagi and other important parts of the Solomons were to be taken.

At the same time, the Army and Navy would strive to establish selected stable operational points in New Guinea near Lae, Salamaua, and Buna. More relay and operational airfields for New British Island and New Guinea were to be established.

On 27 November, the Army General Staff ordered the 6th Air Division to support the 8th Area Army. The 6th Air Division commander was to be in joint command, under the 8th Area Army, in charge of air units.

Many difficulties were encountered in making preparations. Transportation of munitions and reinforcements by destroyers and smaller craft became very difficult, due to enemy air superiority.

Our supplies steadily decreased. This situation caused a great difference in strength to develop between our units and those of the enemy on Guadalcanal.

The 8th Area Army had expected munitions to be transported for Guadalcanal operations. They were needed for use in recapturing important positions on the Solomons according to the operational outline. However, the Navy was constantly encountering enemy air and sea attacks. At the same time, the Army had difficulty in establishing airfields. Meanwhile, the enemy increased its air and sea strength, daily. Imperial General Headquarters found it very hazardous and difficult to carry out its prearranged plan.

If Imperial General Headquarters were to go ahead with the operation according to the old plan, it was indicated that a ship tonnage of 3,000,000 tons must be newly requisitioned. This was not possible because of the effect it would certainly have on the overall National Economy. Past and predicted future losses would have a disastrous effect on the balance in the National Mobilization of Materiel. These were statistical facts. From the appearance of things, important points in the rear areas would be left in very vulnerable positions if strength were diverted from them to the front line. This could be a continuing and dangerous drain on our reserves.

Taking into consideration these difficulties, Imperial General Headquarters decided on 31 December to give up the recapture plan for the Southern Solomons.

Before the above change was made, on 21 December, the Army General Staff changed the order of battle for the 8th Area Army. The 41st Division, and the 21st Independent Mixed Brigade were assigned. The 6th and 20th Divisions were assigned to the 17th Army and the 51st Division was assigned to the 18th Army.

Changes in Other Area Operations Caused by Solomons Difficulties

During the middle part of November, Indo-China Army headquarters had been established. Plans were drawn up to strengthen the defense in French Indo-China and the South Pacific area by revoking the return order for the 5th Division to the Homeland.

Since attacks against India had been suspended, we anticipated difficulties in the program for the Southwest area. This made it essential to adopt a plan to tighten defense there. The necessary personnel and fortifications were increased at major points along the Indo-Burma Border, and in Andaman, Nicobar, Sumatra and Java. This was a move to fill a void caused by the transfer of Army-Navy Air and Navy Surface Forces from the Southwest area to the Southeast. Patrol of the Indian Ocean was assumed by the Army Air Force. Burma Area Army headquarters was established to strengthen the command system.

From a defensive viewpoint, the Lesser Sunda Islands, Tanimbar, Aroe Island and Western New Guinea (near Australia) were vulnerable spots. On 15 October, to cover these weak spots, the Army General Staff ordered the Southern Army to divert personnel to these areas. The 48th Division was transferred from Java to Timor and Soemba Islands. The 5th Division was transferred from Malay to the Tanimbar-Aroe area. 19th Army headquarters was established at Timor and Western New Guinea. This reduced the defensive area responsibilities of the 16th Army stationed in Java.

Public order in the Philippines area was extremely disorderly. Its continuance would not help the situation if the enemy began a counterattack. An Independent Garrison Unit was stationed there to take steps toward straightening out the public disorder by spring.

Miscellaneous Actions During Second Stage

Order of battle for the 3d Air Army was issued on 10 July attaching it to the Southern Army. This was the result of the general reorganization.

After the Chekiang Operation on 28 July, the China Expeditionary Army had been ordered to take the strategic points of Chinhua Vicinity. On 3 September, Army General Staff had ordered the China Expeditionary Army to prepare the start of the Chungking Operation previously mentioned. Later, on 10 December, it was ordered to suspend the preparation.

On 23 September, the Northern Army had been ordered to dispatch, temporarily, part of its force to Central Chishima Archipelago to strengthen that garrison.

The Northern Army was ordered to secure the strategic points in the Attu Island Vicinity, with a part of the Chishima Fortress Infantry Unit on 20 October. That unit was placed under the 5th Fleet commander.

The order of battle for the North Sea Detachment was revoked on 24 October and the order of battle for the North Sea Garrison (composed mainly of the main force of one Infantry Fortress Unit and three Infantry Battalions) was drawn up. The North Sea Garrison was to come under the 5th Fleet commander, and was to occupy and secure the strategic points in the Aleutians.

Line of Communication (Logistical Support) During First Phase

During the first stage of the First Phase, operations of the Line of Communication were excellent and very few interruptions were noticed. It was not necessary for Imperial General Headquarters to watch the transportation activities directly because things were working out so smoothly. However, about the beginning of the second stage of the operation, Imperial General Headquarters was compelled to take over the Line of Communication as described, previously. As the Southeast Operation became more critical, the Line of Communication to and from the Southeast Operation became practically another main role for the Army Line of Communication.

Difficulties encountered included such things as: a way to transport supplies in view of enemy air superiority; study of special field rations; way of counteracting Malaria; and establishment of local self-support. These were all difficult problems. The biggest was to avoid enemy attack due to their air and sea superiority. Such enemy interruptions made Palau a much more important intermediate supply base. Due to heavy losses encountered by our transport ships of various types, we were having difficulty in finding a way to produce enough ships to replace the losses. During November and December of 1943, the increased requisiton for more ships began to affect the stability of the National Economy. This also affected the capacity of the Line of Communication to the China Expeditionary Army and caused suspension of attack operations toward the interior of China.

At the close of the 1st Phase of Operations in the Southern area, we realized it was necessary to complete our supply situation for Manchuria. The necessary requirements for battle were to be stockpiled. About the end of October, the Inspectorate of Supply for the Kwantung Army was established. A Munitions Transport Control Detachment was established at important harbors of Southern Korea, Northern Kyushu, Seto Island Sea, and Hokkaido to strengthen the main transportation lines to the continent.

CHAPTER V

Second Phase of the War

(January - August 1943)

Situation Estimate Regarding Enemy Offensive Potential

The estimate by Army General Staff of the situation at the end of 1942 concluded that several potential enemy offensive areas existed.

In the Southeast area, it was anticipated that the enemy planned to attack Rabaul since it was the operational base for our Army, Navy and Air Forces. To accomplish this task the enemy would start in the Solomon Islands area by trying to drive our units off Guadalcanal Island and then advance northward through the other Solomon Islands. In the Eastern New Guinea area, the enemy would secure the Buna Vicinity and attack Lae and Salamaua from the sea. After penetrating Vitiaz Strait, they would attack Rabaul in a joint operation coordinated with forces from the Solomon Islands. After this, it was estimated the enemy would attack the Philippine Islands by using the northern coast of New Guinea as a route of advance.

In the area North of Australia, centering around the Dutch East Indies, the enemy was expected to make a synchronized attack on Aroe and Tanimbar Islands. At the same time, they probably would take action to advance along the western coast of New Guinea to attack and control that area.

In the India area, the enemy was expected to try immediately for recapture of Akyab and to strengthen air operations. It was anticipated that toward the end of the rainy season they would plan to capture Burma by a coordinated attack from the east and west, with the main force of the British-India Army operating toward the Imphal area and the Chungking Army operating toward the Shan Sector. Meanwhile, the enemy was expected to attack the strategic points on Andaman Island and secure sea superiority in the Bay of Bengal and the Andaman Sea.

Expansion of submarine operations throughout the entire South Sea area was anticipated. Attempts at bombings of our important natural resource areas were expected from the enemy in an effort to check any strengthening of our fighting power.

In the general situation of the Southeast area (center of future operations), sea and air superiority over Guadalcanal and Southeastern New Guinea Islands had been captured toward the end of 1942 by the enemy. This was due primarily to losses suffered by our Navy, especially in air strength and auxiliary ships. At the same time, the enemy increase in Navy and Air Forces had affected control of the sea and air. It became increasingly difficult to send men and munitions to the various Army and Navy Units on Guadalcanal and Eastern New Guinea. After mid-December, even transportation of minimum quantities of badly needed supplies by small craft on moonless nights became difficult. The units on Guadalcanal and Eastern New Guinea struggling against starvation, combat fatigue and superior enemy forces were in a serious predicament.

More and more ships were needed due to the longer sea supply routes, but the total number of available ships was decreasing daily due to an unexpectedly high ship loss. This caused a sharp decrease in the number of ships to transport raw materials which were needed for the National Mobilization Program and were vital to the basic requirements of the nation's fighting power.

In Europe, Germany was entering its second winter of war against the USSR and was no longer able to carry out its operations in the Stalingrad area. It had turned to defensive tactics after discontinuing its offensive drive. At the same time, the fighting power of Allied Forces increased in both the east and west of the European Theater as well as the Far East.

Faced with these facts Imperial General Headquarters concluded it would have to abandon all thoughts of recapturing Guadalcanal Island and postpone all immediate plans to secure Eastern New Guinea, especially Port Moresby.

Amendments to Operational Plans for Southeast Area

Solomon Island Operations for the recapture of Guadalcanal Island were to be stopped. All units there were to be evacuated between the end of January and the beginning of February. Later, the Solomon Islands north of New Georgia and Isabel Islands were to be secured.

In the New Guinea area, the operational bases at Lae, Salamaua, Madang and Wewak would be rapidly reinforced or established. Important positions in Northeast New Guinea (generally north of the Stanley Mountain Range) were to be attacked and secured. Preparations were to be made there for future operations. According to the situation, units in the Buna area were to withdraw to the Salamaua area and secure necessary positions.

Under this operational plan (established 31 Dec 42), the front line on the Guadalcanal Islands was to be withdrawn. However, there was no change in the plan to secure a string of operational bases connecting the important positions between the Solomon Islands (Rabaul as the center) and Northeast New Guinea (Lae, Salamaua, Madang, etc as nucleus positions). The new plan was organized to avoid a disadvantageous battle on the remote islands in view of the trend of the war. By this new plan, the Japanese force yielded the offensive and assumed defensive positions in the Solomons area. It was a major turning point of the war in this area.

During the Second Phase of operations, enemy counterattacks became increasingly active against the outer boundary of the operational areas such as the Southeast area, Burma, the Aleutian, etc.

Meanwhile, the strength of the Japanese Navy and Air Force was declining continuously, a fact true since the outbreak of war. This forced us to switch to defensive tactics and strengthen the important positions captured in various East Asia engagements.

In the Southeast area and in the Solomon Islands, plans for the recapture of Guadalcanal had been abandoned. Units on the Island were withdrawn during the early part of February 1943. In the New Guinea area, units in the Buna area withdrew to the Salamaua area to prepare for a counterattack. Rabaul and other strategic points in Northeast New Guinea were to be used as operational bases. In June, the enemy landed near Rendova to attack our air base at Munda. After stubborn resistance, the Japanese Force retired to Boungainville Island.

In the New Guinea area, forces at the important Lae and Salamaua areas were withdrawn during mid-September since there was no hope of maintaining those positions. The forces began to concentrate in the Finschhafen area on the west coast of Vitiaz Strait.

In the Burma area (Southwest Area Front) an element of the enemy in the Akyab area had planned an offensive operation to begin about the middle of January. Our Army, however, took the initiative and upset those plans. There was no change for the Northern and Central part of Burma except the enemy preparations for a general counterattack scheduled to begin at the end of the rainy season.

In the North-of-Australia area, there were no immediate plans for an enemy offensive before the end of August. However, the enemy was interfering with our defensive preparations by pushing air and submarine warfare. Transportation to these isolated islands became increasingly difficult.

In the Northeast area, the US Army landed on Attu Island on 12 May. Although our Army and Navy units resisted stubbornly, they were annihilated by 29 May. All units on Kiska withdrew safely to Paramushiro on 1 August.

In South China, the China Expeditionary Army attacked strategic points on Haikang Peninsula and entered the French Concession at Kuangchou Bay during the middle part of February. Our forces had anticipated the enemy intention to increase activities of their air force in China and to start a drive into South China with their Chungking Army.

Orders and Operational Principles for Southeast Area

Orders issued on 4 January to the 8th Area Army commander stated:

1. Imperial General Headquarters plans to establish a more favorable situation in the Southeast Pacific area to carry out the war.
2. The 8th Area Army commander will occupy and secure important positions on the Solomon and Bismarck Islands in cooperation with the Navy. He will do the same to obtain important points in New Guinea and begin preparations for future operations in that area.

The Army General Staff ordered the 8th Area Army to conform to the following Army and Navy agreement regarding the operations in the Southeast Pacific area: the objective of the Southeast Pacific Operations was to gain a more favorable situation in that area; the Army and Navy would first cooperate in making coordinated attacks and occupying selected important positions; in the Solomon Islands area, those islands north of New Georgia and Isabel Islands must be occupied; and, in the Eastern New Guinea area, important positions in Northeastern New Guinea must be occupied for use in future operations.

All Army and Navy units were to withdraw from Guadalcanal Islands between the end of January and the beginning of February. All available facilities were to be used in accomplishing this.

Defense of important positions mentioned in the preceeding paragraphs was to be strengthened. Responsibility for this was to be divided between the Army and the Navy. The Northern Solomon Islands (Shortland, Bougainville, and Buka Islands) were to be controlled by the Army. New Georgia and Isabel Islands were to be controlled by the Navy.

In the Guadalcanal Islands area, Navy units were to continue air warfare and attempt to cut off enemy supply lines in cooperation with submarine operations.

Operational bases at Lae, Salamaua, Madang, Wewak, etc were to be strengthened and important positions north of the Stanley Mountain Range in Northeastern New Guinea were to be attacked and occupied. Preparations for future operations, especially against Port Moresby, were to be made. In the Buna area, units were to withdraw toward Salamaua at the proper moment to occupy vital positions.

The Army Air Force was to cooperate with units in New Guinea in ground operations and defense, to protect ground transportation of supplies in the New Guinea area, and to obtain air superiority by annihilating the enemy air force in the Eastern New Guinea area. The latter was to be done in close cooperation with the Navy.

The Navy Air Force was to carry out air operations in the Solomon Islands and New Guinea. In the withdrawal from Guadalcanal Islands, the Army and Navy Air Forces were to cooperate in destroying the enemy air force regardless of former orders.

Working with the Southeast area Fleet, 8th Area Army made the necessary preparations to comply with these orders.

General Operational Progress During Period

Between 1 and 8 February, the entire Army and Naval strength, consisting of some ten thousand men, withdrew to Bougainville Island by destroyer. The evacuation required three separate trips, each under extremely hazardous conditions.

Previously, on 5 January, the 8th Area Army commander had transported an element of the 18th Army (part of the 51st Division) from Rabaul to Lae to attack important points in the Lae and Salamaua area. This unit landed and attacked the enemy at Wau but the attack failed due to lack of men and munitions. The commander realized it was imperative to reinforce the Lae area. To fulfill the requirement, he committed 18th Army headquarters and the main body of the 51st Division which had been located at Rabaul. In transit, on 3 March, this group was attacked by approximately 130 enemy fighter planes and bombers at Vitiaz Straits. There, the majority of the convoy ships were sunk. After this, it was impossible to send men and munitions to the Lae area by surface transport. They had to land at either the rear bases in Hansa Bay or near Wewak. Then they advanced to the front line area by either march on foot or small boats even though interference by enemy airplanes, torpedo boats and the lack of roads in the uncivilized areas made it difficult.

Units in the Buna area withdrew by sea and land to Salamaua simultaneously with units from Guadalcanal Island. During mid-March, the 2d Division which had suffered heavily from operations on Guadalcanal Island was ordered to withdraw to the Philippines to reorganize.

During the first part of April, elements of air forces from each area were dispatched to the Southeast area in an effort to strengthen the combat capacity of the 6th Air Division.

In June, the Army made plans to capture the enemy air base which was under construction at Bena-Bena, Eastern New Guinea. To carry out this operation it was necessary to further strengthen the air force. Accordingly, the main force of the 7th Air Division (previously stationed in the North-of-Australia area) and the 1st Raiding Brigade (a paratroop unit stationed in Japan Proper) were dispatched to the Southeast area.

In late July, the 4th Air Army headquarters was organized to strengthen the air command structure in the Southeast area. This headquarters was established to be in charge of the 6th and 7th Air Divisions and operated under control of the 8th Area Army commander.

In the Solomon Islands area, the enemy landed near Rendova (Central part of the Solomon Islands) toward the end of June and attacked Munda Airfield. In the same area, Army and Navy Units (with the Southeast Detachment as a nucleus) fought bravely but due to inadequate strength were defeated and forced to adopt guerrilla operations. They withdrew to Bougainville Island from Colombangara and Vella Lavella Island toward the end of September.

If our forces were to attack Bena Bena in the New Guinea area, according to the basic plan, the 18th Army commander considered the attack would not be successful because of enemy air superiority. It would be impossible to hold this area after ground forces made an attack. 8th Area Army and the Army General Staff acknowledged this. As a result, the attack was not carried out. Since units at Lae and Salamaua seemed to be unable to hold their positions, they were ordered to withdraw toward the Finschhafen area, west of Vitiaz Strait at the end of August. The New Guinea force was also ordered to strengthen the defense of Madang area.

Important positions in Northest New Guinea area and near Rabaul were located ideally to serve as interrelated operational bases which would allow us to make full use of Navy and Air fighting power in the defense line. Although the Army and the Navy did their best to hold these positions, the strategic points along the front lines gradually fell into enemy hands. The general situation for the Southeast area became critical when it appeared that Rabaul would be isolated as a result of the heavy reinforcement of enemy air bases at Lae and Salamaua.

Central Pacific Area Operations

When the situation in the Southeast area turned for the worse, there was an increased possibility of an enemy attack on the isolated islands in the Central Pacific area, such as the Gilberts, Marshalls, Marcus, etc. The Army dispatched troops to the following places to reinforce Navy maintained defenses. The 1st South Sea Garrison Unit for the Gilbert Islands and the 2d South Sea Garrison Unit for Marcus Island were sent by orders issued in mid-April. The 3d South Sea Garrison Unit for Wake Island and the 4th South Sea Garrison Unit for the Gilbert Islands were sent by orders issued in mid-June. Units at Marcus Island were under the command of the Yokosuka Naval District. Other units in the Gilberts were under the 4th Fleet commander.

On 17 July, the destination of the 4th South Sea Garrison Unit was changed to Bougainville Island while en route to the Gilbert Islands because of the war situation which required additional troops for the defense of Bougainville in the action progressing there.

Orders and Operational Principles for Southwest Area

Toward the end of February 1943, the Army General Staff decided upon an Army operation plan for the Southwest area to be used during the year. It provided that important positions in the Southwest area were to be secured in cooperation with the Navy. Collection of intelligence informmation was to be stressed. Strengthening of military preparedness was vital in this area. If the enemy attacked, the Army, Navy and Air Forces were to concentrate their fighting power wherever necessary to destroy the enemy and their fighting morale. If the general situation were favorable, ground operations against Northeastern India were to be carried out. Main efforts for operations and defense were to be concentrated on Burma and important natural resources areas. Public order was to be enforced in the Philippines.

To accomplish the objectives of the operational plan, areas occupied currently in the Southwest area were to be maintained and safe-guarded. In Burma, the Tenasserim area and the area from the Salween River and to a line on the west linking Myitkina, Kamaing, Kalewa, Gangaw and Akyab were to be secured.

Battle preparedness should be strengthened, immediately, in the sectors having sea supply routes where enemy planes could attack (Burma and Banda Sea areas). Also, the Palembang and the Pangkalan-Brandan areas were to be strengthened, immediately.

Counterattack operations in the Akyab area provided that enemy units attacking along the Akyab front were to be destroyed by a force organized from elements of the 55th Division. This unit was to proceed toward the Buthidaung and Kaungdaw Lines. To assure the security of Akyab, ground supply routes were to be established. Also, protection of sea supply routes was to be increased. The fortifications in the area were to be strengthened and work on air bases completed.

Our counterattack operation against the anticipated main enemy attack in the Burma area called for a strong element of forces to secure important lines along the border area. The main forces were to concentrate at the Mandalay and Toungoo Road area and take the offensive at necessary points by rapid movements designed to achieve the separate destruction of the Chungking and British Indian Armies. It was considered especially important to carry out a major decisive battle with the British Indian Army and to annihilate it in the defile of the Arakan Mountain Range. To execute this operation, special attention had to be paid to the completion of transportation facilities, fortifications and safe-guarding of important communication points. This operation was expected to take place after the start of the dry season. Total military strength scheduled to participate in the Burma Operations was to be about six or seven divisions.

After the rainy season, if conditions were favorable, a ground offensive was to be launched against the Tinsukia area, northeast of India. Objective of this was to cut off air transport (Flying the Hump) reinforcement of the Chungking Army.

In the field of air operations, before the start of the rainy season, an element of the air force was to carry out surprise attacks against the enemy air force surrounding Burma at opportune moments and make every effort to minimize losses. This was to be an effort to eliminate enemy air superiority over Burma. At the same time the air force was to cooperate with offensive operations in the Akyab area.

After the rainy season, the main force of the Air Army was to destroy the enemy air force in East India and check future reinforcements. Whenever the enemy took the ground offensive, the main force of the Air Army was to cooperate with the 15th Army.

Every effort was to be made to strengthen reconnaissance patrols and equip intelligence units adequately to provide full information regarding enemy intentions. If the enemy made moves to attack, they were to be destroyed by our Air and Navy forces before they could land. Air bases were to be equipped as completely as possible to support this operation. Independent garrison units were to defend sectors in which possible enemy landings were anticipated and were to fortify these vital positions. Strategically located mobile divisions were to be moved in rapidly as reinforcements, where needed, to crush any enemy landings.

Even if the situation turned for the worse, the main groups of air bases, operational bases, etc were to be held and developed to facilitate air operations and future offensive operations. All transportation facilities were to be utilized in sending necessary reinforcements to key areas. It was of major importance that main communication lines be protected from enemy air and naval attacks.

Operations for Malay, Sumatra and Java, called for our forces to be prepared to combat enemy attacks. Special emphasis was to be placed on the defense of the Palembang area. Enemy plans must be intercepted and clearly interpreted. Their aircraft carriers and air bases were to be destroyed before an offensive operations by the enemy could be mounted. The Japanese Army and Navy Air Forces were to accomplish that. All fighter plane units were to be deployed to repel any enemy air attacks.

In other areas, especially Malay and the Philippine Islands, mopping-up operations were to be speeded up. In defense operations for North French Indo-China, if the Chungking Army moved to attack, offensive action was to be taken in the important border areas and the enemy was to be destroyed. Our forces were to have cooperation of the French Indo-China Army.

Troop Activities in Southwest Area Operations

The 54th Division was sent to Java from the Homeland in March and placed under the command of the 16th Army.

At the end of March, as operational conditions in the Burma area became more complex, a Burma Area Army headquarters was established and placed under command of the Southern Army. At the same time, the 31st Division, newly organized in Thailand, was sent to Burma and placed under the command of the 15th Army.

During the middle of January, an element of the enemy along the Akyab Front tried to recapture Akyab but they were repulsed. During the middle of February, the 55th Division took the offensive, defeated the enemy and occupied the Buthidaung area. The enemy plan to recapture Akyab during the dry season was unsuccessful. There were no great changes in the Central and Northern areas of Burma, except for enemy counterattack preparations. This was expected to begin at the start of the dry season.

19th Army Headquarters was organized and placed under command of Southern Army General headquarters on 7 January when it became necessary to strengthen military preparedness for the North-of-Australia area. This was caused by the change in the war situation in the Southeast area at the beginning of 1943. 19th Army headquarters took charge of various units, mostly from the 5th and 48th Division.

On 30 January, the 7th Air Division headquarters was organized and placed under command of the 3d Air Army. It commanded the 3d Air Brigade and other units and was responsible for defense of the North-of-Australia area. In that area, there were no indications of active enemy plans before the end of August. Then, influenced by the strengthening of our military forces and positions, they began taking precautions against potential offensive plans of ours. The enemy began to upset our plans by cutting off sea transportation, causing difficulty in supply and personnel movements to isolated islands.

In Southwestern China, enemy activities were quiet although there were indications they were planning to send a strong force to Burma and Yunnan areas from the Chungking and Changsha areas.

At the end of August, the 54th Division was moved to Burma from Java since operations in Burma were to start at the beginning of the dry season.

Troop Activities in Other Areas

At the end of 1942, the 1st Air Division under the command of the 1st Air Army had been organized to strengthen air preparedness in the Northeast area. During the early part of February, it was placed under control of the North Area Army.

The Army General Staff began strengthening defense preparations in the Northeast area, believing that the recapture of Attu and Kiska Islands by the enemy indicated plans for increased activities in that area. On 20 May, the 7th Division was placed under command of the North Area Army commander. On 24 May, Hokkaido was placed on war time defense. In August, the 3d and the 4th Kurile Islands Garrison Units were placed under command of the North Area Army commander and deployed in the Kurile Islands.

In French Indo-China, enemy air raids from China bases increased and an advance by the Chungking Army against French Indo-China was expected. About the middle of January, the Army General Staff decided to solidify control of French Indo-China. At the end of January, orders were issued for the attack and capture of important points on Haikang Peninsula. Also, the French Concession in Kuangchou Bay was to be occupied. These actions were accomplished in mid-February by the China Expeditionary Army.

At the end of February, the China Expeditionary Army was ordered to destroy enemy plans to continue combat and to check activities of the enemy air forces.

In March, the 61st Division was dispatched from Japan Proper to Central China and placed under command of the 13th Army. In June, the 17th Division was assembled at Shanghai to prepare for shipment to the Southeast area.

In the Manchuria area about the middle of June, the 27th Division was transferred from North China and placed under command of the Kwantung Army.

Line of Communication (Logistical Support) During Second Phase

In this phase of the war, it became difficult to manage the Line of Communication because of the unfavorable turn in operations and the increase in ship losses.

In the Southeast area, units were withdrawn from Guadalcanal Island, Burma and Munda Island etc, because of shipping supply difficulties. Our forces tried to transport supplies by establishing land routes and by using small landing craft for supply. Landing craft for this purpose were fitted with fire arms so as to fight enemy torpedo boats. If Rabaul, which was the most important base in the Southeast area, should be isolated it would be necessary to support the fighting strength by a system of self-sufficiency. The Army decided to stockpile operational material immediately in Rabaul. The Army put this plan into effect from the end of August 1943 to the middle of November. The plan for the most part was successful. Because of the serious situation in the Southeast area, it became necessary to strengthen military preparedness in the Western New Guinea and Moluccas areas. The Army General Staff ordered the Southern Army to establish a base in the Halmahera area.

At that time, the various plans of the Southern Army relative to the Lines of Communication and especially the system of self-sufficiency were progressing smoothly. With the development of the critical war situation in the Southeast area and as it became difficult to send out war supplies from Japan Proper, it became necessary to send them from the Southwest area to the Southeast area and to establish a special transportation route for this purpose. The Philippine Islands became even more important as an intermediate base between the Southwest area and Southeast area. Ships from Japan Proper which were to go to the Southeast area via Palau were ordered to use the Philippines harbors as relay points.

CHAPTER VI

Third Phase of the War (September 1943 - June 1944)

PART I First Stage (September 1943 - February 1944)

Situation Review and Estimate of Potential Enemy Plans

During the month of September 1943, considerable activity took place in connection with the war. On 8 September, Italy capitulated, breaking the Tri-Partite Alliance provisions. With development of the critical situation in the Southeast, the shipping losses, aircraft losses, etc, a complete review of the total war picture was made by Imperial General Headquarters and a revised operational plan drawn up. All matters affecting the war were discussed and the final plans were approved through a Council in the Presence of the Emperor on 30 September. General details regarding adjustments in military and governmental policies are included in the following text.

The enemy situation, as interpreted by Imperial General Headquarters in September 1943, concluded that prospective enemy counterattacks would be extremely severe. In the long run, it was estimated that attacks by Allied Forces would be launched against the Axis countries and their satellites. Between the latter part of 1943 and spring and summer of the following year, it was believed the attacks would reach their peak. In the Far East, Britain and the United States would increase pressure on Japan in cooperation with India, Australia and China. Sharp counterattacks were expected in the Southeast. Pressure would be applied at the same time against our Southwest and Northeast areas. Our important occupied areas would be subjected to intensified enemy air and navy attacks. Enemy planning, apparently, was designed to terminate the war in the Far East as quickly as possible.

The Nationalist Army in China, most likely, would continue its fight against us. Activities of China-based enemy air forces would be intensified. The chances of averting war with Russia continued favorable. At the same time, the possibility that the United States would be provided air base facilities in Eastern Russia could not be overlooked.

The Anglo-American front line force was composed of (Sep 1943) approximately 2,500 planes and approximately 23 divisions. Including the strength of its reserves, it was estimated the air force had approximately 6,000 planes and ground force strength of from 70 to 80 divisions.

Estimated Disposition of Enemy Air and Ground Forces

Area	Air Force Strength (No of Planes)		Ground Force Strength (No of Divisions)	
	Frontline	Total Strength	Frontline	Total Strength
Northeastern area	Approx 300	Approx 800	From 2 to 3	Approx 6
Central Pacific area	Approx 200	Approx 1,000		Approx 3
Southeastern area	Approx 1,300	Approx 3,000	Approx 10	Approx 33
Southwestern area	Approx 600	Approx 1,000	Approx 10	Approx 37

Enemy reinforcements in the Pacific Theater would depend largely on the degree to which the enemy expected to establish and maintain a second front in Europe. Also influencing this would be the enemy shipping situation and the degree of progress in the various phases of their preparations for battle. As of September 1943, the enemy was expected to continue concentrating on the European Theater.

Projected Estimate of Enemy Pacific Theater Strength

Period	Air Force Strength (No of Planes)		Ground Force Strength (No of Divisions)	
	Frontline	Total Strength	Frontline	Total Strength
End of 1943	Approx 4,000	Approx 7,700	Approx 35	90 to 100
Middle of 1944	Approx 5,300	Approx 9,000	Approx 43	100 to 110
End of 1944	Approx 7,000	Approx 12,000	Approx 60	110 to 120

The main force of the United States Navy was operating in the area between Hawaii and the Southeast Pacific area. It was divided into several Naval Task Forces. Total strength of the main enemy force included approximately 6 aircraft carriers, 15 battleships and 15 cruisers. Besides these, there were small task-force type units in the Alaska-Aleutian area and in the vicinity of Australia. Approximately 10 converted aircraft carriers were performing the duty of escorts as their principal task.

It was estimated that the United States would have 12 carriers on hand at the end of 1943, and this was expected to increase to 16 in the middle of 1944 and to 18 at end of 1944. Since America's ship building was moving along very smoothly, there could be quite an increase in the number of ships. The enemy's excess shipping tonnage amounted to 2,000,000 tons. The annual increase in shipping tonnage was estimated to be in the vicinity of 4,000,000 to 5,000,000 tons.

The British Navy in the Western Indian Ocean was composed of 1 carrier, 2 converted aircraft carriers, 4 battleships and 10 cruisers as its main strength. Since Italy had capitulated, the possibility of a timely reinforcement of this force by 4 or 5 carriers, a few converted carriers, 2 or 3 battleships and 10 cruisers from the European Theater was expected.

Hawaii, Dutch Harbor (Aleutian), Brisbane and Perth (Australia) were being used as bases for approximately 80 American submarines. About 10 British submarines were located in the Ceylon area with Ceylon as the base.

Beginning about the end of 1943 and extending into 1944, it was estimated the enemy would plan to conduct combined attacks from the east and west in the Pacific area and capture strategic points such as Rabaul in the Southeastern area and Burma, Andaman, Nicobar and Sumatra in the Southwestern area. As part of the over-all Rabaul area operations, following capture of Rabaul the enemy would direct assaults against the South Pacific Mandated Islands and the Philippines area.

As of September 1943, it was believed that the enemy had intentions of launching attacks against the Kurile and Banda Sea areas, of repeatedly bombing Japan and our occupied positions, and of increasing their attacks against our shipping. Probability of large scale enemy assaults, considering their current available carrier force strength, against the Central Pacific Islands was considered unlikely. However, toward the end of the year, enemy attacks in the Gilbert and Nauru areas or in the Wake and Marcus Islands areas in conjunction with attacks in the Rabaul area were quite probable.

Army General Staff Operational Plan Changes

After reviewing and studying the various situations, the Army General Staff considered it necessary to alter its operational plan. This was done on 15 September.

The Army was to cooperate closely with the Navy and direct the operations according to the following plan:

1. From our positions in the Southeastern area, we would strive to destroy the approaching enemy. Our plan would be to carry on a strong delaying action. During this

time, we would complete the construction of defenses extending from the Banda Sea area to the Caroline Islands and increase our counterattacking strength. Powerful attacks were to be thrown against the enemy, and their military intentions were to be anticipated and crushed beforehand.

2. Our positions in the Southwestern area were to be held firmly. For this purpose, the complete destruction of any advancing enemy in the Burma, Andaman, Nicobar and Sumatra areas was essential.

3. While maintaining our positions in China, we would increase our pressure against the enemy and destroy their will to fight. In the north, preparations for battle would be expanded extensively as a threat against any Russian idea of granting air base privileges to the United States. Also, steps would be taken against the United States sea aid route. The Russo-US relationship was to be played down and steps taken to prevent any joint overt action. War with Russia was to be avoided.

4. Defenses of our Homeland, oil regions of the Southwest area and maritime shipping routes were to be strengthened to assure a satisfactory execution of our operational plan.

5. We would make destructive attacks by using raiding tactics deep behind enemy lines extending through numerous areas.

6. Every effort would be made to carry out operations using all available forces in combined efforts, including the Army, Navy and Air Forces strength plus surface transportation facilities.

The above-mentioned plan was necessitated by the foreseeable loss of the zone including eastern New Guinea. Also, in spite of tremendous effort to hold it as a security line, loss of the Northern Solomon Islands in the Southeastern area was expected. Finally, the unfavorable trend of the war in the Southeastern Region, of which Rabaul was the central point, would weaken our position in the Marshall and Gilbert areas. Realizing the uncertainty of holding these areas for a lengthy period, the defensive sphere was contracted to a line extending from the Banda Sea area to the West and East Caroline Islands and Mariana Islands. The line was to be defended using all strength possible. Strength for effective counter-attacks, especially that of the air force, was to be deployed. The aims of these actions were to destroy the enemy completely. The war plan in the Southeastern area was designed as a delaying action.

Following decision on this new operational plan, a Council in the Presence of the Emperor was held on 30 September 1943. The operational concept of Imperial General Headquarters was approved with emphasis on the importance of its successful accomplishment. Military operations were to be as already discussed. Special emphasis was to be placed on a rapid increase in plane production. It was also decided to move for mediation between German and Russia to bring peace. At the same time, ties with Germany would be gightened within limits which would avoid provoking Russia.

Existing International and War Conditions

It was believed the American Army completed its base in the vicinity of Munda (Solomon Islands area) during September 1943. In the latter part of October, the enemy landed in the vicinity of Mono Island (off Bougainville Island). The vicinity of Finschhafen on the western bank of Vitiaz Strait (New Guinea area) was invaded in the latter part of September. At about this time, air and naval operations of both sides reached a climactic stage throughout the

Southeastern area. In ground actions, the enemy met our 17th Army on 1 November when they landed in the vicinity of Torokina (Bougainville Island). At about this time, the naval battle off the shores of Bougainville had begun. During the period between 5 November and 3 December, a naval surface battle, and five great aerial battles were fought in the vicinity of Bougainville Island. Between mid-December and late December, the enemy made landings in the vicinity of Cape Markus and Tuluvu (New Britain Island). On 21 November, the enemy attacked Makin and Tarawa (Gilbert Islands) and by 25 November annihilated our naval land units there. On 1 February 1944, they attacked Kwajalein and Roi (Marshall Group) and destroyed our naval land units by the 6th. On 17 February 1944, an enemy carrier task force struck at Truk and attacked our ships anchored there. Our losses were quite heavy. The US Navy became exceedingly active, and the situation in the Central Pacific area looked very serious. On 29 February, the enemy landed on the Admiralties.

The enemy in the Buthidaung and Maungdaw areas of the southwestern coastal area of Burma was active in offense. Our 55th Division mounted a counterattack but was forced back to the defensive. Since the beginning of February, a newly activated Chinese Nationalist 1st Army, having advanced from the Assam area to Hukawng Valley, was battling our 18th Division.

There were no changes in regard to battle situations in other areas. The numerous penetrations made by the enemy in the different sectors of the Southeastern area had caused operations of the 8th Area Army to be ineffective. With the decline of naval strength and the state of our army operations, future campaign planning for this area appeared useless in relieving the difficult situation facing us.

On 8 September 1943, Italy had surrendered. The capitulation greatly affected the European situation. From November through December, the United States, Britain, Russia and China held the

Cairo Conference and the Teheran Conference. In the Far East, from September through October, the following political agreements were concluded: the signing of the Burma-Japan Alliance Pact; the Declaration of Independence of the Philippine Republic; signing of the Philippine-Japan Alliance Pact; establishment of a provisional government for Free India[1]; and, the signing of the China-Japan Alliance Pact. Within our Homeland, the Ministry of Munitions was established in September, and General Tojo and Admiral Shimada were appointed as Chiefs of Army and Navy General Staff, respectively, in February 1944.

Southeastern, North-of-Australia and Central Pacific Areas Operational Strategy

As a result of a Central Agreement of Imperial General Headquarters, the Army General Staff in accordance with the new operational plan fulfilled its responsibility by issuing necessary orders to the Southern Army and 8th Area Army commanders on 30 September for future operational guidance.

The plan for operations in the Central and South Pacific areas called for a prolonged tactical war in the important regions of the Southeastern area and to complete fortification of positions for counterattacks in the area extending from the North-of-Australia area to the Central Pacific area. At the same time, units were to check any enemy intention of launching an offensive in the area.

---

1. This Free India Provisional Government was an opportune organization with possibilities of furthering the advancement of the Co-Prosperity Sphere. Chandra Bohse, a leader in the India Independence movement, came to Tokyo from Berlin in May 1943. He earnestly requested the Japanese government to support his Independence movement and his plan to establish a provisional government for Free India. Upon getting support from the Japanese government, he flew to Malay and established his government on 21 October 1943. This was recognized by the Japanese two days later. Purpose of the Bohse government was to encourage anti-British movements in India and to establish the independence of India. As the result of Japanese support in his end objectives, his forces cooperated with the Japanese forces in the Burma-Malay Theater. It was his influence with the Indians and the Free India National Army which was made use of by the Japanese to make their operations easier.

The 8th Area Army commander was to cooperate with the Navy and crush the advancing enemy in important sectors of the Southeastern area. This would make an effective delaying action and our over-all operations would be helped considerably. The Southern Army commander was to cooperate with the Navy in expanding preparations for counterattacks in the North-of-Australia area.

Objectives for each responsible Army commander were pointed out to him on the same day as the Central Agreement was concluded which included the previously outlined facts.
The general over-all objectives of the plan included four points:

1. The enemy advancing through the front extending from Eastern New Guinea to the northern part of the Solomon Islands in the Southeastern area was to be crushed, and an all-out delaying action was to be carried out.

2. By about spring of 1944, defenses for the operational bases in important regions extending through the North-of-Australia area and the Caroline and Mariana Islands were to be strengthened. Operational bases in the Philippines area were to be constructed. Preparations by the Army and Navy of air, ground and surface forces for counterattacks were to be speeded up.

3. Bases in the above-mentioned zones were to be used as fortified positions in coordinated counterattacks by forces from the various branches of service in order to defeat any offensives launched by the enemy on its principal fronts. We would make every effort to attack the enemy in advance to prevent the enemy from conducting counterattacks.

4. If the over-all situation permitted, an offensive operation was to be launched from the North-of-Australia

area after the middle of 1944. As to the direction of such an offensive, special studies were to be made and the necessary preparations arranged for.

In the North-of-Australia area, about spring of 1944, the Army and Navy were to cooperate in expediting preparation of operational bases, strengthening of defenses, stockpiling of war supplies, increasing the shipping and constructing a line of communication. These preparations were to be carried out along with defensive action in the area. Urgency in completing preparations as fast as possible was emphasized by the war situation in the Southeastern area.

In the Central Pacific area, about spring of 1944, the Navy was to speed up operational preparations on the Caroline and Mariana Islands. Necessary Army units were to be dispatched along with part of a line of communication unit to the Central Pacific area. They were to cooperate with the Navy in expediting these operational preparations. They were to be placed under Navy officers.

Army General Staff directives were issued to Army commanders concerned covering orders and the Central Agreement. Principles in these directives were to be followed exactly in expediting the operational preparation. Operational preparation was to be approximately completed by about spring of 1944. The entire project was to be completed by the middle of 1944.

A few of the essential matters that had to be carried out for the operational preparation were; construction of air bases, deployment of essential troops, increase of reconnaissance and patrolling against the enemy, construction of fortifications, stocking of munitions, establishment of shipping bases and small boat transportation routes along the coast, installation of communication apparatus and a general bolstering of the system for self-subsistence at occupied positions.

Allocation on areas of responsibility for the supply system provided that Halmahera would serve as the intermediate supply base for the Banda Sea area and northwestern New Guinea. The terminal points for supplies from the Homeland and the Southern Army would be Sorong for the Banda Sea area; Manokwari for northwestern New Guinea; and, Macassar for the Flores Sea area.

To strengthen defenses of the Central Pacific area, Imperial General Headquarters sent the 52d Division from Japan to Truk in the latter part of October 1943. On 16 November, the 1st Amphibious Brigade and the 1st through the 5th South Pacific Detachments were placed under the 4th Fleet commander. The 6th South Pacific Detachment was placed under the 8th Area Army commander. These units were deployed throughout the various islands in the Central Pacific area. The 29th Division was sent to Saipan from Manchuria in early February 1944.

Until early February 1944, progress of defensive preparations in the South Pacific area indicated they were reaching approximate completion. However, isolation of the 8th Area Army and fall of the Gilbert Islands contributed to a speed-up of the inevitable enemy operations. It became necessary to hurry the strengthening of our defenses. During the latter part of February, the 31st Army received battle orders and was attached to the Navy for joint operations.

Outline of the Order of Battle for the 31st Army

    31st Army headquarters
    29th Division
    52d Division
    1st Amphibious Brigade
    South Pacific Detachments (1st, 2d, 3d, 4th and 5th)
    South Pacific Garrison Units (2d and 3d)
    Chichijima Fortress Unit

5th Independent Mixed Regiment

Expeditionary Detachments (1st, 2d, 3d, 4th, 5th, 6th, 7th, and 8th)

Note: The 1st through 8th Expeditionary Detachments were units urgently organized and transferred from Manchuria and Korea. Each was composed of 3 to 6 infantry battalions, one artillery battalion, one engineer company and service units.

Army-Navy Central Agreement Regarding Central Pacific Operations

Objectives were to defeat the advancing enemy, secure the important zones in the Central Pacific area and crush enemy operations in the area.

By the end of spring 1944, the Navy was to rush completion of operational preparations in the Caroline, Mariana and Ogasawara sectors. The Army was to cooperate with the Navy in preparing for and carrying out ground operations by sending necessary units to the Central Pacific area and placing them under command of appropriate Navy officers.

The 31st Army commander was to be placed under the Central Pacific Area Fleet commander and take charge of ground operations throughout the central and western parts of the Caroline and Mariana Islands and in the Ogasawara sector. Regarding ground operations on the various islands, the respective local senior army commanders were to assume command of all Army units (excluding air and air defense units) on the islands.

Involved discussions were held before a final decision was reached on the Central Agreement. While preparations were being made to issue orders for the 31st Army according to the tentative agreement on unified operations under command of the Navy, the Navy requested (in mid-February) that the Army strength in the Central Pacific area be kept separate and that the operations be carried out by normal cooperative methods between Army and Navy. However, Army authorities insisted on the original plans for several reasons, which were recognized finally by Navy authorities. It was necessary to coordinate the entire Army and Navy strength in the area because operations in the Central Pacific area were the most important. The Navy Air Force which was being deployed was to be main defensive force in the operation. The Army would have to hold airfields which the Navy Air Force would use. And, most important, from past experiences of cooperative operations on Attu, Kiska and Guadalcanal, it was considered essential that the Army and Navy operate under a unified command. It was considered very difficult for the Army units on each of the islands to carry out their missions without dominate help from the Navy in regard to transportation, escort, supply, intelligence and communication. These were the supporting reasons for selection of the Navy to handle the unified command.

Operational Conduct for North-of-Australia Area

The Army General Staff decided to increase the troop strength in the North-of-Australia area and establish a functional command to complete operational preparations in the area. At the end of October, the 2d Area Army headquarters and the 2d Army (both in Manchuria) received an order to move to the North-of-Australia area.

The 2d Area Army was made up of miscellaneous logistical units; 2d Area Army headquarters; 2d Army (mainly the 36th Division); and, the 19th Army (the 5th, 46th and 48th Divisions).

Mission given the 2d Area Army commander by the Army General Staff was to repel enemy counterattacks in the North-of-Australia area and hold the strategic areas. In cooperation with the Navy, preparations were to be rushed for our counteraction to hold the North-of-Australia area.

Operational boundary line between the 8th Area Army and the 2d Area Army was to be longitude 140° east. Between the 2d Area Army and the Southern Army, it was to be the line which connected Macassar Strait with Lombok Strait. Between the 2d Area Army and the 14th Army it was to be latitude 5° north.

The front lines which had to be held were strategic areas of Western New Guinea and Aroe, Tanimbar, Timor and the Lesser Sunda Islands.

The 2d Area Army headquarters moved to the operational area in mid-November and assumed command on 1 December. The headquarters was in Davao, but later it was moved to Menado.

Prior to this movement, the 36th Division had been transferred from China to the North-of-Australia area in mid-October and placed, temporarily, under the 19th Army commander. The 46th Division was transferred from the Homeland to Soemba Island and placed, temporarily, under the 16th Army commander. The 19th Army (5th, 46th and 48th) and the 2d Army (mainly the 36th Division) were placed in the new Order of Battle for the 2d Area Army effective 30 October.

Also, the 7th Air Division, in the operational area, was placed under the 2d Area Army operational command.

On 10 February, the 14th Division, which had been in Manchuria, was placed in the Order of Battle for the 2d Army on a shipping schedule dispatching it to the North-of-Australia area. The destination of the Division was changed to Palau after transportation was begun because of urgent necessity to strengthen the defense of the Palau area.

Efforts to Strengthen Shipping and Transportation

Since the outbreak of war, the number of transports sunk by the enemy had increased sharply and it seemed to be developing more seriously.

The Army General Staff had, in December 1942, first presented a recommendation that it be allowed to requisition 300,000 tons more of available civilian shipping facilities. Normally, the War Minister had supported all requests of the Army General Staff in his position as member of the Cabinet. In this case, for the first time, he flatly refused because of his views regarding the over-all total economic picture and its supporting requirements in meeting the needs for war production. The Army General Staff had supported its request by stressing its belief that shipping requirements for immediate operations should be given priority. Thereafter, each time the Army General Staff submitted a request for more ships to carry out its operations, a heated discussion occurred. Continuous efforts were made but only small gains in allowed ships were realized.

Imperial General Headquarters planned to greatly increase shipping units and strengthen defensive measures to protect shipping. The sea escort (Navy responsibility) and the area around ports (Army responsibility) were to be bolstered by increasing fire power and adding necessary air force units for the job, especially in the area in which the enemy had air superiority.

During the latter part of September 1943, the Army General Staff carried out a reorganization and strengthening plan for its shipping units. The reorganized units were stationed at Ujina, Shanghai, Singapore, Rabaul, Halmaherea and Otaru. In part, the added strength was gained through consolidation of units from other areas plus special attention to the development and addition of small craft (such as landing craft and small fishing boats) as a means of transporting supplies in the local areas. In the latter part of December, further reinforcements were accomplished.

Steps Taken to Combat Submarines

Our losses to submarines on the main routes between Japan and the Southern area (Japan to Formosa and the Philippines, and the Philippines to French Indo-China and Malay) were quite heavy. Losses suffered in the Central Pacific area were secondary. Also, it seemed that the losses suffered from enemy air actions were increasing gradually. As a result, the Army and Navy made a joint study and decided to cooperate in protecting shipping.

To accomplish this purpose, on 1 November 1943 the China Expeditionary Army commander and the 14th Army commander were ordered to have their air units cooperate with the Navy in anti-submarine operations. In mid-February 1944, the air units of the Northern Army (1st Air Division) were deployed in the Kushiro, Nemuro and Muroran areas and to the Tsugaru and Soya Straits. Elements of the 1st Air Army were located in Southern Kysushu, the Southwestern Islands and Formosa. The Commander of Homeland Defenses received an order to reinforce protection of sea transportation in the vicinity of the Korean Strait. He was to use air units from the Western District Army and the Korea Army.

Strengthening of Sea Bases

Shipping in the Solomons and New Guinea areas where the enemy had air superiority was very difficult. Our losses from enemy air and sea attacks increased sharply and the area under enemy control became larger. On 15 February 1944, the Army General Staff directed the Southern Army commander, the 2d Area Army commander, and the Northern Army commander to take special precautions to protect the sea bases in Bengal Bay, the North-of-Australia area and the Kurile Islands. Objective of this directive was to make sea movements and counter-operations easier in the zone of enemy superiority and to retain the supply lines for the strategic points in our perimeter. This was a recognition of the vital necessity for fortifying harbors and bases against air and sea attacks.

The items with which the bases had to be equipped were sheltering installations for small boats; small boat maintenance units; communication installations; base units (anti-aircraft units, if possible); navigation markers; necessary line of communication installations; and stockpiles of munitions and fuel. The sea bases would be classified as sea combat bases and sea line of communication bases. They were to be used by torpedo boats and force which were to take part in short range sea combat. Also, they were to be used as stand-by and assembly points for amphibious groups.

Enemy attacks on shipping had forced us to rely on railway transportation. The railroads of Korea, Manchuria, China, French Indo-China, Siam, Malay and Burma had to be improved. On 10 February, the Army General Staff decided and initiated a reorganization plan for reinforcement of railway units to strengthen railway transportation.

Approval of Imphal Operations ("U" Operation)

The Burma area was of strategic value because of the Burma Road. If we cut it off, it would be advantageous both politically and strategically. It had also a great value as the northern wing of the Southern area. Therefore, we estimated the British and Chinese Armies would use their main forces in this area. In anticipation, the Army General Staff and the Southern Army attached importance to this area and planned to reinforce its strength. By the beginning of 1944, the Burma Area Army commander had under his command; the 15th Army (15th, 18th, 31st, 33d and 56th Divisions.); the 28th Army (2d, 54th and 55th Divisions); and, the 24th Independent Mixed Brigade. In November 1943, the 53d Division (in Japan) was ordered to leave for the Burma area to be under the Southern Army commander.

These forces proved to be insufficient to take command of such a wide area. Due to the concentration of the Bristish Army (approximately 3 divisions) and their operational preparations in the state of Assam, the intense air transportation between India and China, the situation of a newly organized 1st Chungking Army (2 or 3 divisions) in the Bukawng River Valley area, and the strength of the Chinese Army in the Yunnan area (approximately 10 divisions), it became necessary to keep a close watch on Northern Burma Operations.

At the end of December 1943, the Southern Army commander sent his Assistant Chief of Staff to Tokyo to make a recommendation to the Army General Staff concerning a contemplated offensive operation ("U" Operation) in Imphal. Ever since the completion of the 1st stage of the Southern Operations, repeated studies had been made by the Southern Army commander and Army General Staff regarding such an operation. The operational plan presented by the Southern Army commander called for launching attacks from the east and south during the spring of 1944 using the 15th Army, composed of three divisions. The objective was to annihilate the enemy in the Imphal Basin.

The Army General Staff brought up several questions regarding the proposed operation. There was a high possibility the enemy would attempt a landing on the coast of Southern Burma from Bengal Bay. If the "U" Operation were carried out, would we be able to carry out countermeasures satisfactorily? After capture, the Imphal area would require a large force to hold it. Would this weaken the defense of the entire Burma area? Could ground operations be carried out successfully even though our air strength was inferior? Would we be able to maintain our supply lines? Lastly, was the "U" Operation sound?

The Southern Army commander felt it was unnecessary to worry. He insisted that capture of the Imphal area would make the general defense of Burma easier. It was his belief that the terrain features of the area would allow us to defend Western Burma with a smaller force than was being used currently. The Army General Staff recognized the necessity of a strong defense for Burma. The "U" Operation was approved. On 7 January, directives were issued.

The Southern Army commander was authorized (as an operational method in the defense of Burma) to launch an offensive operation against the important area of Northeastern India centering on Imphal. After crushing the enemy, the area was to be secured.

The "U" Operation was begun on 8 March.

Instructions Concerning "Ichi-Go" (Hunan-Kwangsi) Operation

Beginning in the autumn of 1943, the Army General Staff made studies regarding future operations to capture key points along the Hunan-Kwangsi and Canton-Hankou railways. Also included was the southern part of the Peiping-Hankou railway. This operation was to be called the "Ichi-Go" Operation. There were four objectives studied for the proposed operation.

1. We were to seize potential American B-29 bases at Kweilin and Liuchow. This would help in the defense of our Homeland.

2. By consolidating forces in the Kweilin and Liuchow areas, we would engage the enemy moving into the South China area via India, Burma and Yunnan.

3. Because sea transportation was deteriorating, the railroad running north and south via French Indo-China would be repaired to establish a reliable land transportation system for the Southern Army.

4. We would plan to weaken the Chungking Government by crushing the Nationalist Army.

After several investigations, item 1 was the only one accepted. The decision to carry this plan out was made in January 1944.

On 24 January, the Commander in Chiefs of the China Expeditionary Army and the Southern Army were issued orders which stated; plans had been made to destroy important enemy air bases in Southwest China; the China Expeditionary Army commander would make attacks against the Hunan-Kwangsi and Canton-Hankou railroad; the Southern Army was to cooperate.

Outline of the Peiping-Hankou Operation provided three items.

1. In April 1944, the North China Area Army would begin the operation from North China. It would crush the

enemy and seize the southern portion of the Peiping-Hankou railroad south of the Yellow River. These operations were expected to take about a month and a half.

2. Strength to be employed was established as the 12th Army (composed of four divisions) of the North China Area Army and a part of the 5th Air Army.

3. After termination of the operation necessary units from the above-mentioned forces would be used in the Hunan-Kwangsi Operation.

Outline of the Hunan-Kwangsi Operation included six points.

1. In June 1944, the 11th Army would begin operations from the Wuchang-Hankou area. In July and August, the 23d Army would begin operations from the Canton area. These two Armies were to rout the enemy and occupy the vicinities of Kweilin and Liuchow. Remnants of the enemy along the Hunan-Kwangsi and Canton-Hankou railroads were to be mopped up. These operations were expected to take approximately five months.

2. According to the situation, an operation to destroy enemy airfields in the Suichuan and Nanhsiung areas would be carried out as soon as possible after the above operations.

3. If the situation permitted, the 23d Army would make another attack against Yungning during January and February 1945 and clear the road between Kweilin and Langson.

4. Prior to the launching of the 11th Army's operation, the 5th Air Army would carry out operations to destroy the American-Chinese Air Force, thus gaining air superiority. While suppressing the

rise in enemy air power, the 5th Air Army would support ground forces directly at critical times with the necessary forces.

5. Strength to be used for the operation was to include:

> 11th Army (from seven to eight divisions)
>
> 23d Army (two divisions)
>
> Forces directly under the Expeditionary Army (from one to two divisions)
>
> 5th Air Army

6. The Southern Army would carry out operations with a part of its strength in the Burma and Indo-China areas to help the China Expeditionary Army in its campaign.

During the early and middle part of February, the strength was increased. The 3d Air Division under the China Expeditionary Army commander was reorganized into the 5th Air Army. It had approximately 250 planes. The 27th Division in Manchuria, the 116th Division and miscellaneous units from the 13th Army were placed in the Order of Battle for the 11th Army. The 22d Division and miscellaneous units from the 13th Army were placed under command of the 23d Army.

This operation was to be conducted under difficulties such as the lack of gasoline and ships and was to cover an area of 1,500 kilometers. It was to be carried out with 400,000 men, 70,000 horses and 12,000 vehicles. The way in which the line of communication operated would have a great influence on the outcome.

The importance of transportation brought about the following special points of operations as directed by the Army General Staff; For the preparation and start of the operation, use of large type ships would be kept to a minimum. Water routes were to be used to their utmost advantage. Railroads would be repaired as soon as possible to economize on fuel. Hospitals in China and Southern Manchuria would be enlarged and measures to prevent malaria and combat pests would be carried out. The Motor Transportation Units which were transferred from Manchuria would be regrouped as soon as rough completion of the operation was assured to prepare for future operations.

The Peiping-Hankou and Canton-Hankou Operations were started on 18 April and 27 May, respectively.

Instructions for Various Areas

When Italy surrendered on 8 September, the Army General Staff ordered the Commanders of the China Expeditionary Army, the Southern Army, the 14th Army, and the Governor General of Hongkong to halt Italian activities in their operational areas and to disarm Italian Forces. These included some Italian Naval Landing Units stationed at Shanghai and Tientsin; the consulates in China, Thailand and French Indo-China (the latter two are not confirmed for this action); and a small number of merchant ships and Italian nationals in China, the Southern Area and the Philippines. All Italian citizens were placed under close Military Administration surveillance.

To strengthen forces in the Southwest, the 4th Division (in Japan) was placed in the Order of Battle for the 25th Army in late September 1943. On 10 December, the Indo-China Garrison Army was organized (21st Division, 34th Independent Mixed Brigade and various units under the direct control of the Army). On the same date, the Siam Garrison Army was organized (29th Independent Mixed Brigade and units under direct control of the Army). In mid-January 1944, the 29th Army was organized (several independent garrison units). The 29th Army was given an assignment in Northern Malay.

In late 1943, defense of the Sumatra oilfields was considered very important. To help this situation, the 9th Air Division was activated. The Bangkalang-Brandon Defense Unit and Palembang Defense Unit were incorporated into the Order of Battle of the 9th Air Division which was placed under the 3d Air Army.

In the early part of January 1944, 7 guard units, 55 special guard units, 64 special guard companies and 15 special guard engineer units were organized in order to strengthen the guard of the Homeland and Korea. These units were placed under appropriate commanders.

The 42d Division was sent to the Kuriles area to reinforce defenses there. It was placed under the Northern Army commander.

Additional Construction and Maintenance Plans for Air Bases

Considering past experiences in amphibious defensive operations, the Army General Staff realized that the best defense came from the Air Force situated in the network of air bases along the main line of defense. In the latter part of January 1944, orders were issued to construct and maintain air bases covering the entire defensive zone until the end of 1944. The main purpose was to coordinate and perfect air defense. This was done by grouping several airfields into a system of centrally organized air base areas. As a result, a concentrated air force could be mounted more quickly and effectively. For proper functioning of the system, an effective communication, repair and supply system had to be provided. The large air base areas would be used by one air division. The ordinary air base areas were to be fortified. Locations were to be fixed in depth, as much as possible, in accordance with the ground force operational area policy. Also, to be taken into consideration on locations was the relationship with the air base areas in the front lines of our outer defensive sphere. In addition to this system of air base areas, emergency fields to support the military air routes and air strips were to be constructed speedily.

PART II Second Stage (March - June 1944)

Situation Review and Estimated Enemy Plans

Because of the penetration of Vitiaz Strait by enemy forces, the 8th Area Army at Rabaul was isolated completely. Sea transportation to the 18th Army in eastern New Guinea was endangered seriously. This became more critical in late April when the enemy landed in Hollandia and Aitape. The enemy landed on Sarumi and Biak Islands in the middle and latter part of May. Eastern New Guinea was cut off from the North-of-Australia area. It seemed the Southern area defensive sphere was beginning to collapse in this corner.

On 8 March, the Burma Area Army had started the "U" Operation according to the plan. In its first phase, it progressed smoothly. Munipur was invaded in the latter part of March. Kohima was captured on 6 April and the attack against Imphal was commenced. Before Imphal was captured, enemy planes cut off our rear and severed our supply line. The enemy was able to support its units through air transportation and our operation was checked.

In the Hukawng River Valley area, our 18th Division encountered enemy counterattacks and was forced to retreat. Due to the invasion of Northern Burma by enemy airborne troops and the failure of the "U" Operation, the situation in the Burma area was at a standstill.

The enemy attacked Palau in the Pacific area in the latter part of March and inflicted heavy damages on our ships. Powerful enemy land, sea and air forces began an offensive operation against Saipan on 15 June. The 1st Mobile Fleet took part in the naval battle off the Marianas on 19 June. Our Air Force suffered heavy damages. In early July, the main force of the unit of Saipan was annihilated and the island fell into the enemy's possession.

Our forces in the China area began the 1st Phase of the "Ichi-Go" Operation in mid-April according to the prearranged plan.

The 12th Army in North China executed the Peiping-Hankou Railway Operation and successfully completed it on 9 May. The first phase was completed and the Hunan-Kwangsi Operation was begun the early part of May as the second phase.

The United States Air Force based in China made its initial air raid against Northern Kyushu in mid-June.

The enemy commenced landing operations in Europe to open the 2d Front in the early part of June.

After conclusion of the first stage of the first phase (the Southern Operation), our Army had made preparations for defensive warfare, expecting enemy attacks from five directions:

1. From the Aleutians against the Kurile Islands
2. From the Central Pacific against the Homeland or Formosa and the Philippines
3. From New Guinea against the Philippines via the North-of-Australia area
4. From the Indian Ocean toward Java and Sumatra
5. From Burma toward Malay and Siam

Reviewing the situation following the middle of 1943, it had been assumed that an American attack from the Pacific area and a combined American-British-Chinese attack from the Burma area would be the most probable.

From autumn of 1942, enemy attacks in the Southeastern area being directed from the Pacific area were successful because they were consistent. The enemy tactics had been to advance against the Gilbert Islands during autumn of 1943 and the attacks against the Marshall and Truk areas in February 1944, they changed their tactics to leapfrog operations using the strength of their fleet. The enemy's strength reflected their materiel power and could not be ignored.

We were unable to judge, definitely, whether the enemy would attack Japan directly or wait until after invading the Philippines and Formosa. Considering the strategical value of the Philippines and the difficulties involved in making a direct attack against Japan, it was more than probable the enemy would attack the Philippines first. In this way, the Southern area would be cut off from the rest of the Empire. In such case, the enemy probably would conduct a diversionary operation in the Kurile area. It was unpredictable whether the enemy would attack the Philippines and Formosa from the direction of the Marianas, or the Southern Philippines from the direction of New Guinea and the North-of-Australia area. According to logical analysis, however, the enemy probably would carry out the latter operation.

Contributing to our problems in the Burma-Thailand-French Indo-China area was the weak situation which confronted us in Thailand and French Indo-China. In each of these countries, we were operating by mutual agreement with the governments concerned. In neither of the countries did we have a military administration. Our presence was based on diplomatic agreement. With the trend of the war becoming unfavorable for Japan, there was some evident dissatisfaction on the part of the people. This unstable political situation was a complication to be considered in future operations and could be disadvantageous to us in case of an enemy counterattack through Burma. If such an enemy attack were successful, it was anticipated that it would encourage the Chinese to new efforts against our forces in China proper.

Disregarding the battle situation in Europe, the United States Army was expected to concentrate its main force in the Far East area. The decisive campaign was considered close at hand.

Even under these circumstances, it was unnecessary for our Army to alter the operational plan established in September 1943. However, preparations for the decisive battle had to be pursued diligently including such things as reinforcing defensive positions in the Central Pacific area; establishing defensive positions on Formosa, the Nansei Islands and the Philippines; strengthening the defense of the Homeland; bolstering the protection of our shipping; increasing the production of airplanes; and, making research on and producing radar equipment.

North-of-Australia Area Instructions

Communication between Rabaul and New Guinea had become difficult due to the enemy's penetration of Vitiaz Strait. The Army General Staff realized it would be difficult for the 8th Area Army commander, under such circumstances, to command the 18th Army. After studying the system of command in this area, the Army General Staff issued an order on 14 March 1944 for the 18th Army and the 4th Air Army to be transferred from the 8th Area Army to the 2d Area Army. Duties of the 2d and 8th Area Armies were revised.

1. The Army General Staff planned to hold the Rabaul and Marshall areas as long as possible, while establishing fortified positions in the area extending from the North-of-Australia area to the Central Pacific area in order to repulse enemy counterattacks. It was planned to take the offensive when and if the situation permitted and to disrupt the enemy's war plan.

2. The 8th Area Army commander would cooperate with the Navy and hold the important Rabaul area as long as possible to make operations easier in the area extending from the North-of-Australia area to the Central Pacific area.

3. The 2d Area Army commander would carry out his original duties. With newly assigned units in eastern New Guinea,

he would also plan to hold the area west of Wewak and would make an effort to check any enemy advances toward the western New Guinea and western Caroline area.

4. The operational boundary between the 8th Area Army and the 2d Area Army was to be longitude 147° east passing through the New Guinea and Bismarck Archipelago area. The Admiralty Islands were to be included in the operational zone of the 8th Area Army.

In connection with these orders, the Army General Staff issued a three point directive to the 2d Area Army commander.

1. The 2d Area Army commander would withdraw the main force of the 18th Army to the area west of Wewak to strengthen defense of the air bases at Hollandia, Aitape and Wewak. The 18th Army, also, was to check the enemy advancing against western New Guinea and the western Carolines. If enemy landings were made during the above-mentioned redeployment of the 18th Army, an effort would be made to annihilate them.

2. The 2d Area Army commander would accumulate the maximum amount of munitions in the Hollandia, Aitape and Wewak areas.

3. The 18th Army's operation was not to be allowed to interfere with completion of the 2d Area Army's operational preparations.

In accordance with previous instructions, the 2d Area Army had already decided to hold the line extending from Tanimbar through Aroe to Sarumi in Western New Guinea, with the area surrounding the Geelving Bay as its center. It was planned to establish the region around the Gulf of Geelving as an air base and the 2d Area Army was endeavoring to complete operational preparations. The Army General Staff had no intention, at this time, of altering the front line although the 18th Army was attached to the 2d Area Army. Its mission was to hold the area outside the 2d Area Army's front lines.

First and Second Modifications of 2d Area Army Front Line

On 15 April 1944, the 2d Area Army (on order from the Army General Staff) was placed under command of the Southern Army. In the latter part of April, enemy forces landed unexpectedly in the vicinity of Hollandia. As soon as our 6th Air Division in this section lost its fighting ability, the area of enemy air superiority, again, increased. Regardless of this fact, the 2d Area Army desired to attack the enemy beyond our front line with its ground forces. However, the Army General Staff could not send any additional air and ground forces into the area. The operation in this area assumed the position of a delaying action to be carried out by existing forces. It seemed impractical to employ the troops and materiel being transported to this area for an offensive operation in the forward area. In order to accomplish the Army General Staff plan, establishment of a new defense line in the rear had to be set after considering the total area covered by enemy air superiority. It was the responsibility of the Army General Staff to advise the front line troops regarding this rear line.

On 2 May, orders issued to the Southern Army commander relieved him of his responsibilities in the eastern New Guinea area. The 18th Army and other units in eastern New Guinea were to be transferred to western New Guinea.

Instructions for the Southern Army commander included three points;

1. The front line to be held in the western New Guinea area would be the line linking the innermost sector of Geelving Bay with Manokwari, Sorong and Halmahera. Important positions in the vicinity of Biak Island were to be held as long as possible. Necessary troops would be sent to the island from units in the Sarmi area.

2. A part of advanced units of the 35th Division which were transferred from China in early April and were to be located on the St Andrew Islands could still be sent to such places as the Mapia Islands.

3. The 18th Army and other units in eastern New Guinea were to be transferred, immediately, to western New Guinea. Any enemy landings in the area would be checked to make all operations easier.

The enemy air force having extended its operational area to the west had caused shipping transportation to the Manokwari area to become more difficult. The 2d Area Army commander had been planning to send the main elements of the 35th Division (stationed in Sorong at this time) to Manokwari. The Army General Staff decided it would be better to leave the division in Sorong for its defense. Stopping the movement of the 35th Division brought about the second change. Instructions issued on 9 May stated that the front line to be held in the key sectors of the western New Guinea area was to be the line in the vicinity of Sorong and Halmahera. The important positions of Biak, Manokwari and near Geelving Bay were to be held as long as possible.

After the enemy landed on Biak Island during the latter part of May, communication between the 2d Area Army and the 18th Army by either land, sea or air became impossible. It was then impossible for the 2d Area Army commander to command, effectively, the 18th Army. Also, the withdrawal of the 18th Army to the Western New Guinea area (ordered by the Army General Staff) became impossible. As a result, the 18th Army was detached from the 2d Area Army and placed under the direct control of the Southern Army on 20 June. The Army General Staff had the Southern Army commander order the 18th Army and units in the eastern New Guinea area to "hold to the end" the important regions in this area. This was directed to make over-all operations easier.

Northeastern Area Instructions

Considering possible enemy attacks against Hokkaido from the Aleutian area, defensive positions on Hokkaido and the Kuriles had been reinforced. As a result of studies made on the character of the Northern Army in spring of 1944, it was deemed necessary to change it from a district army to a complete operational army. It was designated the 5th Area Army and was responsible to the Chief of Army General Staff. Operational boundary between the Eastern District Army and the 5th Area Army was changed to the Tsugaru Strait. The 27th Army headquarters was organized for defensive purposes in the Kurile area and placed under the 5th Area Army commander along with the 1st Air Division. In mid-March, Army General Staff issued battle orders for the 5th Area Army and the 27th Army.

Orders for the 5th Area Army

1. Plans for the Northeastern area provided for rendering the enemy plan of attacking the Homeland impracticable and for prevention of a war with Russia.

2. The 5th Area Army commander would cooperate with the Navy, in expediting operational preparations for the purpose of intercepting any enemy attacks against the Homeland in the Northeastern area.

3. Operational boundary between the 5th Area Army and the Commander of Homeland Defense was to be the Tsugaru Strait. This strait and the Tsugaru Fortress area in Aomori Prefecture were to be under the command of the 5th Area Army.

Formosa and Nansei Islands Instructions

Anticipating future enemy attacks from the Marianas and Philippines areas and surprise attacks from other directions, the Army General Staff realized the necessity of speeding up preparations in the Formosa and Nansei areas. In the latter part of March 1944, the battle order for the 32d Army was issued. It and the Formosa Army were ordered to rush operational preparations. This was called the 10th Operational Preparation.

Organization of the 32d Army

    32d Army headquarters
    Amami-Oshima Fortress Unit
    Nakagusuku Bay Fortress Unit
    Funafuchi Fortress Unit
    Units under the direct command of the Army

Orders issued to the Formosa Army and 32d Army commanders included four points:

1. The Army General Staff planned to strengthen defense of Southern Japan.

2. The 32d Army commander would cooperate with the Navy in expediting operational preparations. He would be responsible for defense of the Nansei Islands.

3. The Formosa Army commander would cooperate with the Navy in expediting operational preparations. He would be responsible for defense of Formosa.

4. The boundary between the defensive areas of the 32d Army and the Commander of Homeland Defense was to be latitude 30°10' north. The boundary between the 32d Army and the Formosa Army was to be longitude 122°30' east. The boundary between the 14th Army and the Formosa Army was to be latitude 20°10' north.

Objectives of the operational preparation which was to be executed by the Formosa Army and the 32d Army were to maintain defense and transportation between Japan and the Southern area. They were to be prepared first to repel any enemy surprise attacks and then to meet orthodox enemy landings.

Air operational preparation was to have top priority. Other items were to be considered secondary. Countermeasures against unexpected attacks were to be carried out, immediately. General operational preparations were to be completed by about July 1944.

In connection with air operational preparation, several air bases were to be constructed in the area extending from the east coast of Formosa to the Nansei Islands in order to make air operations easier. Enough bases were to be developed so that approximately one air division each could be deployed on Eastern Formosa and the Nansei Islands. The amount of materiel to be stockpiled before July was expected to be sufficient for two air divisions. After that, it was to be enough to fill the needs of one air division.

Ground forces were to be developed to protect air bases and main anchorage points. Part of the troops were to be dispatched to the Daito Island area to cooperate with the Navy in building airfields. Part of the Formosa Army was to be sent to Batan Island for its defense.

Two Independent Mixed Brigades and the 28th Division (from Manchuria) being assembled in Shanghai were assigned to the 32d Army in the early part of May and in the latter part of June, respectively. The 50th Division and newly organized 8th Air Division were assigned to the Formosa Army in the early part of May and in the early part of June, respectively.

To consolidate supply operations, the Army General Staff assigned and transferred from its direct command the 32d Army to the

Western Army in the early part of May. This was done because the 32d and Western Army's supply situations were closely related.

Southern Area Command System Unification

In June 1942, the 14th Army was placed under direct control of the Army General Staff. At the beginning of 1944, it was recognized that a unified command by the Southern Army was necessary in the Philippines and North-of-Australia areas. Steps were taken in the latter part of March. Reasons given for the unification included three points.

1. It was certain the American Army would direct attacks against the area extending from the North-of-Australia area to the Philippines. The most urgent countermeasures against the enemy attacks would be made by our air forces within the defensive sphere. It was necessary to unify the command system to get the right concentration of the entire air strength at the right place and at the right moment.

2. Because shipping had to be carried out by a limited number of ships, it was necessary to transfer materiel within the Southern area through local transportation. This system had not been developed effectively due to opposition by the chain of command.

3. In order to enable the Army General Staff to command effectively the over-all operations against enemy attacks from all directions around our defensive sphere, it was necessary to reduce the number of area army command organizations.

Change of Mission and Instructions for Southern Army

The Army General Staff plan was to hold the strategic regions of the Southern area and the Northern and Central Pacific areas, to destroy the enemy's fighting power and to render the enemy's intentions impractical. The plan also required every possible effort to destroy the Chungking Government.

The Southern Army commander was to cooperate with the Navy in hastening operational preparation and maintaining security of strategic areas in the south. The advancing enemy was to be annihilated. Defense was to be enforced in the Andaman and Nicobar Islands, Malay, Sumatra, Java, and the Dutch East Indies areas. Burma, Thailand, French Indo-China and the Philippines were to be secured in cooperation with their governments. An air offensive against the India, China, Australia and New Guinea areas was to be carried out at an appropriate time.

The program of self-subsistence in the various areas would be strengthened to cope with the development of the war situation. Defense of the regions having an abundance of natural resources would be reinforced. Completion of military administration would be rushed. Also, the Southern Army would cooperate with the Navy as much as possible in protecting sea transportation.

The operational boundary between the Southern Army and the 8th Area Army was to be longitude 147° east passing through New Guinea and the Bismarck Archipelago (the Admiralty Islands were to be under the 8th Area Army). The operational boundary between the Southern Army and the Formosa Army was to be latitude 20° north.

Palau Island was to be in the operational zone of the 31st Army. The St Andrews Islands were to be in the operational zone of the Southern Army.

In connection with the line of communication, the Southern Army commander was to concentrate on the adjustment of the relation between air and ground supply routes so emphasis would be placed on meeting needs of the Air Force. These were expected to increase sharply. In addition, steps were to be taken to assure unrestricted exchange of materiel in the entire southern area. Local self-subsistence was to be applied more completely. The Philippines were to be established as the supply base for the Southern area, especially the North-of-Australia area.

Terminal supply points of the Army General Staff:

TERMINAL POINT	AREAS SERVED
Manila	Philippines
Saigon (this point to be transferred to Singapore if necessary for Burma area)	Burma, Thailand and French Indo-China
Singapore	Malay, Sumatra, Java and Borneo
Halmahera and Palau	North-of-Australia

If circumstances permitted, supplies for the North-of-Australia area were to be sent directly to Manokwari, Sorong and Amboina. Materiel hitherto under direct control of the Army General Staff in the Philippines was to be transferred to the Southern Army. In general, the Army General Staff would not deliver war supplies directly to subordinate units of the Southern Army, but would deliver exclusively to the Southern Army.

Headquarters for the Southern Army was moved to Manila from Singapore, and the command system became completely unified.

As part of the reorganization of the command system in the Southern area, the 7th Area Army headquarters was newly organized in Singapore to assume command of the 16th, 25th and 29th Armies. The 2d and 7th Area Armies, the 14th Army and the 4th Air Army were assigned to the Southern Army.

To conduct air operations within our defensive sphere, it was necessary to organize a unified Air Force headquarters. However, this was estimated as being a complication in the command system. Thus, Southern Army headquarters assumed command of the air force. The 3d Air Army (5th and 9th Air Divisions) was stationed in the Singapore area on the Western Front. The 4th Air Army (7th Air Division) was stationed in the Philippines area on the Eastern Front. Expecting the decisive campaign to take place in the Philippines, it was planned to increase air strength. The 2d and 4th Air Divisions were transferred to the Philippines from Manchuria in mid-May.

At this time, an unusual split in the organizational structure and responsibilities of the 2d and 4th Air Divisions was ordered. All flying units of the two divisions were placed under the command of the 2d Air Division commander. All service units of both divisions were placed under the 4th Air Division commander. Thus, the 2d Air Division became a flying division, exclusively. And, the 4th Air Division became an air service unit, solely. Purpose of such reorganization has been expressed as a solution to the control and concentration of air attacks and to expediting air base construction in specific operations. The 2d Air Division (flying units) was assigned directly to the Southern Army while the 4th Air Division (service units) was placed under the 4th Air Army. The mission assigned the 4th Air Division was the construction of air bases in the Philippines. On its arrival in the Philippines (late May), the 2d Air Division was placed under the 4th Air Army by the Southern Army commander.

To strengthen the defense capacity in the Southern area, the 32d Division (from 12th Army in North China) was placed under the 14th Army commander. The 35th Division which had been transferred from China and placed under the 31st Army commander was reassigned to the 2d Army in the early part of April.

The 33d Army (18th and 56th Divisions) was newly organized under the Burma Area Army commander on 11 April. It was activated for the purpose of establishing a strong command structure in the important Hukawng River Valley and Yunnan areas. By this move, it was planned that the 15th Army could be relieved of some of its responsibilities in those areas. In this way, the northern flank would be made secure and the 15th Army and the Burma Area Army could concentrate on the projected "U" Operations.

The 32d Division, recently assigned to the 14th Army, was reassigned to the 2d Area Army in the latter part of April and sent to the Halmahera area. The 30th Division (from Korea) was assigned to the 14th Army and sent to the Mindanao area.

Due to the battle requirements in the Burma area, it became necessary to reinforce troops in the Southwestern area. The 49th Division (in Japan) was assigned to the Southern Army in the latter part of May.

As an aid in future operational preparations and to ease the burden of responsibilities for the line of communication in the Burma area, the Army General Staff organized the following units in the early part of June:

    Southern Army Line of Communication Inspectorate Section
    Burma Area Army Line of Communication Inspectorate Section
    2d Area Army Line of Communication Inspectorate Section

These sections were assigned to their indicated respective Armies.

In order to reinforce the defense forces in the Philippines, independent mixed brigades and other units which had been sent to the area were reorganized. The 100th, 102d, and 103d and 105th Divisions and two independent mixed brigades were organized and assigned to the 14th Army in mid-June.

Over-all preparations (No 11 Operational Preparation) for the possible decisive battle in the Philippines had been put in motion by an Army General Staff Directive in May 1944. Preparations were to be roughly completed by the end of summer.

Central Pacific Area Instructions

The 14th Division (from Manchuria) had been ordered to move into the North-of-Australia area to come under the command of the 2d Army. Because of enemy operations in mid-March, it was necessary to rush the defense of Palau. As a result, the destination of the 14th Division, already en route, was changed to Palau on 20 March and it was placed under the 31st Army.

Using practically all available shipping, the Army and Navy conducted a prompt and effective deployment of strength in the Pacific area during the spring of 1944. In spite of heavy damages resulting from enemy submarine attacks, our defensive positions gradually were improved. The Mariana Islands and the Ogasawara Island areas were of vital strategic value and it was considered essential to further strengthen them. The 29th Division was transferred from Saipan to Guam in the early part of April. The 43d Division was shipped to Saipan from Japan. The 109th Division was organized from troops on Ogasawara Island.

Outline of the 31st Army's order of battle in the latter part of May:

    31st Army headquarters

    Group in the Truk area: Gp Cmdr -- 52d Div Cmdr

        52d Division

        51st Independent Mixed Brigade

        52d Independent Mixed Brigade

        11th Independent Mixed Regiment

        4th South Sea Detachment

        Miscellaneous units under the direct command of the Group Commander

    Group in the Northern Mariana area: Gp Cmdr -- 43d Div Cmdr

        43d Division

47th Independent Mixed Brigade

9th Independent Mixed Regiment

Miscellaneous Units under the direct command of the Group Commander

Group in the Southern Mariana area: Gp Cmdr -- 29th Div Cmdr

29th Division

48th Independent Mixed Brigade

10th Independent Mixed Regiment

Miscellaneous units under the direct command of the Group Commander

Group in the Ogasawara area: Gp Cmdr -- 109th Div Cmdr

109th Division

12th Independent Mixed Brigade

Miscellaneous units under the direct command of the Group Commander

Group in the Palau area: Gp Cmdr -- 14th Div Cmdr

14th Division

49th Independent Mixed Brigade

53d Independent Mixed Brigade

Miscellaneous units under the direct command of the Group Commander

Miscellaneous Groups for other areas: Command -- 31st Army Cmdr

50th Independent Mixed Brigade for Yap

1st Amphibious Brigade for Marshall and Eniwetok

1st South Sea Detachment for Marshall

2d South Sea Detachment for Ponape and Kwsaie

13th Independent Mixed Regiment for Wake

Miscellaneous units under the direct command of the 31st Army

"A-Go" Operations in Mariana Area

During March and April 1944, Imperial General Headquarters planned to fight a decisive battle with the enemy advancing from the Pacific area and conducted surveys which were called the "A-Go" Operation. This was known as the naval battle off the Marianas (Philippines Sea Battle). The enemy situation as estimated by Imperial General Headquarters in the early part of May indicated the enemy's operational preparations in the Central Pacific and Southeastern areas were being carried out steadily. A direct attack against Japan was not expected until after the capture of powerful offensive bases in the Philippines.

We could not determine whether the enemy was planning to advance in the Central Pacific area after extending General MacArthur's offensive line to the North-of-Australia area, or begin the Marianas and Caroline Operations at the earliest possible chance regardless of the progress of MacArthur's operation. There was a good possibility that both operations would be conducted simultaneously. In either case, it was certain the enemy would conduct operations with their main fleet in the waters surrounded by the Mariana and Caroline Islands and New Guinea. Under such circumstances, our force (especially the Navy) would have to operate in spite of inferior strength.

Strength from various areas was to be concentrated in the area against which the enemy attack was anticipated. Although areas from which the strength was taken would suffer, it was thought best to carry out this plan in order to turn the tide of war in our favor. It was decided the area for the decisive campaign would be in the waters surrounded by the Mariana and Caroline Islands and New Guinea.

For operational preparations, the Army endeavored to strengthen its defense and to increase its fighting strength on the islands surrounding the anticipated battle area.

The Navy sent the main strength of its naval land based air units, mostly from the 1st Air Fleet (approximately 1,000 airplanes; 650 were immediately available), to the Mariana Islands area. Part of these planes were sent to the Caroline Islands area. The 1st Mobile Fleet (main strength of the Naval surface force) was preparing for sorties toward the Mariana area from Sulu Archipelago.

While deciding on the operational plan, a discussion took place as to what steps would be taken if the enemy were to attack Biak Island before attacking the Mariana Islands. At the time, strength of our land based air units in the Mariana and Caroline areas was insufficient for a decisive battle. If part of the strength were deployed to the Biak Island area, it would further endanger the "A-Go" Operation. The Navy decided to withhold its air strength though it meant loss of the Geelving Bay area.

During the latter part of May, the enemy launched an attack against Biak Island. The Navy reversed itself and decided to hold the island. This was done after an investigation had been made on the effect which loss of the island and its use by the enemy would have on the "A-Go" Operation. The Navy immediately sent one-third of the land-based air strength in the Central Pacific area from Palau to the Halmahera area. Shortly after arrival in the North-of-Australia area, the majority of the combat personnel in the air units were attacked by malaria.

On 15 June, the enemy began attacking Saipan with the main force of its fleet. Though the defensive installations on Saipan were constructed hastily and were incomplete, they were stronger than any used before in the Southeastern and Central Pacific areas. The Army General Staff believed the island could be held and that the enemy attack plan could be checked for a long time. However, the actual battle situation proved the installations were inadequate to stand up under furious enemy bombing and naval bombardment. As a result, contrary to the expectation of the Army General Staff, Saipan fell after a brief engagement.

At this time, the 31st Army commander was on his way back to his command from a conference at Palau. Due to the enemy landings at Saipan (his headquarters) and Tinian, he flew to Guam. The Group Commander for the northern Marianas and his subordinates fought against the enemy according to the prearranged plan. On the first day, however, heavy casualties resulted and the situation became critical. Efforts of our land-based Navy air units were unsuccessful and strength was depleted.

To aid in the battle, our 1st Mobile Fleet began moving out from the Southern Philippines area, arriving on 19 June in the waters off the Western Mariana Islands. Attacks were carried out with the carrier-based air units. These attacks proved to be unsuccessful due to interception by enemy air planes and anti-aircraft fire. Loss of the major portion of our carrier-based air strength and several carriers forced the Fleet to withdraw. The foregoing was the "A-GO" Operation.

Meanwhile, Army units on Saipan had been conducting effective counterattacks, but by about the 28th, suffered losses of the major portion of their strength. On 5 July, the entire unit was wiped out and the battle of Saipan came to an end. As a result, the strategical situation in the Pacific area changed completely. Imperial General Headquarters planned to conduct an operation to recapture the Marianas but due to the inferior strength of our carrier force abandoned the idea.

The Army General Staff emphasized the importance of the Ogasawara Islands area due to the changed situation in the Mariana Islands area. Command structure for the 31st Army became a problem because command of the Ogasawara Islands by the 31st Army actually became impossible. In the latter part of June an order to reorganize the Ogasawara Group under direct control of the Army General Staff was issued. It was planned to ship troops and munitions to this unit whenever the transportation situation permitted.

Instructions Strengthening Homeland Defenses

Due to the situation in the Pacific area, it became necessary to strengthen defenses of the Homeland. The Army General Staff issued necessary orders in the early part of May as a result of studies which had been made since late January 1944. Influencing the beginning of these studies were the enemy actions during November 1943.

The Commander of Homeland Defenses had been responsible for the command of armies in the Homeland in regard to Homeland defense only. In view of the increasing critical situation, his centralized command authority over most of the armies was strengthened thus improving the coordinated effort of the various Homeland Armies in training, guard and defense efforts. The Eastern, Central and Western District Armies (main ground forces in the Homeland) and the 10th (Tokyo), 18th (Osaka) and 19th (Northern Kyushu) Air Divisions (main defensive air units) were placed under complete command of the Commander of Homeland Defenses. The 1st Air Army commander and the Korea Army commander were also placed under him for defense operations. The 5th Area Army (Hokkaido) remained under the Chief of Army General Staff.

Homeland defense duty assignments issued by the Army General Staff were to accomplish adequate reinforcement. The Commander of Homeland Defenses was to cooperate with the Navy in carrying out the military preparations. Primary objective was to repel enemy air attacks, and protect the strategic region of the Homeland. Defenses of key points along the coast of the mainland and outlying islands were to be reinforced. The Army was to cooperate with the Navy in protecting sea transportation. Effective precautionary measures against air raids were to be developed.

Instructions issued in connection with orders stated that air defense was to protect the Imperial Palace and military installations in Tokyo-Yokohama, Kokura-Yawata, Nagoya and Osaka-Kobe areas. The China Expeditionary Army, Kwantung Army, the 5th Area Srmy and Formosa

Army commanders were to cooperate with the Commander of Homeland Defense in maintaining communication for intelligence reports on enemy air raids. Various strategic military positions and movements were to be protected against enemy attacks. An effort would be made to maintain public order. As a limit to his authority, the Commander of Homeland Defenses had to obtain approval from the Chief of the Army General Staff before changing the location of troops except in cases of emergencies and very minor movements.

In the over-all reorganization, the line of communication in the Homeland became extremely important. The supply depots in the Homeland were unable to maintain the job of supplying materiel requirement abroad because it became difficult to schedule military industrial production. This was caused by the possibility of enemy air raids, rapid increase in the number of troops in our Army strength, loss of munitions while being shipped, and difficulty of transporting essential natural resources from abroad. It was planned to disperse the munitions stored at the supply depots. This plan was undertaken and it was speeded up after the Mariana region was captured by the enemy. The munition plants were not moved in order to avoid lowering the current production rate.

The Army had mobilized strength amounting to approximately 3,650,000 by the end of March 1944. After reviewing the situation, it was believed this could be expanded by approximately 1,000,000. Due to shipping difficulties, it was considered impossible to send troops abroad after summer. Thus, the required strength was being mobilized during the first part of the year.

Line of Communication (Logistical Support) During Third Phase

The supply of operational materiel became inadequate. At this time, the decisive battle was beginning and shipping became difficult due to enemy air and submarine attacks. Shipment of supplies to strategic areas would be continued but it was to be reduced to a minimum in other areas. The quality and quantity of munitions and shipping did not always fill operational needs due to the changing battle situation which necessitated changing troop dispositions. The increased number of ships being lost caused our supply system to become inadequate. As a result, each operational Army received orders to establish a system of self-subsistence. Strength of the line of communication could not be employed effectively under prevailing shipping conditions and because of deteriorating equipment.

CHAPTER VII

Fourth Phase of the War

(July - December 1944)

Operations Summary for Fourth Phase

The 43d Division on Saipan was defeated and annihilated completely on 5 July. The enemy landed and recaptured Guam on the 21st and Tinian on the 24th of the same month. Garrisons on both islands were forced to cease organized resistance in early August.

The enemy started to attack Morotai and Peleliu on 15 September and despite desperate resistance, enemy superior strength gained control of positions on Peleliu Island.

In the Burma Theater, the "U" Operation had ended unsuccessfully, and on 4 July the Southern Army stopped operations according to instructions from Army General Staff. Along the eastern boundary of the Yunnan area (in Burma) units of the 56th Division continuously carried out bold defensive tactics and inflicted heavy casualties on a superior enemy. However, the Myitkyina and Lameng Garrisons were overwhelmed and annihilated on 4 August and 7 September respectively. The situation in north Burma became increasingly critical and was considered to be hopeless.

In China, the Hunan-Kwangsi Operation ("Ichi-Go") was progressing smoothly. Our Army captured Hengyang on 8 August. After a month of consolidation, the attack was resumed and Kweilin and Liuchow were captured on 10 November. The Army then pursued the enemy toward the Tuhshan area and occupied it for some time. In order to prevent the US Army from using coastal bases in China, our Army decided to secure those bases. Yungchia was occupied during the early part of September and Fuchou was occupied during the early part of October.

During this period, enemy air raids on Japan Proper with large bombers increased. On 8 July Kyushu was raided, and on 29 July, Dairen, Anshan, and Mukden were raided. Since August, enemy B-29 attacks were directed chiefly against Kyushu, Manchuria and Korea. On 24 November, Tokyo became the objective. The enemy apparently, had started using the Saipan Air Base.

A strong enemy task force attacked Okinawa on 10 October, and Formosa on 13 and 14 October. The main force of our Navy Air Force (with an attached element of the Army Air Force) counterattacked the enemy off Formosa inflicting heavy damages. On 19 October, the enemy landed on Leyte. Our Army fought decisive major engagements both on the ground and in the air and, on 25 October, the main force of our Navy fought major sea engagements with the main force of the enemy fleet in waters east of the Philippines. We suffered heavy losses, and our counterattack ended in failure. In mid-December, we had to abandon the scheduled plan for the major Leyte Operation. On 15 December, the enemy began to land on Mindoro.

The No 1 "Sho" Operation in the Philippine area was the decisive battle in which the greater part of our Imperial Air and Navy Forces and an element of the Army participated. This battle took place in the Philippines where preparations had been made for the past several months to recover from our unfavorable situation. The failure of this operation narrowed our sphere of influence to Japan Proper, the area north of Formosa and China.

The important international events during this period were the election of the US President for the fourth term on 9 November and the public speech made by Stalin, Premier of USSR on the same day. This speech attracted world wide attention when he declared Japan an agressor nation.

Development and Preparation for "Sho" Operations

Loss of the Marianas area, the most important strong point in the Central Pacific, and heavy losses suffered by our Navy in the Battle of the Philippines Sea made it easier for the enemy to attack the Philippines, their next operational objective. Also, it allowed them to carry out offensive air bombardment against Japan Proper. As the enemy tactics succeeded, capitalizing on close cooperation of their Army, Navy and Air Forces and without aid of land based planes, they advanced rapidly, leaping distances as great as 1,000 nautical miles. As the situation became increasingly worse, our weakness in defensive preparations for Japan Proper was clearly revealed. At this time, our "U" Operation on the continent had failed and recovery from this appeared hopeless. In northern Burma, our Army repeatedly withdrew under difficult circumstances, and developed an unstable troop disposition.

Furious enemy attacks from the east and west, together with intensified interruption of our sea transportation, not only separated Japan Proper from the Southern area, but also gradually isolated each district in the Southern area. This rapid breakdown of our strategic situation, acute shortage of materiel caused by the isolation of Japan Proper, delay in personnel and materiel reinforcements, deterioration of our political influence upon nations in the Co-Prosperity Sphere, and growing unrest within interior Japan, brought about the most serious crisis since the outbreak of the war. It finally resulted in the retirement of the Tojo Cabinet and formation of the Koiso Cabinet in July 1944.

After careful investigation and consideration, Imperial General Headquarters proceeded with preparations for subsequent operations. The defense of the line linking the Philippine, Formosa, Nansei Islands, Japan Proper and Kurile Islands was to be strengthened against enemy attacks from the ocean. Preparations to counter-attack and defeat any enemy attacking any sector on this line would be made by concentrating our land, sea and air forces. This plan was called "Sho" Operation. The Hunan-Kwangsi Operation would be completed as planned, reducing the problem of sea transportation through the change to continental traffic. At the same time, efforts would be made to protect sea transportation along the coastal route.

During the latter part of July, the Southern Army, the China Expeditionary Army, the Homeland Defense Command, the Formosa Army and the 5th Area Army were issued an order covering future operational preparations. It stated that in decisive operations during the latter part of the year, the Army General Staff intended to defeat attacks by the main force of the US Army. The Imperial Army would carry out decisive operations in the Philippines area, Japan Proper, and the area in-between. The exact battle sector and starting date would be decided by the Army General Staff. The Armies concerned would make preparations immediately in cooperation with the Navy.

Supplementing this order, the following directives were issued and Commanders of the Armies were to complete basic preparations according to the schedule listed below.

No 1 "Sho" Decisive operation in the Philippines area -- by the end of August.

No 2 "Sho" Decisive operation in the area between Japan Proper and the Philippines -- end of August.

No 3 "Sho" Decisive operation of Japan Proper (excluding Hokkaido) -- by the end of October.

No 4 "Sho" Decisive operation in the Northeastern area -- by the end of October.

Each Army commander was to make plans and preparations for the deployment of ground troops, according to the following:

Southern Army commander was to deploy a unit, with a brigade as its nucleus, to the northern Philippines area to be ready to fulfill levies at any time for shipments to Formosa or the Nansei Islands (for No 2 "Sho" Operation).

Formosa Army commander was to deploy a unit, with a brigade as its nucleus, to Formosa to be ready to fulfill levies for shipment to the northern Philippines area (for No 1 "Sho" Operation) or the Nansei Islands (for No 2 "Sho" Operation).

The Homeland Defense commander was to deploy one detachment (three infantry and one artillery battalions as its nucleus) to the Kagoshima area (for No 2 "Sho" Operation) to be ready to fulfill levies for shipment to the Nansei Islands area, and another detachment (same strength as the other) to the Himeji area to be ready to fulfill levies for shipment to the Ogasawara Island area.

Army General Staff was to deploy approximately one division in the Shanghai area to be ready to fulfill levies for shipment to the Philippines (for No 1 "Sho" Operation). Nansei Islands or the Formosa area (for No 2 "Sho" Operation).

Army General Staff was to deploy the 47th Division to the Hirosaki area to be ready to fulfill levies for shipment to the northeastern part of Honshu (for No 3 "Sho" Operation). or the Hokkaido area (for No 4 "Sho" Operation).

The 36th Army, probably, would be put under the command of the Homeland Defense commander when it carried out the No 3 "Sho" Operation.

As part of the above-mentioned plan, a Central Agreement on air operations was made between the Army and the Navy at Imperial General Headquarters. Army and Navy Air Forces would complete preparations for the decisive battle by the end of August. In the event of an enemy attack, both Air Forces would concentrate their strength against the enemy at the decisive battle sector.

Basic disposition of the Army and Navy air strength was arranged according to the following outline:

Northeastern area: 12th Air Fleet
                            1st Air Division

Japan Proper (excluding Hokkaido):
                            3d Air Fleet
                            Air Units of the 3d Fleet (whenever in the Japan Proper area)
                            Air Instruction Army
                            10th Air Division
                            11th Air Division
                            12th Air Division

Nansei Islands and the Formosa area:
                            2d   Air Fleet
                            8th Air Division

Philippines, North-of-Australia and Central Pacific area:
                            1st Air Fleet
                            4th Air Army

Other areas: Same as the present.

Depending upon which of the "Sho" Operations was the battle sector, air strength to be used was established as shown on Chart 10.

The operational policy for air units prior to actual start of "Sho" actions called for our air strength to exercise flexible air tactics to decrease enemy fighting strength. At the same time, steps were to be taken to prevent any reduction in our fighting strength. To do this, our air force would conduct short surprise raids upon enemy air bases and use opportune intercepting air tactics. Air units were to be deployed in depth. Antiaircraft fire was to take care of air defense at our air bases.

If an enemy amphibious task force were found to be advancing by sea, an element of our air force would launch a surprise attack on it to inflict damages on its aircraft carriers. The enemy was to be allowed to approach freely near our air base. Then, the combined strength of our Army and Navy Air Force was to attack boldly and destroy both carriers and transports, maintaining a continuous day and night attack.

Against enemy carrier-plane raids on strategic districts in Japan Proper, special efforts would be made to strengthen our air defense disposition. Disregarding the instructions stated in the preceding paragraph, our air force was to attack the enemy carriers before they took the initiative.

As a part of preparations for the "Sho" Operation, the following adjustments in the distribution of strength were made:

No 1 "Sho" area:

    During the early part of August, the 14th Army was deactivated and reorganized as the 14th Area Army. Also, the 35th Army was newly organized. This enlargement was in compliance with an Army General staff order. The 14th Area Army commander was placed under the Southern Army commander and located at Manila. He was responsible for defense of the Philippines area. The 35th Army was placed under the 14th Area Army and was responsible for the defense of the southern Philippines. The 26th Division (in Mongolia) was assembled for transfer at Shanghai. The 8th Division and the 2d Tank Division (in Manchuria) were assembled for transfer at Pusan and its former location, respectively. All were placed under the 14th Area Army during the early part of August.

Order of battle for the 14th Area Army:

    14th Area Army Headquarters

        35th Army (essentially the 16th, 30th, 100th and 102d Divisions, 54th Independent Mixed Brigade and miscellaneous supporting units)

"Sho" Operations Air Strength

Area	Stationed Unit	"Sho" No 1	"Sho" No 2	"Sho" No 3	"Sho" No 4
Northeastern area	1st Air Division	Reserve	Reserve	Reserve	Total Strength
Japan Proper	10th Air Division			Total Strength	
	11th Air Division			Total Strength	
	12th Air Division	2 fgtr regiments 1 heavy bomber regiment	Main Force	Total Strength	
	Air Instructor Army	1 fgtr regiment 1 light bomber regiment 1 heavy bomber regiment		Total Strength	
Formosa	8th Air Division	Total Strength	Total Strength	1 hq ren regiment	Reserve
Philippines	4th Air Army		2 fgtr regiments 1 aslt regiment 1 heavy bomber regiment 1 hq ren regiment	2 fgtr regiments 2 aslt regiments 1 heavy bomber regiment	Reserve
China	5th Air Army	2 fgtr regiments	2 fgtr regiments	2 fgtr regiments 2 light bomber regiments	Reserve

    8th Division

    26th Division

    103d Division

    105th Division

    2d Tank Division

    55th, 58th and 61st Independent Mixed Brigades

No 2 "Sho" area:

In mid-July, the 32d Army was transferred from the Western District Army to the Formosa Army. The 62d Division (in China) was assembled for transfer at Chingtao while the 24th Division (in Manchuria) was assembled for transfer in Northern Kyushu. Both were placed under the 32d Army during the latter part of July. The 66th Division (in China) was transferred to the Formosa Army during the middle and latter part of July. The 10th Division (from Manchuria) had assembled for transfer in the Shanghai area and was placed under the Formosa Army during the early part of August.

No 3 "Sho" area:

During the latter part of July, the 36th Army was organized (essentially the 81st and 93d Divisions and the 4th Tank Division). Its main force was assembled in the Kanto District and at the foot of Mt Fuji. During the early part of July, the 47th Division was put under the direct command of the Army General Staff and kept at its current location.

During the early part of July, the Ogasawara Group was reinforced with an Independent Mixed Regiment and tank, mortar, trench mortar units, etc. In the latter part of July, three Independent Mixed Brigades were newly organized in the Izu Islands area to strengthen defense there.

On 15 July, all Army Districts in Japan Proper were put under a wartime alert condition, and the maintenance of this alert was strengthened.

In the middle of July, the 11th and 12th Air Divisions were organized in Japan Proper, and together with the 10th Air Division which was already established, comprised the main force of air defense units in the Homeland.

In June, all air training schools were reorganized into Air Instruction Divisions. Simultaneously, to order and instruct air operations in the Homeland, the Air Instruction Army headquarters was established. This was organized from the Air Inspectorate General. Personnel served in dual capacities of Headquarters Staff and Air Inspectorate General Staff. These transfers represented the completion in troop adjustments for the "Sho" areas.

We had lost confidence in our island defense operation and its effectiveness in beach combat since the loss of Saipan. A dispute raged pro and con regarding frontal and rear disposition of our troops against enemy landing operations. The Army General Staff formulated a plan to standardize general tactics for island defense. An improvised pamphlet, "The Main Points for Island Defense", was published for temporary use. Then, "The Instruction Manual for Island Defense" was compiled and published to familiarize our Army with new coastal defense tactics. As a general rule, beach and checking positions were to be prepared in the front of main positions. The former was intended to inflict losses upon the enemy by using beach fire power. The latter (to the rear of beach positions) was intended to prevent the enemy from establishing a solid beachhead position. Behind the beach and main line of resistance positions, an additional last line of entrenchments was to be prepared. All positions, especially the main line, were to be constructed to withstand furious enemy bombing and naval bombardment. Following full use of all positions and fire power for inflicting heavy casualties, a counterattack was to be launched at the appropriate time to annihilate the enemy in a single blow.

Since the use of automatic cannons in beach combat was highly regarded, many Independent Automatic Cannon Units were organized and attached to various units in the "Sho" areas, after August, as part of preparations for the "Sho" Operation.

Preliminary Actions Leading to No 1 "Sho" Operation

Enemy invasion of Morotai and Peleliu on 15 September was judged as a preparatory operation for the Philippines. It was estimated the enemy would launch its attack soon against the Philippines. This was clear because recapture of the Philippines would provide a great opportunity for the enemy, politically and strategically. The situation inside and outside the Philippines area was favorable for such a recapturing operation. Apparently, the enemy had made the Philippines their main objective since beginning their counterattack. There were few possibilities of an enemy attack on Japan Proper during the remainder of 1944 since no bases were held from which to launch such a landing operation. Also, a deterrent to such an attack would be their difficulties in maintaining their supplies. Finally, from the stand point of the enemy and our strategic dispositions, a landing on Japan Proper appeared improbable. Enemy air raids against Japan Proper were expected to be intensified. It was probable that the enemy would attack the Ogasawara Islands area. In view of seasonal atmospheric and sea conditions in the Northeastern area, no enemy attack was expected there until Spring 1945. There was a greater possibility of an enemy attack on Formosa and the Nansei Islands than against Japan Proper.

Enemy acticities in the North-of-Australia area were not expected to be too great. However, an operation was anticipated by the Dutch-Australia Army as divisionary support for the main enemy force in the Philippines.

Coincident with offensive operations by the American Army in the Pacific area, the British Army was expected to take the offensive after the monsoon season in the Burma and Indian Ocean area. We considered that a defeat of the American Army on our Eastern Front would keep the British Army from carrying out a large-scale operation alone.

In the early part of September, the United States Task Forces attacked the southern Philippines. On 21 September, the main force of the US Task Force attacked the northern Philippines. In both areas, the attack was directed chiefly on our air strength and naval fleet. Our losses were heavy. When the enemy captured Morotai, they were expected to construct a powerful air base from which to upset our operational preparations and activities in the Philippine area. Both the Army General Staff and the 14th Area Army studied a plan to recapture Morotai. But, it was apparent that if our Air and Navy strength were depleted in such a recapturing operation it would be detrimental to the decisive operation in the Philippines. We decided to abandon the idea and use only an element of our air force to harrass the enemy.

Considering the general situation estimate, the Army General Staff issued the following order on 22 September:

1. Imperial General Headquarters expected to carry out the decisive operation in the Philippine area in and after the latter part of October.
2. To perform their duties, the Southern Army, China Expeditionary Army and the Formosa Army commander will complete their operational preparations by the latter part of October.

When the "Sho" Operational preparations were planned in July, direction of the counterattack by the main force of the enemy had not been determined, exactly. However, it was expected to be directed, probably, toward the Philippine area. In the latter part of

September, the increasing seriousness of the Philippine situation was sufficient to guess the necessity of the No 1 "Sho" Operation in the near future. The Army General Staff made a preliminary decision that the Imperial Army would carry out the decisive operation in the Philippines. Immediately, it was planned to rush the completion of preparations.

Ever since the "Sho" Operational Plan was formed, the Army General Staff of Imperial General Headquarters had proceeded with the study of tactics for the Army air attack.

Because our Navy Air Force always had concentrated its attack on the enemy fleet, enemy transports were able to approach landing areas without suffering any losses. Thus, they easily succeeded in their operations. The Army Air Force intended to prevent this by inflicting heavy losses upon enemy landing forces. Efforts were made to study enemy tactics and carry out the necessary training. The Navy Air Force planned to press its attack on the enemy fleet. This responsibility division was believed to be correct when the performance of our Army Air Force flights over the seas were taken into consideration. In September, the Southern Army expressed its opinion that the principle objective of the Army Air Force attack should be enemy aircraft carriers. The Army General Staff did not change its original plan.

In the middle of September, the Southern Army commander dispatched his operational staff officer to Tokyo to set forth his opinions concerning the start of No 1 "Sho" Operation. The Southern Army commander was convinced that the enemy would land in the Philippines very soon and felt that the concentration of our ground, air and sea forces as provided in No 1 "Sho" Operations Plan should be started immediately to avoid delays in meeting the demands of a last minute decision to repel an enemy landing force in the Philippines. By beginning the concentration of these forces, immediately, he felt the transfer of strength could be accomplished more easily and surely because it would be underway before the full enemy sea and air power was operating in the area. The Army General Staff reply was that orders for the start of No 1 "Sho" would be issued following a thorough investigation then being carried out.

The principle air forces objective of the "Sho" Operation was to annihilate enemy aircraft carrier groups and transport convoys. Tactics to be used were to allow enemy freedom of movement and close approach to our bases. When the enemy was close enough to make quick retreat difficult, the "Sho" Operation was to be put into effect. The entire strength of our Army and Navy Air Forces was to be concentrated in attacking the enemy carrier groups and transport convoys, instantaneously. If our Army and Navy Air Forces attacked too early, our inferior air strength would be annihilated before the decisive battle. If too late, the enemy would escape our attack and the objective of our operation would be lost. The Army General Staff was waiting for the right opportunity and considered the time suggested by the Southern Army commander as too early.

On 22 September, the 1st Division was transferred to the 14th Area Army and sent to the Philippines area. Many sea raiding units were attached to the 14th Area Army, the Formosa Army and the 32d Army. On that same day, the 23d Division was ordered to assemble in Southern Manchuria under direct command of the Kwantung Army commander.

Start and Conduct of No 1 "Sho" Operation

With the beginning of October, enemy planes again became very active in the Philippine area and the situation rapidly shifted to a crisis. Moreover, the enemy seemed to be advancing toward the Leyte area. In the middle of October, the 30th Fighter Group was organized from picked strength of fighter units in Japan Proper and put under command of the 4th Air Army. The Manila Defense command was established at Manila. On 18 October, taking advice given by the Southern Army commander, the Army General Staff finally decided to start the No 1 "Sho" Operation and issued the following order to start the 1st Stage beginning the following day, 19 October.

1. The decisive operation of the Imperial Army would be carried out in the Philippine area.

2. In cooperation with the Navy, the Southern Army commander would start the decisive operation to defeat the main force of the enemy attacking the Philippine area.

3. The China Expeditionary Army commander and the 10th Area Army commander (Prior to 22 September called the Formosa Army commander) would cooperate in every way possible to make the operation easier to accomplish.

According to the prearranged plan, air strength began to concentrate in the Philippine area.

On 20 October, an element of the US Army began landing on the eastern coast of Leyte and following a fierce air battle, combat actions on land were steadily expanded and intensified. When the original "Sho" Operational Plan was drawn up in July by the Imperial General Headquarters it called for execution of the full-scale decisive operation in Luzon by the Army, Navy and Air Forces. In the central and southern Philippines, it was to be carried out only by Air and Navy Forces. In other words, decisive ground operation had been planned only for Luzon. This was planned because ground strength of the 14th Area Army was considered too weak to cover the entire Philippines area in the decisive operation.

The Army General Staff changed its plan. It was believed that the main part of the enemy task forces had been destroyed during the Navy Air Battle off Formosa just prior to the Leyte landing

Also, our Army air operations seemed successful in the early stages of the enemy landing. Therefore, the original plan was revised and the decisive operation in Leyte was established to be conducted by the Army, Navy and Air Forces as had been planned, originally, for Luzon alone. The revised plan to carry out full-scale ground operations was supported and carried out through command authority. Shortly after operations began, there were some evident expressions by the 14th Area Army staff officers which took exception to the revised plan, but command authority settled these quickly. Throughout the Philippines operation, there were several differences of opinion regarding tactics. However, they were resolved through the chain of command.

With Leyte as the center of the operational theater, fierce battles were fought both on land and in the air. Reinforcements were dispatched from various areas according to the "Sho" plan to defeat the enemy. The 14th Area Army and the 4th Air Army assembled their entire combat strength to carry out the decisive operation.

About this same time, the Navy General Staff of Imperial General Headquarters planned an offensive advance using the main force of our fleet in a movement to the Leyte area. Estimating little possibility for success and serious adverse strategic consequences in case of failure, the Army General Staff earnestly urged abandonment of the idea. The Navy was not pursuaded. The main force of our Combined Fleet moved from the Singapore area to the Eastern Sea off the Philippines to carry out its plan. Although we inflicted some losses upon the enemy in the resulting sea battle of 25 October, we suffered far greater and were forced to retreat. This critical loss in our Navy strength seriously lowered chances for success not only in the Leyte area operation, but also in the overall operational situation existing between the enemy and our forces. Following this, enemy task forces dominated the sea surrounding Japan Proper and the East and South China Sea.

On 28 October, a restatement of tactical principles in the form of an Army and Navy Agreement for air operations to defeat the enemy landings was concluded at the Imperial General Headquarters. This strengthened the high command's tactical unity through the chain of command. Outline of the Central Agreement on air operations concluded on 28 October provided:

1. The Army and Navy would dispatch a majority of their air units, replacement personnel and manufactured planes to the Philippines area for use in the No 1 "Sho" Operation.

2. Principle duties of the Army and Navy Air Forces were to be as follows:

    The Navy Air Force was to be responsible for interception of enemy sea transportation and reinforcements of Army Groups already put ashore. This included destroying enemy transports near the anchorage. Also, defeat of enemy task forces, including the enemy fleet supporting the landings, was to be accomplished by the Navy Air Force.

    The Army Air Force was to be responsible for attacking enemy air bases and air control over the anchorage area. Also, it was to destroy enemy transports in the anchorage area, including attacks during debarkation from enemy transports. Additionally, it was to cooperate directly with the ground operation.

3. Special Suicide Attack Units were to be used to perform the above-mentioned duties.

4. The Army and Navy commanders in the operational theaters were to make every effort in performing these duties

and securing air supremacy in operational areas. According to the situation, they were to take advantage of every opportunity to cooperate in accomplishing the objectives.

During its early stages, the Leyte Operation progressed very favorably as the 4th Air Army, with its entire strength using suicidal tactics, repeatedly attacked and inflicted heavy losses upon the enemy convoys. However, our reinforcements from Japan Proper did not arrive as necessary which caused our strength and the enemy's to become almost equal.

On 1 November, a second order for No 1 "Sho" Operation was issued. The Army and Navy made strenuous efforts to transport replacements for both planes and air personnel. Difficulties were encountered and the operational situation gradually became worse. Together with this unfavorable air situation it became difficult to send ground forces to Leyte. By the latter part of November, it was impossible to recover from this difficult position. In the middle and latter part of November, the Army General Staff transferred the 10th and 23d Divisions from the 10th Area Army and the 19th Division from the Korea Army to the 14th Area Army. It ordered the Kwantung Army commander to assemble the 12th Division. In the early part of November, the 2d Raiding Brigade was placed, temporarily, under the Southern Army commander. In the latter part of November, the 1st Raiding Group was put under the command of the 4th Air Army commander. When both were dispatched to the Philippines, the 2d Raiding Brigade was made an organic unit of the 1st Raiding Group.

As soon as the general situation in Leyte was settled, the enemy secured a landing base on Mindoro Island on 15 February and accelerated construction and repair of bases in Leyte in preparation for the Luzon Operation.

Sea Transportation was a critical element in the preparations for the No 1 "Sho" Operation. It was hindered, continuously, by enemy interception from sea and air. Since August, enemy interception had increased sharply, and our losses increased enormously. Local transportation within the Philippines was also cut off. Operational preparations, especially those for the smallest advanced units did not go well. Special efforts were made to guard transport convoys. Essential war materiel was divided and loaded on several transports to avoid any total loss of materiel by the sinking of a single transport. The quickest possible unloading of transports was stressed to avoid enemy air attacks during debarkation. Priority was given to transportation of essential war materiel and to technical training. Even with these efforts, the Leyte Operation had started with only 50 to 60% of our planned operational preparations completed.

Operational Conduct in Other Areas

In the Central Pacific area during the latter part of July, the enemy landed on Guam and Tinian. No word had been received from Guam since the end of July or from Tinian since the early part of August. The enemy appeared to have started a large scale construction of air bases in the Marianas. Keeping pace with this construction, air raids on the Ogasawara Island area were intensified. Consequently, reinforcement for the Ogasawara Group became increasingly difficult.

Previously, when the command for all units in the Southern area was unified, the Southern Army headquarters was moved to Manila. In August, the Southern Army commander expressed his opinion that his headquarters should be situated at Saigon or Singapore. His reason was that these places were more convenient than Manila for commanding all troops in the entire Southern area. The Army General Staff did not approve this advice. It was considered improper to change the Southern Army headquarters location when the Philippines Operation was about to begin. In November, after some disputes, this request from the Southern Army commander was granted. Then, the Southern Army headquarters was transferred to Saigon.

Following the unsuccessful Imphal Operation ("U" Operation) and failure of the operation in the Hukawng Valley area, the disposition of our troops was undergoing a rearrangement in the Burma area to be completed by the beginning of October. Meanwhile, the Burma Area Army was making preparations for launching its attack in the Salween River area.

The Army General Staff studied plans for subsequent operations in the Burma area after failure of the Imphal Operation. In the middle of September, for purposes of continuing operations there, it instructed the Southern Army commander to secure strategic areas in southern Burma as strong points in the northern flank of our southern sphere and, simultaneously, make efforts to interrupt enemy liaison between India and China. The intercepting operation in Burma to cut off enemy liaison between India and China had been the principle mission of the Burma Area Army. By this, our Empire had been endeavoring continuously to terminate the China Incident. The unsuccessful progress of the war situation in the northern Burma area and the small number of reinforcements we were able to send there forced withdrawal of the missions.

Although the Army General Staff never neglected the Burma area, important operations to be carried out in the Pacific area took precedence. This resulted in no strength being available to send to the Burma area as reinforcement. Since the enemy was expected to attempt a new attack on southern Burma through the neck of the Malay Peninsula, it became necessary to regroup the main force of the Burma Area Army in the southern Burma area. This reduced the strength in the northern Burma area.

Defense of the Celebes, Borneo, Andaman and Nicobar up to this time was the responsibility of the Navy. In the latter part of September, the Imperial General Headquarters revised the Central Agreement concerning defense of the strategic areas in the South. It was decided that the Navy would be responsible continuously for sea operations. Other operations were to be a joint responsibility of the Army and Navy. Both Army and Navy units were to be posted in all these areas. In the latter part of October, the Agreement was revised again making the Army mainly responsible for direct defensive land operations in these areas. The 2d Area Army commander in the Celebes, the 37th Army commander (prior to 22 September called the Borneo Garrison Army commander) in Southern Borneo, and the 29th Army commander of both Andaman and Nicobar Islands were ordered to command the Navy Land Units in their respective sectors in addition to their Army units.

Earlier, in July and August, when an enemy attack on the Philippines and North-of-Australia area had been expected soon, the Army General Staff studied a command system for the Philippines, North-of-Australia, Borneo, and the Java areas. Three alternatives were considered:

1. Present command system would be maintained. In other words, the 14th Area Army and 2d Area Army would be responsible for the Philippines and North-of-Australia area, respectively. The 7th Area Army would be responsible for Borneo and Java.

2. The Philippines and northern Borneo would be put under command of the 14th Area Army, while the North-of-Australia area, Celebes and Java would be put under command of the 2d Area Army.

3. The Borneo Garrison Army would be transferred from the 7th Area Army to the direct command of the Southern Army.

Among these proposals, the second was judged best under normal conditions from a strategic standpoint for defensive operations in the Philippines since the Philippines and Borneo were closely related and separated only by the Sula Sea. Also, it would be the 2d Area Army's advantage to have a deep rear zone behind its responsible sector. However, any large scale change in responsible sectors evidently should be avoided since the strategic situation had become increasingly critical. Thus, the 3d suggestion was adopted and the order was issued in September. This plan was advantageous since the Southern Army commander could easily control the strategic relationship between the Philippines and Borneo.

In October, the newly organized 94th Division was put under the 29th Army commander. A Singapore Defense Command was established and put under the 7th Area Army commander.

In November, the 49th and 53d Divisions (previously under the Southern Army) were put under the command of the Burma Area Army.

In the middle of November, after the Southern Army headquarters had moved to Saigon, both important flanks east and west of the Southern area (the Philippines and Burma) developed unfavorable situations. It looked like these strategic area values we held were in danger of being lost forever.

In French Indo-China, Thailand and Malay we had only a token garrison force. The Southern Army wanted about five new divisions for these areas as reinforcements. The Army General Staff studied the general disposition of all the Imperial strength in the entire operational area. In December, it transferred the 37th Division southward by land from the 11th Army (in China) to the French Indo-China Garrison Army. The 22d Division (in China) was also planned as reinforcement in the near future.

In the Formosa and Nansei Islands area about the middle of October, an enemy task force appeared off Formosa and raided the entire Formosa area plus the Okinawa Island. At first, we refrained from counterattacking to avoid any depletion of our air strength. Army ground units made every effort to maintain efficiency of the air bases through constant repair and anti-aircraft defense activities. Navy air units in Japan Proper area were sent to Okinawa and made a surprise attack on the enemy task force off Formosa. As stated previously, it was believed the main part of the task force had been destroyed.

Since the activation of the 5th Area Army and the 27th Army in March 1944, they had been reinforced gradually by successive mobilization procedures. By July, the 7th and 77th Divisions were both complete tactical divisions, and a 7th Depot Division was placed under the 5th Area Army commander, too. The 69th Independent Mixed Brigade was assigned to the 27th Army in August.

In the China area about the latter part of May, the 11th Army began its Hunan-Kwangsi Operation which was the 2d Phase for the "Ichi-Go" Operation. This progressed smoothly as we captured Changsha in the middle of June, Hengyang in early August, and Lingling in early September. In the latter part of July, according to plan, the 23d Army (two divisions and two brigades as its nucleus) started its operation, moving northward from the Canton area. This was quite successful, too. On 10 November, Kweilin and Liuchow were captured and without rest, the Canton-Hankou Railroad Penetrating Operation was carried out and completed in late January. The "Ichi-Go" Operation was accomplished.

For security against landings by US Troops in this area, for protection of coastal sea transportation and to establish intermediate bases for ships, the Army General Staff ordered the China

Expeditionary Army commander to capture strategic points on the eastern coast of Chekiang Province in July. An element of the 13th Army, in cooperation with the Navy, captured Yungchia in early September and Fuchou in early October.

Since the 11th Army headquarters had been sent on an operational mission, 34th Army headquarters was established in the Wuchang-Hankou sector during July.

Also in July, the following divisions were organized and placed in the Order of Battle of the following Armies:

114th Division -- 1st Army

115th and 117th Divisions -- 12th Army

118th Division -- Mongolia Garrison Army

Simultaneous with the beginning of the Hunan-Kwangsi Operation, China Expeditionary Army headquarters was advanced to the Wuchang-Hankou sector to direct this operation. In August, in order to facilitate the general command and control of the entire China Expeditionary Army, 6th Area Army headquarters was established under the China Expeditionary Army commander to assume direction of the Hunan-Kwangsi Operation.

Order of Battle for the 6th Area Army:

6th Area Army headquarters (27th, 64th and 68th Divisions)

11th Army (3d, 13th, 34th, 40th, 58th and 116th Divisions as nucleus)

23d Army (22d and 104th Divisions as nucleus)

34th Army (39th Division and 5th Independent Mixed Brigade)

In September, 20th Army headquarters (in Manchuria) was transferred to central China to be responsible for command of the Canton-Hankou Railroad Penetrating Operation. It was put under command of the 6th Area Army and the 27th, 64th, 68th and 106th Divisions were placed under its command. In October, the 47th Division was transferred from Japan Proper and placed under command of the 6th Area Army.

In November, the Governor General of the Hongkong Occupied Territory was also placed under the command of the 6th Area Army.

In the Manchuria and Korea areas, as mentioned above, from August to December of 1944 the 20th Army headquarters, 1st, 8th, 10th, 12th, 19th and 23d Divisions, the 2d Tank Division and the 68th Brigade were withdrawn from Manchuria and Korea. The majority were transferred to the Philippines area while some elements were transferred to Formosa and China. During the same period, the 108th, 111th, 112th, 119th and 120th Divisions were organized in Manchuria and Korea.

Since 1943, most of the reserve materiel accumulated in Manchuria had been sent to the Southern area. Later, additional military equipment which had been issued to the Army units in Manchuria was also transferred to the Southern area.

At every opportunity, the Army General Staff repeatedly warned the Kwantung Army commander to prevent any provocation which might start a war between Japan and Russia. In case of a Russian Army attack, a defensive operation was expected to be very difficult due to the greatly reduced strength of the Kwantung Army. Investigations were repeated several times concerning defensive operation in Manchuria against the possibility of Russian attack. Two suggestions were made. One was to conduct a prolonged war of resistance in southern Manchuria from the beginning and the other was to counterattack the enemy in the border line area and later withdraw gradually through successive delaying operations. Final decision had not been reached as yet.

Following the beginning of No 3 "Sho" Operational Preparations, all Army units in Japan Proper were working on the construction of coastal defense positions, especially in southwestern Kyushu, southern Shikoku, Ise, Toyohashi, Sagami, Chiba-Ibaragi, Sendai and the

Aomori areas. By December, construction of fortified positions were completed partially in all areas. Following this, they were strengthened gradually.

Since November, enemy air attacks became more intense resulting in increased losses and damages in the Tokyo, Nagoya, Osaka, and northern Kyushu areas. These air raids seriously impeded various war time activities. The Army General Staff took special steps to strengthen air defenses including replenishing and fully equipping air defense units.

As part of this program in late December, the Air Instruction Army headquarters which had been organized from the Air Inspectorate General was dissolved. The 6th Air Army headquarters was established under the Commander of Homeland Defenses. It was responsible for preparation of homeland defense air operations.

The greatest difficulty in making preparations for the defensive operation in Japan Proper was in supply services. Investigations and preparations were made on a five-point plan which was accomplished, gradually.

1. War materiel was to be accumulated in strategic coastal areas of Japan Proper by the end of September. It was to be used by Coastal Mobile Units in any emergency.

2. Operational war materiel vital to the defense of Japan Proper but not yet produced had to be manufactured, immediately. Locations of accumulated materiel distributed for purposes of storage and air defense would be changed to make execution of the operational plan easier.

3. In Japan Proper, the Army had no operational line of communication units. All supply depots and medical facilities were under command of the military administrative organizations (War Ministry). Line of Communications activities were quite complicated due to

civil rights of the people. It was necessary to correct these relationships.

4. Since sea transportation between Japan Proper and the Southern area was expected to cut off soon, fighting strength from the continent had to be transferred to Japan Proper in spite of sea transportation insecurity. The transportation system between China, Manchuria and Japan Proper should be rearranged.

5. Self-sufficiency of Japan Proper had to be developed.

Army-Navy Discussions Regarding Unified Air Forces Command

Investigations and disputes had been repeated many times between Army and Navy General Staffs of Imperial General Headquarters concerning operational responsibility and cooperation of the Army and Navy Air Forces ever since June of 1942.

Actually, the Navy Air Force (responsible for sea patrol of the Indian and Pacific Oceans, offensive operations in the Northeastern area, and air operations in the Southeastern area) was depleted both in its plane and personnel strength and in efficiency due to long exhausting battles in the Southern area and the Mariana Sea Battle. The Army Air Force (responsible for operations in areas other than the Navy's and defense of Japan Proper) was depleted due to exhausting battles in New Guinea and Burma and operations in China.

In June and July of 1944, a suggestion was made by the Navy General Staff which called for the entire Army Air Force being placed under the command of the Navy to take advantage of possible unified employment of the Army and Navy Air Forces under a single command. Also, it was the Navy's belief it would provide economical use of our air strength. The Army General Staff had no objections to a unified employment of air strength. However, it was pointed out that Army ground operations could not be carried out without supporting air strength. For example, the principle tactic in the No 1 "Sho" Operation was an air operation to be carried out against enemy transports and under command of the Southern Army commander. If the entire Army Air Force were placed under command of the Navy, the Army could not carry out its operation. Also, the Army Air Force was not effective in sea operations and was considered unsuitable for Navy tactics, including the suicide technique.

The enemy fleet had made rapid progress in its air defensive measures. If the Navy persisted in its traditional tactics it was feared our entire air force would be destroyed, shortly. As a result, the Army could not approve the Navy suggestion. After an investigation, agreement on the following plan was reached in late July and the necessary order issued.

1. The 1st Air Division, though in the chain of command for the 5th Area Army, was placed under the 12th Air Fleet commander for operational control. Through mutual agreement, the Combined Fleet Commander was to order the 12th Fleet commander to follow orders from the 5th Area Army commander whenever planes were needed for air operations over land areas. In cases of air operations over sea areas, the 12th Air Fleet commander was to take orders from the Combined Fleet Commander, as before. Thus the 12th Air Fleet commander had a dual responsibility in carrying out orders from both the Combined Fleet commander and the 5th Area Army commander.

2. The 8th Air Division, though in the chain of command for the Formosa Army, was to be placed under the operational control of the 2d Air Fleet commander for operations over both land and sea.

3. The 7th And 98th Air Regiments (heavy bombers and torpedo bombers), though in the chain of command for the 1st

Air Army were to be placed under the 2d Air Fleet comcander.

4. In the Philippines area the 4th Air Army and 1st Air Fleet would cooperate in all operations whether over land or sea. The 15th Air Regiment (torpedo bombers) was to remain under the operational control of the 1st Air Fleet commander.

5. All Navy Air Units in the Homeland which were responsible for operations over land areas only (air defense) were to be placed under the operational control of the Army Air Force air defense commanders.

6. Special attention would be paid to cooperation between the Army and Navy in exchanging technical information which was vital as the result of this realignment of command authority.

Measures to Facilitate Railway Transportation on the Continent

In the middle of December, the Army General Staff planned a method of operation for control of the continental railroad transportation which would be flexible to the needs of various areas involved as well as support the preparations in the Homeland. The Chief of the Army General Staff was authorized to move the available Field Railway units in Manchuria and China to the various commands (China Expeditionary Army, Kwantung Army, or Korea Army areas) according to requirements of the overall transportation planning. The Field Railway unit of the Kwantung Army was deactivated and redesignated the Continental Railway Unit (Hqs, 1st and 3d Railway Units). Field Railway Units of the Kwantung Army and China Expeditionary Army became "floating units" which were assigned duties, when needed, according to decisions made by the Chief of Army General Staff. Command responsibility for these railway units was that of the commander in whose area transportation operations were being carried on (China Expeditionary Army, Kwantung Army or Korea Army areas).

During this period, in order to continue our supply services, efforts were concentrated on reinforcing our fighting strength in the Philippines and Nansei Islands areas. This large-scale transfer of strength necessitated changes in equipment for the troops. Transportation and arrangement of operational war materiel became very complicated. Losses and damages to our ships on the sea and the increase in bombardment of our materiel stockpile combined to make it very difficult to keep posted on the situation and progress of supply operations. No transportation of supplies could be undertaken for areas in the South except those mentioned above.

In the China area, in order to complete the "Ichi-Go" Operation, strenuous efforts were made to establish supply facilities in that large operational area under difficult conditions. Expecting an enemy attack on Japan Proper, in the very near future, various supply activities were planned and gradually put into effect.

CHAPTER VIII

Fifth Phase of the War

(January - August 1945)

PART I Operational Stage Prior to "Ketsu-Gp" (January-March 1945)

Situation Review and Conclusion Regarding US Strategy

In the Philippines, enemy forces landed at Lingayen Gulf on 9 January 1945. Our ground force strength on Luzon was inadequate to carry out a decisive battle. Worse yet, our air forces were hopelessly outnumbered by those of the enemy. Such being the case, the 14th Area Army was not in a position to plan a decisive operation to destroy the landing troops of the enemy. Instead, the Army planned a considered, realistic approach to the problem. Special attack units and raiding parties were sent out to inflict damages on enemy landing units and to harass their advance. Also, a series of delaying actions were planned in scattered areas of Luzon using our main forces. Our preparations even for such an operation as planned were far from adequate and the war situation prospect on Luzon was not bright.

In Burma, our Burma Area Army had finished reorganizing its fighting positions near Namhkam, Mongmit, Mandalay, tracts along the left bank of the Irrawaddy River and other key areas in southwest Burma, at the end of 1944. In the meantime, the Army tried hard to prepare for the coming campaign. Most of the troops under the Army were in such a demoralized state that even by patching up their weakened power, they had no capacity to attempt a major interception operation along the Burma Road.

In other areas of the Asiatic Theater, the war situation had been generally quiet except for intensified bombings of B-29's. From their bases at Chengtu and Mariana, enemy planes aimed at destruction of the vital industrial facilities in Manchuria and Kyushu.

In the European Theater with the successful formation of a second front by the Allied Forces in Northern France, the battle went into a new phase, adverse to the Germans. Failure of the German counteroffensives on the Western Front in December 1944 was followed in mid-January of the following year by a major winter offensive by the Russians on the Eastern Front. Now struggling under doubled pressure from both fronts, the outlook for the Germans was dark.

The general war situation in Asia at the beginning of 1945 could be summed up as growing tense and adverse for the Empire. Collapse of the Axis Power in Europe was foreshadowed and the next move the Russians might take toward Japan following the fall of Germany was a matter of growing concern for us. Undeniably, we stood at the crossroad of defeat. The enemy, despite battle successes, was laboring presumably under many difficulties of its own and seemed anxious to end the war as soon as possible. The course of world events thus definitely pointed to the passing of the war into its final phase in the near future.

The power of the US to carry on the war attained its highest peak at the end of 1944. It was then in a position to fill any amount of requisitions required by its forces in operation. With defeat of Germany in the near future being more than probable, Japan had to be prepared to face the worst when US Forces could come down upon us with additional strength freed from the European Theater.

In sizing up US military power, we had to take into consideration the highly developed equipment of its forces such as large-type planes, tanks, guns, small fire-arms, motorized vehicles and rocket weapons which their Navy designed for use against us. Also, to be considered was the plan of increased production which according to report was underway.

Recruiting of man power, however, was considered one of their major bottlenecks. After having drafted a total force of some 11,500,000, it appeared they would have great difficulty in the future in supplying additional man power to the industrial as well as war fronts. There was a change that a long drawn out battle might in the course of time breed hatred of war among their people who had l ved on optimistic views about the war. If they could be made "tired of war", their determination to continue the operation against Japan might relax.

Since the beginning of 1945, strategy of the US in the Asiatic theater seemed to be based on the following points: advancement of superior air and surface forces in a massive battle plan; encirclement of the Homeland by cutting off all our contacts with the outside thus neutralizing our fighting power; then, as soon as the opportunity presented itself, land forces at strategically vital points in the Homeland to drive the war to the quickest possible finish.

We singled out two alternatives which the enemy would likely take and give them careful examination.

    1. As their invasion in the Philippines progressed they would advance to South China to secure bases for their air forces, moving from there to the Nansei Islands area. Swatow and Hongkong seemed to be the most likely points for their landings. Time of their move was expected to be in late March at which time they would have air units of sufficient strength to operate from Luzon. The land force they would commit for such an operation was estimated as three to four US divisions and three British or Australian divisions. They would attempt invasion of the Nansei Islands in or after June with a force of about five divisions.

2. After completion of their Philippines Invasion, they would attempt to move forward to Formosa, Nansei Islands and Iwo-Ogasawara Islands, instead of South China. Bases would be established there from which bombing groups could operate over Japan. At the same time, their power to launch a major amphibious operation against the Japanese Homeland would be built up.

There was a great possibility the enemy would first aim its drive upon strategic points in Northern Formosa and render all our air bases there useless. By doing that we could no longer delay their operations against the Nansei Islands area. Then, they would push their air forces to the points from which they could assume an active part in executing operations around Shanghai and the Nansei Islands area. The time for their landing operations was estimated to be around March or April for Formosa and May or June for Okinawa. Strength of their invading troops would presumably be four divisions.

After carefully examining the two alternatives, we concluded the 2d alternative was more probable. Main reason for this was that it was estimated the enemy, in its plans to terminate the war quickly, had every intention of taking the shortest route in its steps toward mounting an invasion of Japan proper. Also, it concluded that the enemy was sure it had severed the supply transportation lines between Japan and the Southern area thus making landing and battle operations in that area easier for them because of inadequate support for our field forces. In addition, our radio intelligence units had gathered indications the enemy was concentrating an attack on Iwo Jima in the very near future.

The outlook of the battle in the Philippines was bad. Delaying actions conducted by the 14th Area Army might pin down a portion of enemy forces on Luzon for awhile, but the continuous dwindling of our power (especially the air force and supply of fuel and ammunitions) would soon make delaying actions futile. Thus, the island could be written off from our strategic point of view.

Attitude of Russia and Military Preparations of Chungking Nationalists

The strain between Japan and Russia was near the breaking point. When the Soviet would declare war against us depended upon the progress of their war with Germany and upon the progress of the war in Asia. Very probably, Russia would turn against us in the summer or fall of 1945 at which time the US was expected to have accomplished all preparations for invading the Homeland.

In event of hostilities, the Russian Far Eastern Army was expected to come rolling down upon Manchuria, Korea, North China and Karafuto (Sakhalin) and occupy all vital zones there. They would sweep over us by rallying their superior air force and mechanized troops.

When their troops were thoroughly remodeled after the US pattern, the Nationalist Army would likely embark upon major offensives in the Hunan and Kwangsi zones. Their total strength was estimated to be about 24 or 25 divisions including nine Americanized divisions. The time to assume the offensive was estimated to be about July or August. It was expected they would time their actions with those of the US Forces should the latter land on the China Coasts.

Appraisal of Japan's Man and Material Powers

Ath the end of October 1944, total strength of the reservists, which formed the main reservoir of manpower for military mobilization, was some 6,390,000 men. Of this number, 4,690,000 were ready to take active service. If Imperial General Headquarters required new forces to strengthen defense of the Homeland and this were to amount to 1,500,000 men necessary for mobilizing 40 divisions plus a force to take care of the line of communications for those divisions, the total manpower cited above appeared adequate as far as the number concerned. But when we looked into the qualification of those reservists, we saw that they were not adequate to build up effective fighting strength. For example, there was a lack of personnel trained to handle technical services such as engineering, signal and so forth. Furthermore, some 87% of the total adult population had been drafted into the food and munitions industries which were considered of primary importance in maintaining war supplies and a minimum subsistence for the people. Of this production manpower, 47% belonged to some class or other of the Reservists Army. In summing up, we could say that on the surface we had enought manpower to fill the Army requirements but, actually, their capacity as fighting men would be less than one half or third of what it was before. This meant that unless we adopted some drastic and deliverate measures to regiment manpower and speed up military training, we would be unable to raise the necessary fighting strength. Equally radical steps were needed in planning the total national mobilization, otherwise all industrial activities would come to a halt.

To meet the pressing needs of the tense war situation a large number of ships had been requisitioned throughout the war, but most of them had been lost or damaged and were out of service. Consequently, the natural resources supply from overseas was tapering off and the total national military productive power was in bad way. If we considered the eventual halt of import of raw materials from the Southern area and the intensified bombing by enemy planes aimed at destruction of hour Homeland industrial installations, our productive power would soon be neutralized.

Basic figures of our production as planned for the year 1945 were: 3,000,000 tons of steel; 40,000 airplanes; over 1,500,000 tons of steel ships; and, 1,650,000 kiloliters of liquid fuel from Manchuria.

China and Japan. These figures were far smaller than the one's planned for 1944. For example, in liquid fuel the plan called for half the production in 1945 that was planned for 1944. Yet, the liquid fuel plan for 1945 was still slightly higher than the actual production in 1944. Steel to be available for use by land forces in 1945 was reduced to 260,000 tons, 60% of 1944's total. The only exception was production of airplanes.

With this precarious production situation it was impossible to fill requirements of an army fighting on widespread fronts. We were confronted with many hard problems, such as unified control of requisitions by the Army and Navy, standardizing of designs for weapons, simplification of supply items and exhaustive efforts to find any unexploited resources. In short, we had to stretch what materiel we had as far as possible and use all idle materiel and captured materiel to get the last possible production result. Also, we stressed the importance of conservation of all materiel on hand. Troops were instructed to produce, repair and maintain equipment and materiel as much as possible.

Fundamental Strategy of Imperial General Headquarters

Our attempt to turn the trend of the war in the battle of the Philippines having failed, subsequent events gradually drove us back on the Homeland where we were to make a last ditch stand.

What we lacked in materiel power was to be compensated for by strong determination of the rank and file to sacrifice themselves for the sake of the country, a unique source of spiritual strength. Every terrain advantage and the combined action of the entire population would be used in our struggle to fight to the finish.

The main points of the strategy conceived by Imperial General Headquarters during the period from mid-January until early February included:

1. Whenever opportunity presented itself, the invading enemy was to be crushed, especially the main US Forces. Invulnerable defense was to be established around the Homeland for use in crushing the advancing enemy to such an extent that their determination to fight with Japan would be neutralized. Defense preparations were to be speeded in front of the Pacific and the East China Sea areas which were assumed to form the main battle front against a coming invasion by US Forces.

2. On the Chinese Continent, too, we were to endeavor to strike and smash the US Forces which formed the core of the enemy. At the same time we would continue to drive for destruction of the Chungking domination. For this purpose, the China Expeditionary Army was to be instructed to rearrange its battle fronts so as to face the US Forces. They were to strengthen defensive preparations immediately on the coastline of Southeastern China. Then, those of the strategic zones around the lower stream of the Yangtze River, especially near the Shanghai area, were to be completed by early summer of 1945.

3. To upset the advance of the enemy air and sea bases, we had to hold Formosa and the Nansei Islands. This was essential as an aid to successful execution of the entire defensive operations for the Homeland. Formosa and Okinawa, in particular, were to be defended strongly since they would furnish bases for our air forces to operate in the East China Sea.

4. On the Homeland, the Homeland Defense Army was to be deployed, immediately, in battle positions. All necessary measures were to be taken to destroy the invading

enemy. The Homeland group, consisting of the Kurile Islands, Karafuto (Sakhalin), Hokkaido, Honshu, Shikoku, Kyushu and its neighoring isles (Tanegashima and Yakushima) in latitude 30° north and northward, but excluding Korea, was to be secured firmly.

Chief emphasis of Homeland defensive operations was to be placed on the Kanto, Kyushu and Tokai (Nagoya area) Districts. Air defense installations and activities in those districts and the Osaka-Kobe area were to be given first consideration. In case of air-raids, efforts would be directed to intercepting the enemy at the appropriate time. At the approach of enemy forces the Army was to join with the Navy in striking and destroying them. Efforts were to be made to destroy the enemy landing forces on the ocean before they could reach the beach.

In Korea, the 17th Area Army was to be established and was to have the mission of firmly guarding the peninsula, beating off any invading enemy. Main stress was to be placed on the strategic zones in Southern Korea including Saishu (Quelpart) Island.

In keeping with the changing war situations in the Philippines, our Southern Army was to concentrate its efforts on holding strategic zones in Indo-China, Thailand, Malay and Sumatra, by destroying the attacking enemy. From those positions they were to stop any advance of enemy forces heading for the Homeland or the Chinese Continent. In the Philippines, now that the No 1 "Sho" Objective was no longer possible, our defenders there were to make efforts to hold key positions on Luzon and launch an effective delaying campaigns.

During earlier stages of the war, the center of our military operations had been in the overseas area. Much of our main force had been stationed at strategic points on the continent or in outlying islands away from the Homeland. Subsequent development of battle, however, made it necessary for use to withdraw them toward the Homeland and place them in new defense lines around Japan Proper. The unexpected rapid turn of events, made it hopeless to withdraw our forces from the Southern and Central Pacific area.

Imperial Gneral Headquarters had to solve many difficult problems included among which were how to achieve Homeland defense with a poor fighting potential, and what measures were to be taken in accomplishing necessary operational preparation in a very short period of time. Need for finding solutions was urgent lest a sudden unforeseen turn of the battle denied us any opportunity of saving the situation.

To make matters worse, the future of our relations with the Soviet appeared unfavorable. In anticipation of eventual hostilities, we were forced to reexamine and adjust our basic policy of military operations on the continent. The Greater Asiatic War had now reached such a critical point it was definitely beyond the power of military strategy, alone, to save the situation. We demanded diplomatic quarters make a determined move toward improvement of relations with the Soviets.

With the change on policy for military operation of the Japanese Army in January 1945, we planned on creating an additional operational force consisting of about 40 divisions, about 20 independent mixed brigades and accompanying organic units. Mission of this organization would be defense of the Homeland, exclusively.

Total war power of the Empire seemed inadequate to fight the decisive battle. However, it was absolutely necessary to make up a strong defense force to destroy a combined invasion of British and American forces. This was vital to secure the Imperial Homeland. The Army decided to draw some troops, especially officers, from Manchuria and China. These were to be placed in Homeland defense positions. It was recognized such measures would affect the strength of our overseas forces. We tried to raise the materiel power by taking over Navy surplus materiel on hand. Also, taken over were munitions and materiel stored in Manchuria.

The plan by which we tried to raise our military strength to the desired level included 5 main points:

1. Enlargement and reinforcement of our air attack force and air defense force was to be given first priority in military preparations.

2. Production of special attack weapons plus training and organization of capable personnel to man those weapons.

3. Instead of a large number of loosely knit and poorly equipped troops, we preferred fully trained and well equipped troops even though the number would be limited. Other troop strength would be gathered from the enormous mass of civilians, even though they might be inadequately armed.

4. Our overseas forces in Manchuria and China were to be urged to stabilize their positions of self-supply, so that they could continue to fight independent of any outside assistance.

5. Strong and effective administrative measures were to be adopted to elevate the fighting power of the Army and to correct any disconcerting elements tending to cause unrest among military personnel which might weaken fighting morale.

Establishment of Civil Defense Plan

The District Army headquarters in the Homeland were to be split into Operational and Administrative Army Headquarters. The Commander of Operations (Area Army Commander) was to be responsible for making operational preparations. The Commander of Administration (Administrative District Commander) was to be responsible for all military administrative activities which, necessarily, had close contact with many phases of civil administration. By this devise we planned to relieve operational troops of any non-essential duties which might interfere with full execution of their purely operational activities. At the same time it would consolidate preparedness of the whole country for battle since both military and civil forces would be welded together.

The Commander of each Area Army was to assume a dual responsibility for administrative army units in his area as well as the operational armies. To support him through the chain of command in organizing the civilian reserve forces of the Homeland, a Divisional District commander was to be established. Under him were Guard District commander and Local Defense Unit commander. These Guard District commanders would be of two types, according to area of command. Type-A was to be assigned to suburban or rural prefectures. Type-B was to be assigned to cities such as Yokohama, Nagoya, Kyoto, Osaka and Kobe. Tokyo would be **excluded** from this plan because of its importance as location of the Imperial Palace and government facilities.

Among units which would be thus organized, the first in line of experience were members of the regular guard units who served as full time soldiers in training and actual duty. Next in line of military qualified troops were the Specially Established Guard Units composed of personnel who had combat experience, previously, and had been returned to civilian status. Members of the Specially Established Guard Units would be authorized to work at their civilian jobs as well as being members of the civilian defense forces. Last came the Local Defense Unit personnel who were completely inexperienced. They, too, were to be authorized to work at their civilian jobs in addition to being responsible for military duty.

Another phase of the civilian reserve mobilization was the Replacement Unit under each Divisional District commander. Personnel undergoing training in such units were subject to call for service with operational units. In case of actual ground battles, both types of Guard Units were subject to call for operational army service as units, but not as individuals.

Operational Army Mobilization Schedule

To effect quick reinforcement of battle positions an emergency mobilization plan for Homeland operational forces was established in early February providing headquarters of the 11th, 12th, 13th, 15th and 16th Area Armies at Sendai, Tokyo, Nagoya, Osaka, and Fukuoka. In addition to those armies, four independent mixed brigades were to be activated and placed at likely enemy landing points.

The First Group Operational Army Mobilization plan which was to be accomplished in late February and March (completed 8 April 1945) using depot divisions as a nucleus resulted in 18 combat divisions being activated. These included: 13 for Honshu, Shikoku and Kyushu (140th, 142d, 143d, 144th, 145th, 146th, 151st, 152d, 153d, 154th, 155th, 156th and 157th); 3 for Hokkaido, Karafuto and Kurile (88th, 89th and 147th); and 2 for Korea (150th and 160th). The primary mission of this First Group was to be guarding strategic zones along coastlines and insuring a foothold for operations by rear echelon attack forces. First task to this end was construction of fortifications.

The Second Group Operational Army Mobilization plan was developed in April and carried out in May, mostly. It consisted of eight thoroughly equipped mobile divisions (201st, 202d, 205th, 206th, 209th, 212th, 214th and 216th) of the best personnel possible under the current manpower situation; six independent tank brigades; and five tank regiments. In addition, a force of four strong divisions (1st Armored Division, 11th, 25th and 57th) and three divisions (111th, 112th and 121st) were to be transferred from Manchuria to the Homeland and Korea, respectively. Primary mission of this Second Group was to be the last decisive battle. As part of this mobilization, two General Army headquarters, Air General Army, and nine Army headquarters established. With the activation of General Army Headquarters, the position of Commander of Homeland Defenses was dropped and the country was divided into two areas of command responsibility under the Chief of Army General Staff, 1st (East) and 2d (West) General Army headquarters.

The Third Group Operational Army Mobilization plan was developed in May and carried out during the latter part of May and June. It called for 16 new divisions (221st, 222d, 224th, 225th, 229th, 230th, 231st, 303d, 308th, 312th, 316th, 321st, 322d, 344th, 351st and 354th) for the Homeland. Among the 16 divisions, nine were coastal defense divisions and seven were mobile divisions. Later, two more were activated (234th and 355th), one each of which was coastal defense and mobile. Two divisions (320th and one other which was not realized) were to be activated for Korea. Also, 14 Mixed Brigades were to be formed and 5 Mixed Regiments plus a number of composite units centered around artillery units. The main objectives of this Third Group were reinforcement of coast defenses and mobile fighting strength.

The state of supply potential, both manpower and materiel, was such that simultaneous activation of all operational forces was impossible. Thus, it was split into the three Group Mobilization Plans, giving priority to those vital zones which had to be speedily fortified and strongly manned for strategic reasons. Those zones were also given priority in procurement of necessary war materials.

Lacking necessary materiel, we could not mobilize many line of communication units. We intended to leave this task, chiefly, to some of the units arriving from Manchuria. In mobilizing line of communication units in the Homeland, they were to be limited to only those directly needed by units. Most of the rear echelon services were to be left in the hands of drafted civilians because the coming battle would be fought on the Homeland.

Total strength of line of communication units being considered for mobilization consisted of independent motor transport battalions or companies, independent animal transport battalions or companies and various other duty units as the core force, amounting to some 400,000 men. They would be equipped with 12,000 motorized vehicles, 470,000 heads of horses and 70,000 transport carts. Since the Army had no new motor vehicles to spare for this purpose, it was planned to requisition them from among the total of 35,000 civilian cars, of which 24,000 were known to be in operating condition. Herds of horses were to be requisitioned amounting to about one-seventh of the total serviceable horses in the country. The Army would be able to furnish 20,000 transport carts but the additional 50,000 carts would have to be built or requisitioned by troops in their responsible areas.

Southern Army Operations

Although strategic value of the Southern Army had diminished greatly after the defeat in the Leyte campaign, it was hoped it would still be able to help general operations designed to check the enemy's anticipated plan for invading Japan Proper. To this end, the basic missions of the Southern Army were to be revised. Strong measures were to be taken to secure and stabilize the French Indo-China peninsula which was the most important area for maintaining self-sufficiency of the Southern Army. Personnel and materiel essential for Homeland Defense (fuel, air units and personnel for mobilization of new air units) were to be sent back to the Homeland. After careful investigation, the Army General

Staff revised its basic order for the Southern Army on 27 January. At the end of February, authority was granted to use armed force, if necessary, to settle the unstable French Indo-China situation. Meanwhile, essential personnel and materiel for the Homeland were sent back through joint efforts by the Army and Navy.

In the beginning of February, the enemy in the Philippine Islands attacked Manila from Lingayen Bay and Batangas area. The 14th Area Army continued persistent and vigorous delaying action in Northern Luzon, in the area east of Manila, and in the area west of Clark Air Base. In May, the efficiency of our forces in Luzon showed a marked decline making it impossible to carry out further effective activities.

Enemy forces in the Philippines toward the end of May totalled approximately ten divisions on Luson plus several divisions deployed in Panay, Negros, Masubate, Cebu, Palawan, Jolo, Tawitawi, and Mindanao Islands. In addition, there was an Air Force consisting of some 2,000 first line planes.

Our operations against the Chinese Army in northern Burma were not successful. At the end of February, the Burma Road Operation was abandoned. Fighting power of our Burma Area Army which attempted to beat back the Indo-British Army advancing southward along the Irrawaddy River to Mandalay declined greatly. This made it impossible to hold the front line along the Irrawaddy River by the end of March. The Southern Army ordered the Burma Area Army to consolidate important points of Loikaw, Toungoo and Rangoon on the front line in southern Burma. However, before the Army could change its troop dispositions Rangoon surrendered to the enemy in early May.

In order to strengthen Thailand, French Indo-China and Malay area, the Southern Army transferred the 2d Division (from Burma), the 4th Division (from Sumatra), and the 46th Division (from Flores

Islands) to these places. The Army General Staff also ordered the 22d and 37th Divisions to be transferred from South China to French Indo-China.

On 27 January 1945, the Southern Army commander was ordered to secure all important positions in the Southern area which would facilitate general operations. He was ordered to destroy the enemy attacking our important positions and check enemy advances toward China and the Homeland. Particularly, he was to secure strategically important positions on Luzon and destroy the attacking enemy; secure Indo-China, Thailand, Malay and Sumatra as the important centers of the whole Southern area; also, in other areas, secure strategically important points which the enemy was likely to recapture, especailly those where natural resources and bases were found; destroy the enemy strength as throughly as possible; harass enemy supply lines as much as possible; in case our sea communications were cut off plan to adjust operations accordingly; and, formulate military administrative plans in accordance with existing conditions and indoctrinate the people in the South on the purpose of the war.

The directives based on the above-mentioned orders provided the outline of measures which the Southern Army was to take concerning utilization of the Line of Communication Units and communication facilities. The Southern Army was not to rely on receiving supplies and reinforcements from the Homeland due to the existing situation of sea transportation. Instead, it was to carry out self-supporting operations. Line of Communication and transportation facilities were to be strengthened in French Indo-China, Thailand and Malay areas as supply centers for the whole Southern area. Munitions in the Southern area were to be concentrated in central locations conveniently accessible to units in that area. As much national defense materiel as practicable was to be sent back to the Homeland. Military administrative measures were to support operational plans and were to win the confidence of the people.

The Southern Army, China Expeditionary Army and 10th Area Army commanders through co-operation were to secure the communication lines by utilizing airplanes and small boats. A trans-continental communication route was to be established between the Southern area and China.

After defeat of our forces in Burma and the Philippines, it became imperative to secure the French Indo-China Peninsula (central area of the South).

The relationship between Japan and French Indo-China had been based on the "Joint Defense Agreement" supplemented by a "Military Agreement". Japan had paid full respect regarding the dignity of French Indo-China sovereignty and never interfered in domestic affairs. However, at the beginning of 1945, war situation in Europe became disadvantageous to Germany and with De Gaulle assuming administrative powers of the French Government in place of the Vichy Government, the attitude of the French Indo-Chinese gradually turned against Japan. Finally, they went as far as to refuse the fulfilment of their responsibility provided by the "Joint Defensive Agreement".

As the situation in the Pacific at that time was disadvantageous to us and landing of US Forces in French Indo-China seemed probable, there was danger of the French Army in French Indo-China turning against us. The Army General Staff considered that it was necessary to hold French Indo-China as the central point in the Southern Area. On 28 February, the Southern Army commander was ordered to occupy French Indo-China with armed forces in event the request of the Japanese Government was refused by the French Indo-China Government.

The Japanese Ambassador to French Indo-China presented on 9 March the following request to the Governor-General of French Indo-China.

In view of the general situation, and especially due to the fact US Forces were launching carrier-plane strikes against French Indo-China and their possible landing on French Indo-China, Japan is requesting the Governor-General to resist with his Army the US Forces and to co-operate with Japan in accordance with the "Joint Defensive Agreement". To accomplish that, Japan also is requesting the Governor-General to agree to the following points of demand:

1. The French Indo-Chinese Army and the Armed Police Units must be placed under the control of the Imperial Army for the duration of the present situation. They must obey our command in relation to organization, disposition and movements of units, ammunition and material. All transportation, shipping and communication facilities which are necessary to carry out the military operations must be under command of our Army.

2. The Governor-General must order all governmental agencies and the population of French Indo-China to co-operate wholly and faithfully with Imperial Forces.

The Governor General refused this demand through diplomatic channels. Following the refusal, the Southern Army commander took military action to enforce the demands. Japanese forces began disarming and disbanding the French Indo-China Army, Security and Police Units. Our Army also took control of railway, shipping and communications. In the main areas, these military measures were completed by the middle of March. Then, the Army turned to suppressing elements of the French Indo-China forces which were in the mountains in Northwestern and Central French Indo-China.

Central Pacific, Formosa and Nansei Islands Directions and Operations

Since late January, movement of enemy convoys in Mariana and Ulithi waters grew increasingly active. Taking off on 12 February from their bases in Ulithi and Mariana under heavy cover of their carriers, enemy invading forces approached Iwo Jima on the 16th and on 19 February under cover of naval bombardment landed on the southern shore of the island.

Our total garrison force on the island was (as figured in the middle of February) about 20,000 strong, consisting of:

- 9 infantry battalions
- 6,000 naval land force troops (20 heavy artillery pieces, 170 automatic cannons)
- 1 tank regiment (23 tanks)
- 2 artillery battalions (about 40 guns)
- 5 anti-tank battalions (about 70 guns)
- 3 trench mortar battalions (about 110 mortars)
- 60% of the standard issue of ammunitions sufficient for one engagement by one division.

About four months' rations provisions and forage

At first the enemy landed about one division as the core force and some 200 tanks. However, this force increased during the battle and by the end of February some three enemy Marine divisions were in action.

When the island was invaded, the entire 109th Division from the commander on down put up a bitter and determined resistance from fortified positions. But in spite of desperate and prodigious struggle by our defense forces, gradually our fighting power was overcome by the enormous materiel superiority of the enemy. On the 23d, our powerful positions on Mt Surihachi fell and part of our main defense position was lost to the enemy. An instance taken from one day the latter part of February showed the enemy fired as many as 30,000 rounds and made over 100 air sorties.

Since 25 February enemy forces had opened a general offensive on all fronts. Against it, the heart of the 109th Division fought gallantly sending out raiding parties and repeatedly trying counter-attacks by resorting to all known tactics. However, the efforts were futile. From 27 February on they lost strong main defense positions one after another. Their doomsday came on 14 March when they destroyed their regimental colors. On 17 March all the remaining troops made the last suicidal charge upon the enemy. By late March most of the officers and men had died heroic deaths.

It was regretable that because of increasingly menacing situations on all fronts we could not spare sufficient air support for Iwo Jima to cover our garrison force there. All we could do was let the Commander of Homeland Defenses send out part of the 6th Air Army in a futile attempt to check landing operations of the enemy.

After the fall of Iwo Jima, the commander of the whole Ogasawara Army Group located in the rest of the island group.

After 1 April, the 14th Division which was the garrison force of Palao, made recurrent attacks against enemy sea forces operating in the waters near Peleliu. These attacks continued up to the middle of June and scored many gains.

In view of reverses in our Philippine Operations, the Army General Staff decided at the beginning of 1945 to first of all reinforce battle preparations for Southern Formosa. At Kagi, 40th Army headquarters was created early in 1945. The 71st Division (from Manchuria) and the 9th Division (from Okinawa) were transferred to Formosa. These divisions arrived in Formosa during February. By the end of that month, total strength of the land force in the island rose to five divisions and six brigades.

To fill the gap in the defense of Okinawa caused by withdrawal of the 9th Division, The Army General Staff studied the problem of supplying the 84th Division (from the Homeland) for the island. Some munitions were shipped while the plan was still being studies. Actually, this plan was not materialized because strong opinions arose in the Army General Staff discrediting strategic value of such measures. It was pointed out that lessons learned from battle experience in the past showed we could not rely too much upon the defensive strength of those outlying islands no matter how much they might be fortified. Further, it was suggested we would do better to concentrate our efforts in in **strengthening battle preparations for the Homeland itself.** Homeland preparations were still in a chaotic condition. Even the general plan had not been developed completely.

On 3 February, the Army General Staff issued an order to the 10th Area Army commander giving him the mission of blocking every attempt of the enemy to advance their sea and air bases toward Formosa and the Nansei Islands.

Main points of the order were as follows:

1. Main objective of the operation at this stage was to beat back the advancing enemy, especially the US Forces, on the outlying islands in order to facilitate prosecution of our general operations in all important areas in the vicinity of the Homeland.

2. With this objective in view, the 10th Area Army commander was to hold firmly Formosa and Nansei Islands by smashing advancing enemy forces. In carrying out the mission, the 10th Area Army Commander was to emphasize the chief mission of smashing all attempts by the enemy to advance their sea and air bases toward Formosa and the Nansei Islands. This was to be **done** to prevent them from gaining footholds from

which to operate further drives toward the Homeland, Korea or the coasts of China. Of all the strategic areas to be held, Formosa and Okinawa Main Islands were of primary importance. They were to be guarded at all costs. This was vital so we could hold the necessary bases for conduct of our future air operations over the East China Sea. Operations from the above bases would be co-ordinated with those of our other bases in Kyushu, Southern Korea, and the lower stream of the Yangtze River.

3. In case the enemy landed on the Southeastern China coast, the 10th Area Army would help the operations of the China Expeditionary Army by destroying the enemy convoy on the sea with its air forces.

In support of the above order certain agreements were made between the Army and Navy regarding the principle points of co-operation. As a rule, in Formosa and the Nansei Islands the Army would be responsible for land defense and the Navy for sea defense. In carrying out land operations the 10th Area Army commander was authorized to command as many of the Naval land units stationed in Formosa and the Nansei Islands as he needed. However, necessary negotiations were to be held with the Commander in Chief of the Sasebo Naval District and the Commander in Chief of the Takao Naval Guard District as to how many and which naval land units were to be used for this purpose.

Preparations and Disposition of Forces in Korea, China and Manchuria

To cope with the eventual worst phase of battle, the Korea defense plan had to include a dual strategy, setting up a bulwark in southern Korea against American Forces and another bulwark in northern Korea against the Russians. The various phases of the Operational Army Group Mobilization plans provided the means to this end. Three new divisions were to be created, immediately. Of the three, one was created by reorganizing the 19th Depot Division into the 79th Division. It was placed in northern Korea. Another scheduled to be organized in the Homeland for use in Korea was dropped. In Korea, the 96th Division was created and placed on duty in south Korea. At the same time, five Divisional District headquarters were to be established. During the 1st Group Mobilization in the Homeland, one Army headquarters (58th) and two divisions (150th and 160th) were to be organized. During the 2d Group Mobilization, three divisions (111th, 112th, and 121st) were to be transferred from Manchuria to Korea. In the 3d Group Mobilization, two more divisions (320th and one other for which the 127th Independent Mixed Brigade was later organized and substituted) were to be created.

Generally speaking, it can be said that the disposition of forces in Korea was governed to a large extent by the direction of operations in subsequent stages of battle on the continent. This was especially true considering development of anti-Soviet defensive plans. As a result, efforts were to be made to preserve a certain measure of flexibility readily adjustable for any emergency.

The program of battle preparation in China was extensive and varied. Some of the urgent problems were: to firmly secure a number of strong air bases in China from which to operate in protecting vital bases linking China, Manchuria and the Homeland; to be ready to beat back any enemy attack against Southeastern China; to be ready to make speedy disposition of necessary forces to maintain peace and order; and, to organize and hold ready the entire reserve forces of the Army so they could be moved quickly to the Manchurian Front in case of emergency. Late spring or early summer of 1945, was set as the time when occupation of all captured zones would be completed and foundation for the strategy ahead firmly established. After that, by making whatever required revisions or replacements were necessary in a buildup of forces, we would have by the summer of 1946 such a strong military setup on the continent that it would be invulnerable against any invasion from the outside.

With these objectives in mind, we started raising the strength of the operational group to 20 fully equipped divisions; the force to preserve peace to 20 under-equipped divisions; the special guard force to six divisions; mixed brigades to 17; and, the route guard force to 50 battalions. This was to be completed by the end of 1945. Eight of the above 20 under-equipped divisions were to be strengthened and reorganized into fully equipped divisions by the middle of 1946. At the same time, the number of guard battalions was to be enlarged to 110.

Note: Incidentally, the total strength of forces stationed in China at the close of 1944 was 25 regular divisions, one tank division, 10 independent mixed brigades and 11 independent infantry brigades.

In view of the impeding landing operations by the US Forces on China and the increasing difficulties in surface transportation, intermediate measures were taken toward the contemplated reinforcement of southeastern China. From among units in the Homeland, troops sufficient for about three divisions were gathered, provisionally organized and hurriedly shipped to the China zones concerned. There, they were combined with field replacements units which were used as the cadre force and the three new divisions, 12 mixed brigades, seven guard units and accompanying organic units were activated. Simultaneously, the main body of our China Forces began to coverge toward the triangular zone in Central China. To direct the operation in these sectors an Army headquarters was arranged to be transferred there from Manchuria.

With the development of the battle in the Pacific Theater, some 11 divisions were transferred one after another to the Theater from Manchuria. They were the 1st, 8th, 9th, 10th, 12th, 23d, 24th, 28th, 29th, 71st Divisions and 2d Tank Division. Considerably more forces would need to be drawn from Manchuria to supplement Homeland forces in the near future. Consequently, it was easily predictable the ultimate strength of the entire Kwantung Army would be weakened greatly.

To cope with this predicament, the Army General Staff had to adopt a policy of artificially increasing the number of personnel and divisions. The objective of this policy included three points: to discourage Russia from entering the war against us by creating an impression of a gigantic, strong army; to make available the Kwantung Army troop strength as a reservoir from which the Homeland Army could draw its required reinforcements; and, to make the Kwantung Army strong enough without help from outside to fight Russia whose invasion might be made during the summer of 1945 if the worst situation developed.

In line with the above policy at the beginning of 1945, the 3d Cavalry Brigade and Border Garrison Units were reorganized into eight divisions and four mixed brigades. Simultaneously, an operational group of four fully-equipped divisions was transferred to the Homeland, while two under-equipped divisions were shifted into Korea. About one third of the total equipment and war material on hand for the Kwantung Army together with a force of key personnel required by the Homeland Army were transported to Japan.

Line of Communication (Logistical Support) During This Period

During the past seven years of persistent intensive fighting beginning with the China Indident, Japan's reservoir of materiel power had been depleted, pitiably. All potential resources had been exploited almost to the last iota. Such being the situation in the later stages of the war, we had increasing difficulty in filling even current requirements of our fighting forces. Conservation of the national defense power so that reserves would be available for the last Homeland Defense battle was almost impossible. To make matters worse, reverses in the Philippines nearly precluded the possibility of our having recourse to supplies from Southern regions. Our supply routes stretching both to the Northern and Southern areas were under constant menace.

In an effort to meet this situation, all our overseas Armies were instructed to establish a self-supporting system in their respective areas. This way they could continue fighting on their own resources while living off the land. In the Homeland, we concentrated all of our efforts in preparation for an all-out Homeland battle by building up materiel power with whatever remaining materiel resources we could lay our hands on within the country and assembling all the fighting strength in the strategic zones of the Homeland. Regarding defense preparedness for rear echelons of the Homeland, the groundwork plan was, in outline, as follows:

1. The entire Homeland was to be converted immediately into a state of readiness for all-out defense of the country. The time set for its preliminary completion was the end of June 1945. Its final completion was to be the end of October. Special efforts were to be made to urge completion of the defense preparedness in such vital districts as Kanto, Kyushu, and Shikoku on a priority schedule until the middle part of 1945.

2. Along with the preparations for purely military operations, the war preparedness for civil guard forces and of productive installations were to be urgently reinforced and completed.

3. Fighting strength would be concentrated in the Homeland until the middle of 1945. During the first half of 1945, a giant effort would be made to raise the fighting strength of the Homeland Armies to the highest possible number of men. At the same time, as many replacement forces as possible would be recalled from

the continent of the Homeland.

4. In stabilizing the line of communications for the air forces, chief emphasis would be laid upon increasing the number of fully protected installations for planes; increase in the number of bombs for use by special attack planes; accomplishment of a network of communication for command and information; and, storage dispersal of aviation fuel. These tasks would be accomplished by the end of June.

As practical steps in carrying out the above-quoted policy, each Army administrative district in the Homeland was to be urged to establish an independent self-subsistent colony within its area. The line of communications necessary for operational reasons was to be manned, chiefly, with part of the forces drawn from Manchuria and some provisional units organized for that purpose.

Our groundwork plan for handling war materiel for operational purposes in the earlier stages of the preparation are as shown on Chart 11.

Conduct of Homeland Operations and Strategy

During the early part of February, the Army General Staff laid down the groundwork plan for preparation of operations both in the Homeland and Korea. On the basis of this a series of orders to the Armies concerned were issued, successively, clarifying command operations in Formosa, Nansei Island Group, China, and Southern area and also the command of general aerial operations in the Eastern China Sea area.

On the basis of the emergency mobilization plan, District Army headquarters were deactivated on 6 February. They were replaced by Area Army headquarters having operational missions and Army Administrative District headquarters whose principal functions

Plan of Employment of War Materiel Reimported from Manchuria

Place of Employment	Description		Quantity	Period of Employment						Remarks
				Mar	Apr	May	Jun	Jul	Aug	
The Homeland	Fuels (1,000 kiloliters)	Aviation gasoline	17	12	5					Provisional programs of debarkation being as follows: 40%–Niigata 20%–Tsuruga 40%–Fukuoka
		Ordinary gasoline	20	8	7	5				
		Light oil, Lubricating oil, etc	10	←————→						
	Ground Ammunition		Sufficient for 10 engagements by division	←——————————→						
Southern Korea	Aviation Gasoline (1,000 kiloliters)		3	←————→						Transported to Heijo Area
	Ground Ammunition		Sufficient for 5 engagements by	←——3——→				←—2—→		

Notes:
1. Order of priority in transportation was to be: Fuel, especially aviation gasoline, ground ammunitions.

2. In addition to the materials mentioned in the chart, efforts would be made to reimport, as much as possible, railroad materials, river-crossing materials, materials to be used in close combat, anti-tank materials, and preservable foodstuffs.

3. Estimate of materials weight to be transported indicated that ground ammunitions sufficient for 1 engagement of a division amounted approximately to 2,000 tons.

4. The amount of materials to be reimported was subject to change.

were to be handle all military administrative matters.

Headquarters and their locations (in parenthesis) were as follows:

    5th Area Army and Northern Army Administrative District (Sapporo)

    11th Area Army and Northeastern Army Administrative District (Sendai

    12th Area Army and Eastern Army Administrative District (Tokyo)

    13th Area Army and East Coast Army Administrative District (Nagoya)

    15th Area Army and Central Army Administrative District (Osaka)

    16th Area Army and Western Army Administrative District (Fukuoka)

    17th Area Army and Korea Army Administrative District (Seoul)

    10th Area Army and Formosa Army Administrative District (Taihoku)

Since it was obvious operational preparations could not be prosecuted indepedetnly of general administrative activities, the Commander and staff of one headquarters concurrently held the same posts in the other headquarters. Through this dual-mission of headquarters personnel and mutual exchange of officers between them, we tried to insure interlocking and decisive decisions between the Area Army and the Administrative headquarters.

In prosecution of the above-mentioned missions, the Homeland Defense Army and the 17th Area Army were ordered immediately to move into battle disposition. The Northern, Formosa and Korea Army Administrative District commanders were placed under the direction of the 5th, 10th and 17th Area Army commanders, respectively, in all matters pertaining to operations. The Commander of Homeland Defenses was entrusted with the mission of directing activities of the 17th Area Army in aerial operations and protection of surface transportation. Simultaneously, an order was issued to both the Commander of Homeland Defenses and 17th Area Army commander to beat back any invading enemy and guard the Homeland and Korea.

Main points of the operational order issued to the Commander of Homeland Defenses.[1]

1. In making preparations for Homeland operations, preference will be given to the Kanto, Kyushu and Tokai (the East Coast) districts, with special emphasis to be placed upon air defense of the respective districts and the important Osaka-Kobe district.

2. In case of enemy air-raids, effort must be made to throw them back and in collaboration with the Naval Forces to annihilate any enemy task force operating near the Homeland.

3. As soon as any enemy attempt to invade the Homeland is detected, efforts must be made to strike and annihilate their forces while they are still at sea.

4. Protection of land transportation routes and harbor installations must be maintained thoroughly with special attention paid to guarding key points of surface transportation between the Homeland and Korea.

5. In the protection of surface transportation routes, assistance will be given the Navy as much as circumstances permit.

Main points of the operational order issued to the 17th Area Army commander:

1. In putting into effect necessary preparations for defensive operations against an anticipated Russian attack, the 17th Area Army commander was to come under the delegated command of the Commanding General of the

---

[1] Prior to 6 February, the Commander of the Homeland Defense was identified in Japanese terminology as Boeisoskireikan. Following the order of 6 February, the Commander of Homeland Defenses was identified in Japanese as Naichiboeigunshireikan. The Japanese carries a slightly different shade in its meaning, but for simplification in recreating the proper impression of command authority in this translation the term of Commander of Homeland Defenses is used for each of the Japanese words.

Kwantung Army.

2. Operational preparations were to be effected with emphasis placed on the defense of strategic areas in southern Korea including Saishu (Quelpart) Isle.

3. Key points of the trans-peninsula railroad line, northern Korean railroad lines and Tumen River must be guarded thoroughly.

These orders were delivered, personally, both to the Commander of Homeland Defense and the various Area Army commanders who were summoned to Tokyo in early February. On this occasion, the Chief of Army General Staff emphasized the necessity for a realignment of the groundwork plan in each headquarters for conducting the Homeland battle. He urged thorough training of each Army, speedy accomplishment of all preparations, rearrangement of intelligence activities, maintenance of transportation and communication facilities, careful handling of war materiel and equipment and a diligent application of effort to execution of duties by staff officers.

Following their successful battle achievements in the Philippines, enemy forces began to aim their drive at Iwo Jima in mid-February and then at Okinawa in late March. Despite determined resistance offered by our island defense forces under the protection of Army and Navy Air Forces, the two islands were lost (Iwo Jima in mid-March and Okinawa in late June).

In the Southern Regions, part of our Army forces were shifted from Burma and Sunda Isles to Siam and Malay Sectors. In March our forces stationed in French Indo-China disarmed the French Indo-China Army and occupied French governmental installations to settle an unstable situation and consolidate defense positions in that vital area. By early June a good part of Luzon was lost to the enemy. Our Burma Area Army suffered another reverse in the late campaign along the Irrawaddy River. Early in May, Rangoon fell forcing our

Army there to withdraw its main forces toward strategic areas in southern Burma.

In the China Theater during early February our Canton-Hankou Railroad Penetration Operation had brought the Canton-Hankou Railroad under our control. At the same time, we put the enemy air bases out of action in the Suichuan and Kanhsien regions. To pave the way for subsequent operations in China, we embarked upon two more operations, the Laohokou Operation in March and the Chihkiang Operation in April.

The Army General Staff had been busy since February examining plans for Homeland defense preparations intending to strengthen them. Substantial progress had been made in the new regimentation and disposition of Homeland Forces, completion of a new command system, activation of new Army groups and arrival of replacement groups from Manchuria. In late March, the Army General Staff laid down the basic plan of preparation for the Homeland operation. It was circulated among all Armies to get things underway in preparation for the operation. This was the first step in the "Ketsu-Go" Operational preparation.

At the same time, the Army General Staff studied plans to revise directions of operations on the continent in keeping with the new Homeland defense program. It was decided to contract the lines in southwestern China zones and to strengthen defense preparations in central and northern China, southern Manchuria and Korea in anticipation of eventual intrusion of Russia and United States Forces. The Kwantung Army, the China Expeditionary Army and Korea Army were given the necessary instructions to that effect.

Air Operations and Enemy Bombing of the Homeland

On 6 February 1945, instructions (based on a tentative agreement with the Navy)[2] were delivered to all Armies concerned on general air operation policies against enemy forces invading the East China Sea. Main points of the instructions were as follows:

1. The Commanders of the 10th Area Army, China Expeditionary Army, Homeland Defense Command, Southern Army and Kwantung Army would conduct air operations in accordance with the Army-Navy Central Agreement regarding Air Operations for the 1st half of 1945 and the outline of the Direction of the Army Air Operations, given below.

2. The Homeland Defense commander was to be responsible for air operations over Okinawa Main Island and all areas north of the island.

The tentative Central Agreement concluded regarding air operations for the 1st half of 1945 established a policy of attacking and destroying any premeditated enemy advance into the East China Sea. Combined Army and Navy Air Forces were to be used. At the same time, inner defense positions of the Homeland were to be strengthened. In this operation we were to emphasize the necessity of building up special attack forces and their suicide tactical employment.

Air operations in the area around the East China Sea (Formosa, Nansei Islands, Southeast China, Kyushu and Korea) called for both the Army and Navy Air Forces to deploy immediately to the spot and attack in the event of an enemy advance there. Main targets for attack by the Navy Air Force would be the enemy task force. The

---

[2] The Army-Navy Central Agreement regarding Air Operations, which was delivered on 6 February was a tentative plan. The formal agreement was delivered on 1 March. This was because the Navy could not decide in early February on the air strength to use for the operations.

Army would attack the transport ships. However, the Army Air Force would assist the Navy in its mission as much as circumstances permitted.

In the area of the South China coast, as a rule, Army air units would be responsible for attacking the invading enemy. Air units originally stationed in the area would bear the basic burden. Partial reinforcement was to be made in the event of battle. Navy air units would offer assistance to the Army as much as circumstances permitted.

In the Iwo Jima and Ogasawara Islands area, responsibility for defense would be shared by the Army and Navy Air Forces. They would support the operations of the garrison forces there. Future air operations in the Philippines area would be waged by our air forces in the Philippines as well as those in Formosa. In the Indian Ocean area our air units stationed there would endeavor to blunt any enemy plan of invasion. In the Northeastern Sector, the present disposition was to be maintained. On the Chinese Continent for waging air operation on the western battle fronts we would have to be content with available minimum strength. In the Manchuria area, defensive measures against eventual offensives from the Soviet were to be planned. However, no specific units for this purpose were to be allocated.

Overall air defense planning called for important sections both in Japan and Manchuria to be strongly protected against enemy air attacks. Naturally, this emphasized continuance of attacks on enemy air bases to put them out of action. Also, to prepare ourselves against any unforseen eventualities, we were to endeavor building up of sufficient reserve air forces through an intensive training program which would increase their fighting abilities.

Both the Army and the Navy were to endeavor raising fighting morale among their men by indoctrinating in them the spirit of suicide attacks. Special attack units were to be increased. At the same time supporting units were to be developed so as to have special attack units perform their mission to their fullest extent.

As a rule, air battles both in the Homeland and in the East China Sea areas were to be operated by co-ordination between the Army and Navy. Generally, command posts would be in the same place for the Army and Navy Air Force commanders during the operation so close liaison would be insured. To this end, the Army and Navy air Force commanders in respective areas were to confer immediately with each other and decide on the suitable place from which to command their combined action. Battle fronts for which the Army and Navy were to be responsible remained as before.

Outline of the aforementioned plan is recreated in Charts 12, 13, 14 and 15.

The outline of directions for Army Air Operations established a policy that, to meet the premediated advance of enemy invading forces in the East China Sea areas, preparations for air operations there were to be made and accomplished by the end of March. This air operation was designated as "Ten-Go" Operation.

Main objective would be destruction of enemy convoys. To do this it was considered important to hold our attack force and direct escort fighter force back in full strength until the enemy convoys were well within range for our effective attack.

Although desirable, air annihilating combat, aerial protection of our land operations and similar actions were to be carried out with a certain amount of restraint. This was especially important considering such conditions as the degree of training of our air force (especially air crewmen,) state and efficienty of our equipment, reserve supply prospects, and the critical fuel supply conditions.

Source of Army Air Force Operational Strength in Case of Enemy Attacks

Planned Transfer and Allocation of Army Planes Against Nansei Islands or Formosa

Location and Unit Source for Planes Transferred

Homeland (6th Air Army)		China (5th Air Army)		Hainan & French Indo-China (3d Air Army)	
Fighters	30	Fighters	75	Fighters	25
Assault Planes	80	Assault Planes	30	Heavy Bombers	15
Heavy Bombers	10	Light Bombers	20		
Direct Support Reconnaissance Planes	25	Special Attack Planes	50		
Hq Reconnaissance Planes	20				
Special Attack Planes	300				

Formosa (8th Air Division)	
Fighters	120
Light Bombers	20
Assault Planes	40
Hq Rcn Planes	10
Special Attack Planes	250

Nansei Islands Group

Chart 12

Planned Operations and Strength for Army Air Force (Homeland and China)

Homeland			China
6th Air Army Planes Retained in Homeland		Reserve Forces	5th Air Army Planes Retained
To be used against Sea & Land Bases	To be used in Air Defense		
Fighters 60	Fighters 400	During April and May, personnel to be selected from Training units. As many as possible for "Special-Attack" units to be organized as reserve forces.	Fighters 30
Special Attack (Heavy Bombers) 30	Hq Rcn Planes 45		Assault Planes 70
Special Attack (Hq Rcn Planes) 10			Hq Rcn Planes 16
Hq Reconnaissance Planes 10			Special Attack Planes 150
Special Attack Planes 100			

Note: The number of planes is an estimated one, of those to be prepared by the end of March.

Chart 13

Source of Navy Air Force Operational Strength in Case of Enemy Attacks

Planned Transfer and Allocation of Navy Planes
Against Nansei Islands, Formosa or Iwo-Ogasawara Islands

Location and Unit Source for Planes Transferred

Homeland (a part of 3d Air Fleet)		Homeland (5th Air Fleet)	
Fighters	40	Fighters	200
Carrier bombers	10	Carrier bombers	60
Carrier attack planes	10	Carrier Attack planes	30
Land-based attack planes	10	Land bombers	90
		Heavy bombers	30
		Land-based attack planes	90
		Seaplane bombers	10
		Flying boats	5
		Reconnaissance seaplanes	5

Formosa (1st Air Fleet)	
Fighters	40
Carrier bombers	10
Carrier attack planes	10
Land bombers	5
Land-based attack planes	5
Reconnaissances	5
Night fighters	5
Seaplane bombers	5

Iwo Jima Ogasawara Islands

Nansei Islands

Chart 14

Planned Operations and Strength for Navy Air Forces
(Homeland, Southwestern Pacific Area and Surface Escort)

	Homeland		Southwestern Pacific Area	Surface Escort
Main Force of 3d Air Fleet	Homeland Air Defense Force	Reserve Force (10th Air Fleet)	13th Air Fleet	
Fighters 300		Combat aircraft 700		East China Sea 150
Carrier bombers 80		Training planes 1,300	Fighters 50	
Carrier attack planes 50	Eastern District 60	The fleet was undergoing training for special attack. (This training was to be completed by the end of April).	Carrier attack planes 15	Southwestern Pacific 50
Land bomber 30	Central District 50		Land-based attack planes 15	Homeland area 150
Land-based attack planes 30	Western District 50			
Rcn planes 20				

Chart 15

The following two precautionary rules were to be emphasized, especially:

1. In giving air protection over important areas against enemy air raids, it might be tactically desirable to send our fighter force against the enemy fighters. However, as a rule we would not risk it unless we had a decided advantage and were sure of success, or it was absolutely necessary to do so.
2. To send our air forces out with a mission to overcoming enemy air bases also was to be subjected to similar restraint.

To assist the Navy Air Force in striking enemy task forces, the Commander of Homeland Defenses would use all special attack forces stationed in the Homeland when the enemy attacked the Homeland. Also, a sufficient fighter force would be assigned to act as escorts. If enemy task forces approached the Nansei Islands area, the commander was to send forth part of his special attack forces together with necessary escort fighter force at an opportune time to smash the enemy in co-operation with the Navy. In a similar manner, the 10th Area Army, China Expeditionary Army, and Southern Army commanders would at an opportune time set in action part of their special attack forces and necessary escort fighter force to strike the enemy task forces.

Defensive installations of all air bases would be strengthened immediately. This was to be done in such a way that even under the heaviest fire and bombing by enemy planes, the air bases could maintain their full function. All areas required for maintenance of our air operations, especially our important air bases, were to be guarded strongly by our land forces and held firmly as long as possible.

As is evident from the text of the above orders, in event the enemy approached the Nansei Islands area, counter-air operations would be shared between the Commander of Homeland Defenses (6th Air Army) and the 10th Area Army commander (8th Air Division).

To effect a new alignment of air forces for serial operations around the Homeland, we had transferred air force personnel out of the Southern Regions during January and February where our military position had so deteriorated there was no longer need for them them. The time, destination and names of the army of original assignment are given in the following figures:

Army of Original Assignment	Transfer Destination & Schedule				
	Homeland (January)	China (January)	Formosa (January)	China (February)	Homeland (February)
2d Air Div (Part)	7th Air Brig Hq 62d Air Regt (hvy bmrs) 45th Air Regt (aslt planes)				66th Air Brig Hq 65th Air Regt (aslt planes) 66th Air Regt (aslt planes) 27th Air Regt (aslt planes) 2d Air Regt (Hq Rcn)
7th Air Div		3d Air Brig Hq 24th Air Regt fgtrs	9th Air Brig Hq	75th Air Regt (fgtrs)	20th Indep Air Unit (hvy bombers)
9th Air Div					31st Indep Air Squadron (hvy bombers)
Southern Army					Transp Brigade of 1st Raiding Gp 30th Fighter Gp (fighters)

After deactivation of the 4th Air Army headquarters in late February, parts of the 2d and 7th Air Divisions, 10th Independent Air Brigade and other miscellaneous units were incorporated into the 3d Air Army. The 4th Air Division, 1st Raiding Group and various other air units (all service units) that had been assigned to the 4th Air Army headquarters and stationed in the Philippines were incorporated into the 14th Area Army as ground forces personnel.

In the Homeland, the 30th Fighter Group was reorganized to include tow fighter regiments and one heavy bomber regiment. Its mission was set to attack enemy taskforces operating near the Homeland.

Loss of the Philippines and movement of the scene of battle to Okinawa almost strangled completely our liaison with Southern Regions, making it impossible for us to send more planes to the South. Our Southern Army was forced to conduct a prolonged delaying operation using whatever fighting strength it had available.

Since January 1945, the enemy air forces using carrierborne planes as their main force had been attacking the Eastern District and the Eastern Coast District with increasing intensity. The first large scale bombing was started on 25 February with a force of 600 carrierborne planes and 150 B-29's aiming at destruction of the Kanto District. Since then the enemy seemed to have launched a program of major aerial bombing of all important areas of the Homeland.

The night bombing of Tokyo with B-29's on 9 March was worthy of special mention. In this bombing some 110 B-29's took part and dropped a large number of incendiary bombs, inflicting great casualties and damage. In the middle part of March, persistent air attacks were made daily on Kyushu, Shikoku and Kinki Districts by carrierborne planes numbering about 1,000 a day. Until the close of March, the enemy planes seemed to aim their attacks chiefly against our airfields and harbor installations as a part of their Okinawa Operation.

Until the middle of April main targets of the enemy's bombing were the munitions industries located in Kanto, Shizuoka and Nagoya, especially the aircraft plants. Since late April, the attacks were directed toward the Kyushu area to knock our air bases out of action there. In the middle of April, some hundred small enemy planes arrived on Iwo Jima and started operating raids from bases there.

Also, in April, the Air General Army was put into our battle order. It was to be responsible for all air defense operations to be waged against enemy air units. However, to facilitate protection of vital sections in the Homeland and important installations, air units with exclusively air defense missions were created and placed under the command of the 1st and 2d General Army commanders.

In May B-29's began incedinary bombing of such cities as Tokyo, Yokohama, Shizuoka, Hamamatsu and Nagoya. All suffered heavy casualties and damages as shown on Chart 16.

Casualties and Damages Suffered from Air Attacks

1942 -- 1945

Categories of casualties and damages	1942-1944	January 1945	February	March	April	May
No of raids	76	79	78	91	101	233
No of planes participated	2,079	589	3,193	4,608	2,997	5,462
Bombs dropped: Demolition Bombs	4,980	2,793	4,997	7,263	25,100	14,025
Incendiary Bombs	42,027	36,597	93,352	649,210	112,781	904,018
Mines				770	87	769
Casualties: Killed	2,657	1,515	1,516	89,045	8,957	11,186
Serious Injured	1,729	693	854	8,783	3,749	5,691
Slightly Injured	2,058	1,426	1,852	49,817	7,164	22,013
Total	6,444	3,634	4,222	147,645	19,870	38,890
Building: Destroyed by fire	20,394	3,969	25,178	54,503	283,916	356,560
Damaged by fire	622	682	1,208	5,037	3,025	3,025
Totally demolished	1,017	1,045	915	3,648	7,970	5,558
Partially demolished	1,622	1,865	1,434	4,840	8,441	7,543
No of sufferers	62,498	18,891	85,352	2194,283	169,099	1320,414

Chart 16

PART II   "Ketsu-Go" Operational Stage (April-August 1945)

Operational Preparations Resulting from Situation Estimate

In line with the progress of the battle, the Army General Staff had to revise its appraisal of the general war situation for the year 1945. Careful study was made of the high command system and its adaptation to operating decisive battles on the Homeland. This included main points for conducting battles in various zones and all relevant problems such as army intelligence activities, lines of communication, transportation, communication and training. On the basis of these studies, the Army General Staff formed a tentative plan of strategy (later designated "Ketsu Go") and in March had summoned staff officers of the various Area Armies to explain it to them. In the presence of those officers the Chief of the Army General Staff demonstrated the new strategy by means of a war game to acquaint the audience thoroughly with the new operational policy.

Indications were that the United States was determined to land its forces on the Homeland for an ultimate war victory within a short period. In order to advance their sea and air bases to support the final blow on Japan following the present Okinawa Operation, the enemy was likely to carry out landing operations against strategic points along the coast of the continent, in the Korean Channel and on the islands in the vicinity of the Homeland. This would presumably take place in the summer. Time for the invasion of the Homeland for a final decisive battle appeared to be set for sometime during or after fall.

Prior to the invasion, it was likely an attempt at crippling our fighting power by air operations would be made. After our strength was weakened, the Kanto District would be chosen as the possible ground for a final decisive battle to finish the war by one fatal blow. However, it was highly likely an invasion would be made of Kyushu first as a preliminary move.

The opportunistic strategy of the Russians needed to be watched carefully. They seemed to be waiting for a chance to extend their influence in East Asia, if necessary by force. Indications were that they recently had started moving their forces into East Asia. After summer they would be ready to take the offensive against us any time they thought fit.

The Chungking Army had been strengthened to an appreciable extent through the aid of the United States. With the decline of our military power in China, it was anticipated it would launch offensive actions to reverse the situation. Probably in the fall or winter the Chungking Army would move forward with a considerable force in an attempt at general offensives on all fronts.

In addition, the Yenan Army by tactifully handling the assistance offered by the United States and Russia and particularly under cover of Russian military strength would steadily pursue its increasingly active counteroffensives plan.

To cope with this situation, what we had to do was to speed up the war preparedness of the entire Homeland and to keep military power on the alert so that in the event of the enemy invasion we could rally the main forces of the Army, Navy and Air to smash the enemy. At the same time, every bit of man and material potential must be assigned for use in an all-out homeland battle preparation to establish a firm position for waging a tenacious delaying war. It was also important that measures be taken to confront any sudden adverse turn of the situation in the northern border regions.

Although the groundwork for military operations had been established, in view of the current international situation it seemed imperative that we decide what steps to take in driving a drastic diplomatic offensive immediately. Otherwise, there was danger of losing a change to save the situation. We called on the quarters concerned to take necessary diplomatic actions against Russia.

In April, as the program for Homeland military preparations made much headway, it was necessary to revise the high command structure for the Homeland and on 8 April an order was issued establishing the 1st (East Sector) and the 2d (West Sector) General Armies and the Air General Army, putting them into the order of battle. This eliminated the Commander of Homeland Defenses and each General Army Commander became responsible directly to the Chief of Army General Staff.

The revised system of high command for the Homeland and neighboring areas is shown on Chart 17.

The Army General Staff issued an order on 8 April to the 1st and 2d General Army commanders and the Air General Army, giving them the mission of attacking and smashing any invading enemy operating near the strategic areas of the Homeland.

In order to carry out this mission, the 1st and 2d General Army commander were shown the basic principles to follow in making their preparations.

1. Reinforcement of their state of preparedness was to be rushed for battle and direct decisive action was to be taken against an invading enemy to smash them. Priority was to be given preparations in the Kanto and Kyushu Districts.

2. Against enemy aerial attacks they were to furnish strong protection for vital sections and all important installations in the Homeland.

3. They were to co-operate with the Navy in the task of guarding surface transportation and in conducting all sea operations, especially defense of the channel zones.

4. Operational boundary between the 1st General Army and the 5th Area Army was to be the Tsugaru Straits.

Revised System of High Command

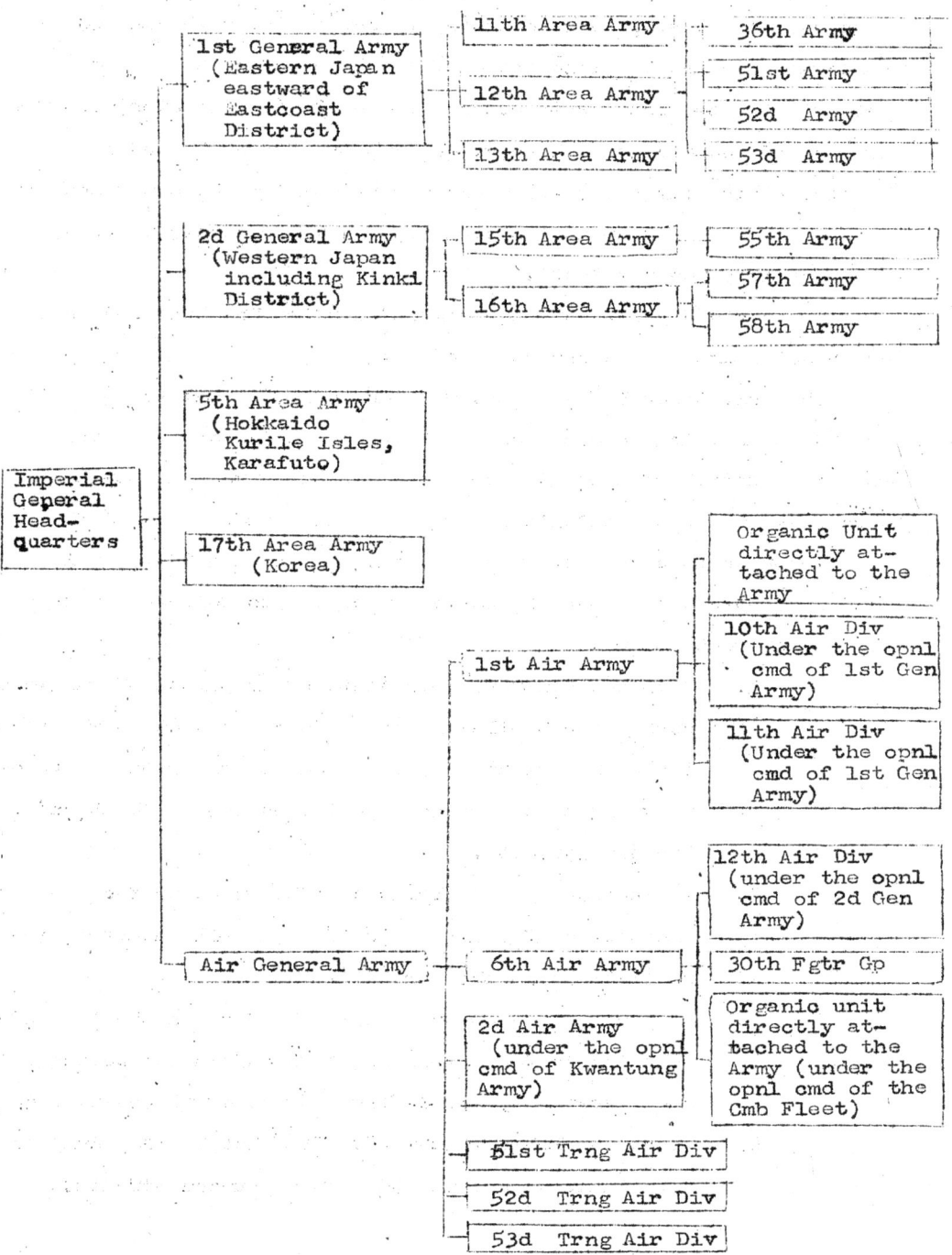

Chart 17

Operational boundary between the 1st and 2d General Army was established along a line following the Suzuka Mountain Range. Fukui Prefecture boundary was the extension line to the North and all of Fukui Prefecture was included in the 2d General Army area. To the South, as an extension of the Suzuka Mountain Range line the prefectural boundary for Mie was used. All of Mie Prefecture excluding Iga province was included in the 1st General Army area.

Operational boundary between the 2d General Army and the 17th Area Army was to be the Korean Channel. Between the 2d General Army and the 10th Area Army it was to be latitude 30°10' north.

For attainment of the same mission, the Air General Army commander was shown the basic principles to follow in prosecuting his battle preparations.

1. His Air General Army must endeavor to attack and smash the invading enemy before they get at vital areas of the Homeland, especially in the Kanto and Kyushu Districts. This was to be done by attacks while enemy convoys were still out at sea.

2. Air Forces must be kept on the alert concerning movement of enemy forces especially the possible direction in which they would attack. Efforts would be made to perdetermine their plans.

3. At the appropriate time, interception of enemy aerial attacks on the vital parts of the Homeland was to be made. Whenever opportunities presented themselves, attacks were to be made on enemy air bases to put them out of action. Also, the same principle was to be used in attacking enemy task forces to check their air

control initiative.

4. The enemy was to be prevented from extending its operations into the Japan Sea.

5. Operational zone for the Air General Army was to cover a part of the 10th Area Army area north and including Okinawa Island, and the zones covered by the 1st and 2d General Armies, 17th Area Army, and Ogasawara Group.

The same day (8 April) the aobve orders were issued to the 1st & 2d General Armies and the Air General Army, the "Ketsu-Go" program was circulated to all armies concerned as the criterion to follow in achieving their battle preparations.

Objectives

The Imperial Army was to rush reinforcement of battle preparations and build up strategic positions which in event of invasion by US Forces would provide the necessary strength in the Homeland to smash the heart of the enemy attack. The premediated main battle front was to be the Pacific and Eastern China Sea Front. Special stress would be laid on battle preparations in the Kanto and Kyushu Districts. Every effort would be made to guard strategic points along the Japan Sea Coast. At the same time, steps would be taken to prevent the enemy from attempting to harass the sea lanes there.

At appropriate times, we had to try overcoming any enemy air activities over the Homeland which were contrary to our wishes or expectations. As a result, Tokyo, industrial installations, transprotation facilities, operational preparations, and similar important spots would be protected.

We would do our utmost to strike and annihilate enemy forces attempting to invade vital areas of the Homeland while they were still at sea. In event of their landing, our land forces would be rallied quickly to challenge them in a decisive battle for our ultimate victory.

In conducting air operations, the primary objectives was to be the prevention of any enemy attempt to land. The main target was to be the prevention of any enemy attempt to land. The main target was to be their convoy. In waging air annihilation combat (those attacks directed against enemy air bases or installations and task forces not including landing forces) or in conducting air defense operation or in giving support for land operations, operations will be conducted only to the extent of not interfering with the stated primary objectives of the air forces. Special attention was to be given the preservation of full fighting strength for use against eventual enemy landing operations.

The main objective of land operation was to be in meeting any enemy attempting landings in decisive battle and overwhelming and annihilating them on the coast. Strategy was to be so designed that even without assistance of air units ground forces could carry out their operation independently and achieve their mission.

The Army would aid the Navy in protecting surface transportation, in launching surface and underwater special attacks and in guarding the channel zones.

We would be determined to drive the operation to final victory by making the most of any and every advantage inherent in fighting on our own homeground. We would inspire the traditional superb morale underlying our system of universal military service and loyalty. In anticipation of the eventual invasion of part of the enemy or any sudden adverse turn of events, the whole nation would be called out for an all-out defense battle. In such case, all measures would be taken to firmly maintain order and stability throughout the country.

Line of Communication (Logistical Support) Preparations

The whole country would make a swift transition into a state of readiness for battle. Preparations of rear echelons were to be roughly completed by about the end of June and fully accomplished by the end of October 1945. Efforts were to be made to complete preparations fully for the important Kanto, Kyushu and Shikoku Districts by the middle of the year. Along with purely strategic preparations, battle-preparedness of the civil defense forces and all industrial activities would be firmly established. Everything in the Homeland would be exploited to the fullest extent to help our Homeland Armies in their struggle for a decisive victory. Operational preparations in the rear echelons would be completed in the shortest possible period by taking advantage of this being a Homeland defense preparation. Emphasis would be placed on training operational troops, construction of fortifications, general dispersion of war materials for protective purposes, speeding up of production for priority war materiel and procurement of provisions.

The Army, acting as the core force, would regiment the entire national power and strengthen battle preparedness of the Homeland. The premeditated concentration of fighting power in the Homeland would be accomplished by the middle of 1945. With this goal in mind, war materiel production would be pushed to the fullest extent during the first half of the year. All unexploited resources having a potential use in our materiel production were to be used in expanding our fighting power. A special effort was to be made to withdraw a large an amount of fighting power as possible from the continent to the Homeland.

Principal points of the preparational program for the air force line of communication would be the strengthening of protective installations for planes, preparation of bombs for special attack planes, establishment of a complete network of signal communications for transmitting orders and intelligence reports, and precautionary dispersal of aviation fuel over separated areas. This program was to be accomplished by the end of June.

The Army was to take over part of the fuel production industry as well as industries dealing with increased food production. Wherever possible liberal assistance was to be given civilian industries in these lines. In the preparation of munitions we would strive to materialize co-ordinated plans which had been prepared, but in view of rapidly diminishing land and sea transport facilities, a new scheme was necessary to enable us to fight the Homeland battle without outside assistance. Each Army Administrative District was directed to build up its own operational potential. In ored to do this, primary attention would be given to self-sufficiency regarding provisions needed by troops in the local, repair of arms and equipment, and prodiction of fuel, weapons and other war implements.

In prosecution of the "Ketsu-Go" war preparations, the Army must closely co-ordinate its activities with those of the Navy.

Transportation Preparations

Transportation formed one of the corner-stones upon which much of the success of the "Ketsu-GO" Operation depended. Therefore, all important transport facilities in the hands of the Transportation and Communication Ministry as well as of the Army and Navy were to be unified with a strong centralized control and were to be put into full operation to facilitate the completion of "Ketsu-Go" Operational Preparation by the middle of 1945. For the latter half of the year, even after the Homeland battle started, we would try by all possible means to preserve at least sufficient transport power to take care of troops movements, concentration and replenishment of munitions, and activities relevant to the maintenance of well being for the whole populace. We would control all transport facilities such as railroads, vessels and small land and water transport power and operate them systematically.

In the "Ketsu-Go" Operation, the Army General Staff would exercise ultimate control over railroads, allowing Homeland railway units to take over all military railway duties. However, administration and operation of railways, at first, would be the responsibility of the Ministry of Transportation and Communication. The Army would offer all-round support, by taking over protection of railways and part of the transportation duties.

A flexible system of command authorization was to be developed to cover critical situations which might develop, especially after the Homeland battle had started. The Army would be prepared to take over all administrative railway work if circumstances required. If necessary, the civil offices of the railways were to be placed under control and command of the Army General Staff or individual Area Army Commanders whichever was more desirable. In the latter case, Army Railway units (under Army General Staff) would be assigned to the Area Armies requiring them in executing railway operation. The areas, time and method of effecting such a transfer of duties would be instructed later by separate orders.

In view of the fact that thorough execution of the shipping transportation during the first half of the year would determine the success of our "Ketsu-Go" Operation and ultimate fate of the Empire, we had to be ready for every possible type of action in strengthening the protection of vessels and harbor installations against bombing and to assure efficient, fast-moving debarkation operations. In addition, we had to try to establish a traffic zone in the Japan Sea which would be secure against enemy intercepting maneuvers.

Communication System Preparation

In order to assure perfect working of communications links even under the most rigorous fire of bombing, all means of communication had to be consolidated into one comprehensive scheme, systematically. Nerve centers commanding operational key junctions were to be rearranged and strongly protected.

In arranging and operating the communication network, main efforts were to be made to insure faster transmission of all intelligence reports required by the Air Force in conducting its operations or by Imperial General Headquarters in putting its operational orders into effect.

In operating government or civilian communication services, all matters relevant to military operations would be given primary consideration, but those official communications necessary to the prosecution of national administrative policies were to be given due regard. These two types of communication would be so regulated that one would not, necessarily, preclude the other.

All communications equipment and installations (Army, official and civilian) would be directed by all means and without delay toward serving the strategic purposes of "Ketsu-Go".

To meet eventual strategic exigencies, we were to encourage improvisation of all kinds in communication devices and vigorous and tactful application of them.

We would start immediately short-term intensive training of additional signal and code personnel. At the same time we would try to increase the proficiency of code personnel already in service with signal units.

Strong measures would be taken to guard electric power plants and sources, adequately.

Land Forces Concentration Plan

Regarding movements of land forces the Army General Staff had formed a provisional plan to follow in the initial stage of the decisive battle.

Concentration of forces to be effected after the initial stages of the battle would be directed later as situations developed taking into account the specific battle situations. In the event the direction of the enemy invasion was detected and a swift shift in basic battle positions was to be carried out in advance, the movement of troops would be effected according to cardinal points established in the basic plan, in most cases. Each General Army would set up its plan of assembly by the end of August along a pattern indicated by the plan shown on Chart 18 and would strive to accomplish all necessary preparations by the end of September unless otherwise specified. As a rule all movements of troops would be completed by foot marches but, if the situation would permit, they could use railways and vessels to speed up their movement. Army baggage which marching troops could not carry was authorized for transport by railways and vessels.

It was to be up to the commandant of each operational zone to assure concentration of troops swiftly and smoothly. Each commandant was to give them all the necessary assistance so fighting strength would not be affected in transit. Should the enemy attempt, simultaneously, to invade a region from which forces were predetermined for transfer to other sectors, the original movement plan could be modified to the extent of leaving sufficient strength behind to confront the invading enemy. In such case, depending upon military circumstances, the whole troop transfer might be cancelled.

Plan of the Army General Staff regarding the Maneuver of Land Forces in "Ketsu-Go" Operation

	Ketsu No 1	Ketsu No 2	Ketsu No 3	Ketsu No 4	Ketsu No 5	Ketsu No 6	Ketsu No 7
5th Area Army							
Forces in the Northeastern Army Admin District (1st General Army)		2 divs → / 3 divs ←	2 divs → / 3 divs ←	2 divs → / 3 divs ←	2 divs → / 1 div	2 divs → / 1 div	
Forces in the East Army Admin District (1st General Army)		2 divs ⇄	Matsumoto, Nagano / 3 divs	2 divs ⇄ Nagoya	3 div / 1 div → Osaka, Kyoto, Nara	3 divs / 2 divs → Osaka, Kyoto, Nara	
Forces in the East Coast Army Admin District (1st General Army)			2 divs ⇄ / 2 divs	2 divs / 1 div ← Osaka, Kyoto, Nara / 2 divs	1 div ← Midland	1 div	
Forces in the Central Army Admin District (2d General Army)			2 divs / 4 divs	5 divs			
Forces in the Western Army Admin District (2d General Army)			1 div ←	1 div ←	1 div ← / 2 divs →	2 divs / 1 div → Northern Kyushu	
17th Area Army							

- - → Movement of forces subject to change according to battle requirments.

Chart 18

Army-Navy Strategic Collaboration

Important problems which called for co-opeartion between the Army and Navy would be the closely aligned areas of commanding responsibility between the Army and Navy in their operational sectors; the co-ordination between disposition of naval surface, underwater special attack forces and land operational forces; and, the tight co-ordination of activities between the Army and Navy in air operations.

Having arrived at a Central Agreement with the Navy regarding command of operations in the waters near the Homeland (except for the Nansei Islands Group), Korea and Karafuto, the Army issued on 8 April the following order:

1. In the event of waging land operations, the 1st and 2d General Armies, 5th Area Army and 17th Area Army commanders were to take over command of naval land forces stationed in their respective operational zones. In this way, the battle in these zones would be conducted under one unified command.

    The command of land operations around naval ports or other important naval bases, within operational zones, would come under jurisdiction of the commanders of the Naval District or Naval Station. He would operate both Navy and Army units stationed in the district under direction of the Area Army commander concerned. During the time for preparation of "Ketsu-Go", however, Area Army commander could give Navy commanders concerned orders relating only to land defense plans and training of troops in defensive missions.

2. Both surface and underwater battles were to be directed by the Commander in Chief of the Combined Fleet. The following named Fortress Units of the Army were to

be directed by the Commander in Chief of the Combined Fleet. The following names Fortress Units of the Army were to receive orders from the higher Navy commanders in each respective area regarding all actions which were to be co-ordinated with surface operations: Soya, Tsugaru, Tokyo Bay, Yura and Hoyo Fortress Units; parts of Shimonoseki, Iki, and Pusan Fortress Units; and, the Units in charge of firing which covered the entrances to Ise and Kagoshima Bays.

General Military Preparations and Disposition of Fighting Forces

On 2 April, as part of the Second Group Army Mobilization Plan an order was issued to create eight well-equipped divisions which were to furnish the core of our mobile fighting strength. This was followed on 6 April by another order for the plan, mobilizing six independent tank brigades and five tank regiments with the special mission of strengthening our counterattacking power. In the meantime, the 11th, 25th and 57th Divisions and the 1st Tank Division arrived in the Homeland in close succession from Manchuria.

On 23 May, as part of the Third Group Army Mobilization Plan, a total of 18 general divisions (originally 16 planned) were activated of which ten were to be located along the coasts and eight were specially fitted as mobile divisions. Also, activated under this order were 14 mixed brigades, five mixed regiments, three independent field artillery regiments, four independent field artillery battalions, nine independent mountain artillery regiments, 32 trench mortar battalions, 10 self-propelled gun battalions, five field heavy artillery battalions, three independent mortar battalions, four independent heavy artillery battalions and 50 independent engineer battalions.

By this time Iwo Jima had already been lost to the enemy, while our defense forces on Okinawa were suffering a series of heavy reverse in battle. The menace of an enemy invasion of our Homeland, especially the Southern Kyushu District, was increasing constantly. In all likelihood, the enemy would drive its spearhead invasion into the homeland during or after the fall of 1945. Faced with this ominous situation, there was no time to be lost in raising battle preparedness to the goal of "Ketsu-Go" plans. However, the available national power was pitiably short of requirements. As a result, we were forced to fall back upon the temporary expedient of further strengthening the regimentation of manpower. Our hopes for replenishment of materiel power rested upon what our production could achieve during the few months up to October. In the meantime, priority measures were taken to replenish equipment and supplies of various army groups stationed in the Kyushu area. This was to be done even at the expense of deferring, temporarily, materiel preparation for forces in Eastern Japan areas. It was considered strategically important that battle preparations in Southern Kyushu should be strengthened immediately.

In addition, some shifts were effected in the general array of forces in the Homeland with a view to filling gaps in defense preparations. From the Northeastern area, the 77th Division and from Formosa the Headquarters of the 40th Army were switched to the Kyushu area. From the Northeastern area, the 147th Division was transferred to the Kanto District.

After two divisions had been withdrawn from the Northeastern area, as mentioned, we found it necessary to give the 5th Area Army a new definite operational mission commensurate with their revised fighting strength. On 8 May the order was issued. It stated that the 5th Area Army commander had a twofold mission: to frustrate enemy attempts to advance their air and sea bases to the Northeastern area, and to overcome their harassing maneuvers in the Japan Sea. In fulfilling this mission the successful prosecution of our Homeland battle plan would be aided.

To do this, main battle preparations were to be established firmly in Hokkaido Island. From this base, counterattacks were to be carried out against advancing enemy forces to prevent them from advancing their air and sea bases.

In a similar manner, the Army was to provide sufficient protection for strategic points in the Kuriles Islands and Southern Karafuto. By firmly holding strategic points on the coasts of the Soya and Tsugaru Straits, the Army would endeavor in co-operation with the Navy to check enemy attempts to dominate the Japan Sea. A swift and complete logistical transition was to be made in such a way as to develop self-sufficiency in provisions, war implements and other supplies. The Army was to be prepared to operate on its own without outside help.

The 5th Area Army commander was to start preparations for defensive operations against eventual attacks from the Soviet. In event of the enemy coming down from the north, the Army was to strike and smash them immediately. The strategic zones in the Northeastern Homeland were to be held firmly. Strategic zones in the Kurile Islands and Soya Strait were to be safeguarded at all costs so we could continue our intercepting operations against the US and the Soviet. Should the Soviet invade Hokkaido Island the Army must strive to destroy them by tactical maneuver with troops attacking from every vantage point to protect and hold all strategic zones in the Island.

Direction of Operations in Korea Area

Since April, there had been indications the Soviet had started transporting their troops from the European Theater to the East and it became increasingly clear that by timing their action with the progress of the US Operation on Okinawa they would eventually attack Japan in or after the summer of 1945.

After concluding the "Ketsu-Go" preparations for the Homeland battle, the Army General Staff took up the problem of direction for subsequent operations on the Continental areas. Toward the end of May, the changing situation on the Continent convinced the Army General Staff of the urgent necessity for quickly strengthening and consolidating defensive preparations in North Korea and Manchuria against the Soviet menace. On 30 May, an order was issued, telling the Commander of the Korea Army Administrative District to operate under direction of the Kwantung Army commander in regard to Anti-Soviet defensive preparations and defensive actions against US Forces in North Korea.

There was a difference in areas of responsibilities for operational and administrative army duties of the 17th Area Army commander. Normally, the concurrent command areas were identical. But in his case, the 17th Area Army commander (as Operational Army commander) was responsible for operational army missions in South Korea whereas in administrative army missions (as Korea Army Administrative District commander) he was responsible for all Korea. In North Korea, the operational army missions were the responsiblity of the Kwantung Army commander. Thus, there was a necessity for close liaison between the 17th Area Army commander and the Kwantung Army commander. In addition, due to a cautious policy in carrying out customary administrative army duties using civilians in North Korea, the 17th Area Army commander was authorized to direct operational army personnel of the Kwantung Army in carrying out his mission in the area. However, this was to be done in such a way as to always avoid affecting the execution of any operational mission of the Kwantung Army troops and units.

Direction of Operations Against Enemy Invasion of Okinawa

From early January to the middle of March, enemy planes had been attacking Formosa and Okinawa with increasing intensity. The overall situation indicated the next move of the enemy would be directed definitely to the Nansei Islands. In late March, enemy task forces operating from their bases in Mariana and Ulithi attacked the Okinawa Main Island (mainly with their carrier groups). Number of sorties amounted to about 500 to 700 daily. This was climaxed on 25 March with their landing on Kerama Island.

The "Ten-Go" air operation had been started on 26 March. In spite of desperate counterattacks by our air forces, the enemy landed on the Okinawa Main Island 1 April. Enemy strength was estimated as about two divisions supported by some 200 tanks.

Operational mission assigned to the 32d Army on Okinawa consisted of turning back any enemy attempt to advance their sea and air bases into the Okinawa Island. Our 9th Division had just been transferred from the central sector (location of the important airfield) to the Formosa theater. When the battle spread to the Okinawa area, the invaders found the island defenses sorely weakened especially in the central sector. The 32d Army had planned to conduct a delaying action by using the fortified zone prepared in southern Okinawa, leaving the airfield substantially unprotected. Whether by coincidence or not, the enemy struck the weakened central sector first when landing their troops. On the following day, 2 April, they captured the airfield quite easily.

The Army General Staff was dissatisfied with an apparent lack of aggressiveness in the operation assumed by the 32d Army. The Staff was convinced that success or failure of our operation in Okinawa depended upon whether or not we could halt the enemy from securing their landing beachheads by using the help of our air attack forces. Therefore, instructions were issued to the defenders to begin more aggressive offensive operations to deny the enemy use of the airfield.

In line with these instructions, the 10th Area Army commander issued an order for an offensive to the 32d Army which accordingly revised its operational plan. The revised plan called for an attack to recapture the airfield. The plan called for the attack to be started on 6 April, but it was cancelled on 4 April because another enemy convoy appeared. Again, strict orders were issued by the 10th Area Army commander. The 32d Army, reluctantly, decided to start the attack on 8 April. But again, the Army gave up its plan fearing the possibility of a flanking attack from the enemy convoy which had appeared off the shore of the Army's rear in the afternoon of 7 April.

Meanwhile, the Combined Fleet including the 6th Air Army as part of a preliminary to the expected ground attack by the 32d Army carried out continuing combined naval and air attacks starting 6 April. By the 9th, it seemed these attacks had gained considerable success. Enemy ships around Okinawa had been reduced in number and the enemy ground attack had been weakened, also. Taking advantage of this, the 32d Army opened an attack on the night of 12 April. But this attack proved unsuccessful from the beginning and the entire plan was abandoned the next morning. Thus, the 32d Army fell back on its original plan of a delaying action.

Toward the end of April, the 32d Army was conducting a desperate defensive battle from fortified positions against the general enemy attack which had been launched on 19 April. The fortified positions were gradually lost to the enemy and, finally, the Army was forced to stand on its last line of entrenchments.

Even after the failure of the counterattack effort on the night of 12 April, the Army General Staff and the 10th Area Army commander had maintained their original intention of resuming a ground attack. Taking this into consideration, the 32d Army commander on 29 April decided to abandon his delaying tactics and launch a general counterattack starting at dawn on 4 May. It began as scheduled. The first line units were the 24th and 62d Divisions. The second line was provided by the 44th Independent Mixed Brigade. The Combined Fleet supported the plan with a general air attack. Initially, the attack was successful, but gradual increases in battle casualties and disruption of our communication network forced the Army to give up the attack toward evening the following day. As a result, the 32d Army again fell back on its final line and the change for a ground decisive battle on Okinawa was lost forever.

Specific features worthy of special mention in the history of our air operations in the Okinawa Campaign were: first, the completely co-ordinated action of the Army and Navy for the attack by consolidating the total strength of their main air units; second, the major adoption of our special attack tactics.

Judging from the general trend of battle during the month of March, enemy invasion of the Nansei Islands in the near future had appeared inevitable. To meet this coming invasion, the 6th Air Army headquarters was moved forward to Fukuoka. On 19 March, an order was issued putting the 6th Air Army under the Commander in Chief of the Combined Fleet for all operations in the Nansei Islands area. This rearrangement of the command system was effected with a view to providing unified Army and Navy air forces in the whole East China Sea zone.

On 26 March, the Combined Fleet issued orders to start the "Ten-Go" Operations. According to the prearranged plan, our 6th Air Army and the 8th Air Division launched an attack against enemy transports around Okinawa. The Navy Air Force attacked the escorting enemy naval vessels. Even after 1 April, the combined Army and

Navy Air Forces made recurrent assaults on enemy convoys in the vicinity and scored much success. Other targets for our attacks were the airfields which the enemy began using after the middle of April.

On 8 April when the Air General Army was activated, the 6th Air Army was placed in the organizational chain of command for the Air General Army but remained under tactical command of the Commander in Chief of the Combined Fleet.

When it became apparent at the close of May that the days of depserate but futile fighting with the overpowering Americans were about to come to an end of the defenders of Okinawa and that there was no reversing the situation, the Army General Staff saw the urgent necessity of immediately putting the whole Army into positions for "Ketsu-Go" Operation. On 26 May, the 6th Air Army was removed from the tactical command of the Commander in Chief of the Combined Fleet.

The operational plan of the Army air forces assigned to the East China Sea area had to be modified under the new situation resulting from the loss of Okinawa. The new plan as it was conceived by the Army General Staff at the end of May included four alternative operational plans.

1. In case the Okinawa Operations continued, the main force of the 8th Air Division (Formosa) and a part of the 6th Air Army (Kyushu) would continue air operations against Okinawa.

2. In the event of an enemy landing on Amami Oshima, the main force of the 8th Air Division (Formosa) and part of the 6th Air Army (Kyushu) would be used against the enemy.

3. In the event of an enemy landing on Sakijima Islands (Miyako and Ishigaki), total strength of the 8th Air

Division (Formosa) would be used against the enemy.

4. In the event of an enemy landing on the Chinese Triangular zone surrounding Shanghai, the main forces of the 8th Air Division (Formosa) and the 13th Air Division (China) would make the attack. In this case, the 5th Air Army (Southern Manchuria and Korea) would send 100 special attack planes to support the 13th Air Division's operation.

Strength of our Army Air Forces and location of units are shown on Chart 19.

Main Continental Operations

The China Expeditionary Army had been investigating major operations in China since the end of 1944 when the No 1 "Sho" Operation ended in failure. Because of success of the "Ichi-Go" Operation (Hunan-Kwangsi Operation) and the existing situation, the China Expeditionary Army judged that the fighting power of the Chungking Government had been weakened seriously. It was estimated the Chungking Government could be made to sue for peace or lay down its arms if a smashing blow were dealt to it through an invasion of the Kweichow Plain.

Being convinced regarding this theory, the China Expeditionary Army commander suggested it to the Army General Staff. But the Army General Staff believed the Chungking Government, bearing in mind that war was nearing its end, would have a sttong will to continue resistance. Chances of success in such an operation were considered unpredictable by Army General Staff. Further, considering the importance of strengthening defenses in strategic areas of the Homeland it was the Army General Staff's opinion that the greater part of the forces in China should not be concentrated for a big scale operation in the interior. Instead, only raids by small forces should be planned to avoid hindering operation of

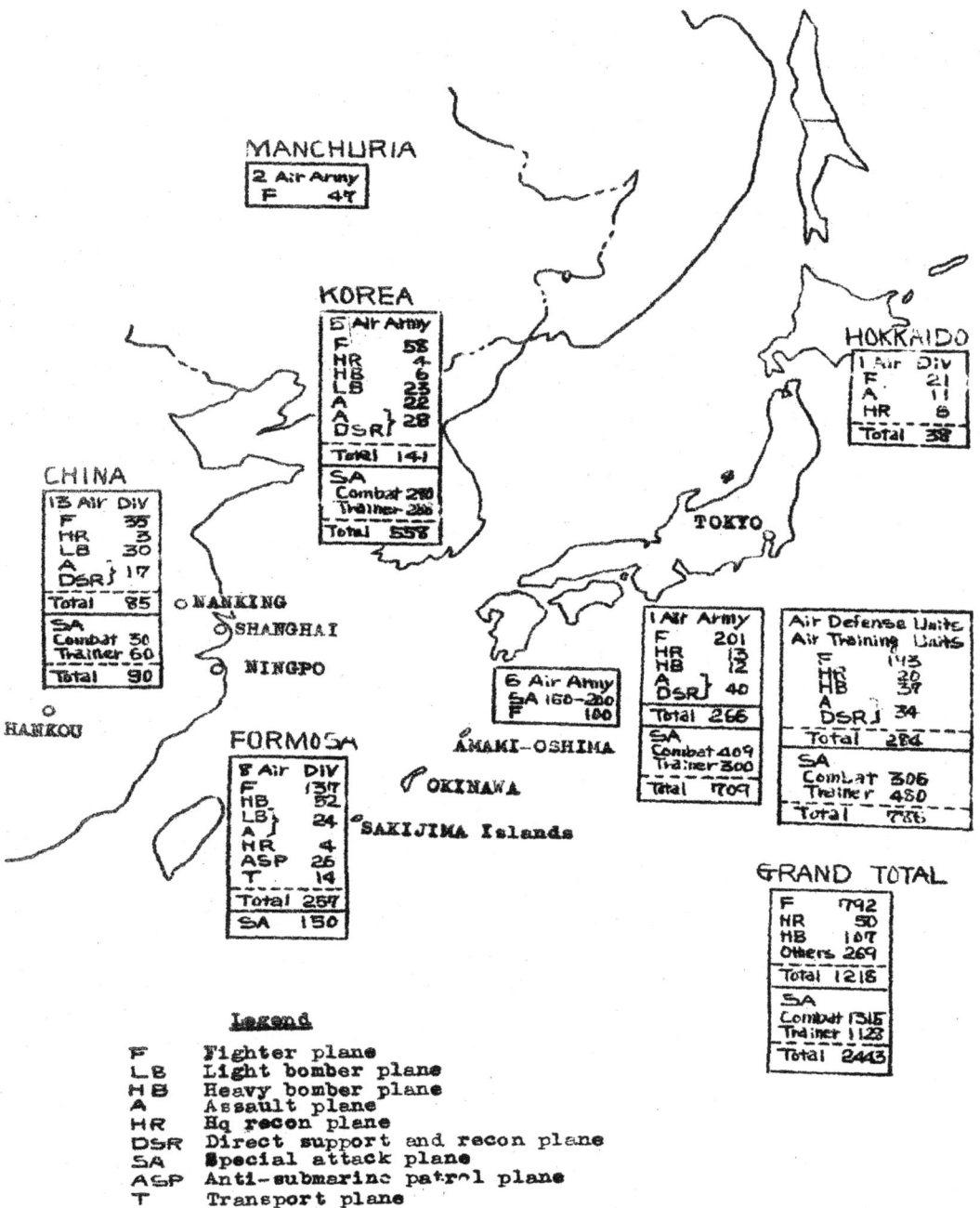

Chart 19 — Strength of Army Air Force (End of May 1945)

the main forces.

The China Expeditionary Army commander was notified on 22 January regarding this conclusion. In its orders, the Army General Staff stressed the importance of strengthening the South and Central China area, especially the lower regions of the Yangtze River. He was ordered to strive to upset enemy plans by first annihilating any American Forces invading the continent and then crushing the Chungking Government by securing strategic areas on the continent.

To upset enemy plans it was necessary to strengthen rapidly the military positions in China; to annihilate the enemy forces, especially the American Forces, invading from both the Eastern and Western Fronts; to secure strategic areas on the continent close to our Homeland placing due importance on operations in the South and Central China area, especially in the lower regions of the Ynagtze River; to crush the Chungking Government through the increase of pressure against them, the destruction of their Army, and political strategy; to strive toward destroying the US-China air force; to establish as soon as possible operation bases; and to maintain order in occupied areas, especially in North China and the lower regions of the Yangtze River, in order to secure the important national defense resources.

All operations, except raids by small forces in the area west of the line running from Hsisunitewangfu through Pailingmiao, Anpoi, Yellow River to the southwestern tip of Shansi, and then through Laohokou, Ichang, Hsiushan, Limingkuan and Pingma were to be carried out only under special definite orders.

The China Expeditionary Army commander, also, was to co-operate as much as possible with the air operations in Formosa and the Nansei Islands and to keep in contact with the important Southern areas.

Essential points of the directives which were issued in accordance with the above-mentioned orders, were as follows:

1. To aid the crushing of the Chungking Government and harassing of enemy aerial activities, the China Expeditionary Army commander was to carry out continuous systematic raids with many small forces in the interior of China.

2. The commander was to take charge of shipping inside China and along the China coast of assuming command of the Second Sea Transport Unit. However, he was not to be concerned with shipping facilities which were under direct control of the Army General Staff.

Essential points of the Central Agreement between the Army and Navy pertinent to the previously mentioned order were circulated. Objectives of the main operations were to be: to strength war preparations immediately in the area along the southeastern China coast, especially in the vicinity of Canton, in order to annihilate invading American Forces; to strengthen, by summer, positions along the lower regions of the Yangtze River, especially in the vicinity of Shanghai to annihilate invading American Forces in a decisive battle; to prevent the enemy from using main harbors and airfields in the Hainan Island area by full co-operation of Army and Navy Units on the Island; to secure the transportation routes between the Southern Sea and the Japan-Manchuria-China sphere; and, to provide coastal transportation protection to insure fullest maneuverability of forces.

The following forces were to be prepared in the following area for embarkation to other areas.

Shanghai area: A force comprised of four infantry battalions as the nucleus.

Canton area: A force comprised of four infantry battalions as the nucleus.

The following forces were to be prepared by the Southern Army and the 10th Area Army for embarkation to the China Theater:

    Northern French Indo-China: A force comprised of three infantry battalions as the nucleus.

    Formosa: A force comprised of three infantry battalions as the nucleus.

The Army and the Navy were in charge of land and sea defenses, respectively. However, the China Expeditionary Army commander and the China Area Fleet commander would co-operate in defense of these islands. The China Expeditionary Army commander and the China Area Fleet commander would command Navy and Army units in the said area of operation, respectively, by mutual consent and agreement.

The China Expeditionary Army strengthened its positions by reinforcing its units along the southeastern coast of China and carrying out mopping-up operations using a part of the 23d Army in the vicinity of Lukfung and Hoifung in the Canton Provinces; completing the penetration of the Canton-Hankou Railroad with conclusion of the Third Stage of the Hunan-Kwangsi Operation on 29 January; and, destroying the Suichuan and Kanhsien Airfields early in February.

Prior to this, and in accordance with the order issued in the beginning of February, three divisions (131st, 132d and 133d Divisions), 12 independent mixed brigades (81st to 92d Independent Mixed Brigades) and seven independent garrison units were organized from among field replacement units stationed in China for strengthening positions in the southeastern coastal area of China. Organization of these units was completed in March.

In order to strengthen positions in the lower regions of the Yangtze River, the China Expeditionary Army planned to concentrate units redeployed from North China and the interior of Central China to the vicinity of Shanghai and Hangchaw. In answer to a request from the Expeditionary Army for a strengthening of the command system in the lower region of the Yangtze River, Army General Staff had transferred the 6th Army headquarters (Khailar area in Manchuria) to China on 26 January 1945.

The French force in China had been disarmed on 9 March. The main force of the 12th Army (110th and 115th Divisions, 3d Tank Division and 4th Cavalry Brigade) and part of the 34th Army (39th Division) had started the Laohokou Operation 11 March, aiming to annihilate the enemy air bases en route to the Hupeh Plain. Due to rapid progress of the Operation, Laohokou was captured early in April. The 13th Air Division was newly activated and placed under the 5th Air Army in March. During the same month, 2d Air Brigade headquarters, 9th, 48th and 6th Air Regiments which had been transferred from Manchuria where they were under the direct command of the China Expeditionary Army was placed under the 5th Air Army commander.

China Operations During the Okinawa Campaign

In April 1945, the Army General Staff anticipated that American and English forces after the Okinawa Campaign and during June and July would transfer their operations to the Northern and Central coast of China, especially the strategic sectors along the lower regions of the Yangtze River, in the vicinity of Ningpo or on the Southern Shantung Peninsula. By such moves, the Allies would be after three operational and political objectives: to capture the above operational bases which were so important in launching a final invasion of Japan; to make the expansion of Soviet influences in Yenan easier; and, to provide encouragement to the Chungking Government.

In April, just after the start of the Okinawa Campaign, the Soviets began transferring forces to the Far East. Thus, Japan was placed in the extremely dangerous position of being encircled by the hostile powers from all directions.

The Army General Staff planned to prepare against a possible invasion of American and Soviet forces in the coastal area of Central and North China and Manchuria and Korea, repsectively. On 18 April, the China Expeditionary Army commander was ordered to transfer and concentrate the 3d, 13th, 27th and 34th Divisions (the most highly trained units in China) from South China to the strategic areas of Central and North China. The plan established to accomplish this was as follows:

    3d Division: To leave the vicinity of Chuanhsien late in July and arrive at Wuhu via Chiuchiang late in September.

    13th Division: To leave the vicinity of Chuanhsien late in July and arrive at Huaining via Chiuchiang late in September.

    27th Division: To leave Huiyang late in May and arrive at Licheng via Kanhsien and Nanchang.

    34th Division: To leave Sinning during the middle of June and arrive in Nanking via Nanchang late in September.

The main strength of the 20th Army (47th and 116th Divisions and the 58th Independent Mixed Brigade) started the Chihkiang Operation during the middle of April. Its purpose was to facilitate the future operations in southwestern China by annihilating the main enemy forces in the Hunan area and by destroying enemy airfields in the vicinity of Chihkiang.

The main strength of the 11th Army (3d and 13th Divisions) began the Tuan Operation late in April in co-operation with the Chihkiang Operation. Its purpose was to deliver a smashing blow on the enemy confronting them to make overall withdrawal easy.

However, the enemy forces being flown in by air transports from the Kweiyang area were far greater in number than we expected.

By the early part of May enemy transport planes numbered 2,500 and had moved 25,000 troops and 30,000 to 35,000 tons of ammunition. Operational progress of the 20th Army, due to the rugged terrain in the Shaoyang area and to reinforcement of enemy troops, fell short of expectation and was discontinued early in May.

Due to the loss of Okinawa and activities of Russian Forces in the Far East, it became imperative as soon as possible to strengthen positions in Manchuria, Korea and Northern and Central China, especially in the strategic areas surrounding the East China Sea. To do this the Army General Staff redeployed the 39th, 59th, 63d and 117th Divisions (from Northern and Central China) to Manchuria and Korea late in May. On 30 May, in order to strengthen strategic areas in North-Central China, the Army General Staff issued the following orders concerning redeployment of units from Hunan, Kwangsi and Kiangsi areas.

The China Expeditionary Army commander was to withdraw as soon as possible forces from occupied areas along the Hunan-Kwangsi and Canton-Hankou Railways in Hunan, Kwangsi and Kiangsi Provinces and deploy them in strategic areas in North-Central China. At the same time, an Army headquarters was to be prepared for transfer to Manchuria as soon as practicable. In addition to his present duties the China Expeditionary Army commander was to carry out operational preparations against Soviet Russia. He was directed to conduct a holding action against the enemy landing in the lower regions of the Yangtze River rather than a decisive battle operation.

Manchuria Operational Preparations

Annulment of the Neutrality Pact between Japan and Soviet Russia, the commencement of transfer of her forces to the Far East during April, and the unconditional surrender of Germany on 8 May unmistakably pointed to the inevitability of Soviet Russia's participation in the war against Japan.

In mid-May 1945, the Army General Staff made an appraisal regarding the position of Soviet Russia. Soviet Russia's intention of extending her influence throughout East Asia was being furthered by her taking advantage of opportunities and transferring troops to the Far East. It was necessary to watch the activities of these troops closely since they could strike at us any time during or after summer.

World War II was undoubtedly an opportune time for Soviet Russia to extend influence in East Asia. Her main and immediate objective would be Manchuria and China. After achieving this, she would place the southern countries which are rich in natural resources under her control in a co-ordinated movement from the West and Middle Asia. For the time being she was expected to leave active operations to the American, English and Chinese Forces. Later, however, she surely would enter the Great East Asia War.

Clearly, USSR was developing hostile feeling toward Japan by propaganda in her press, by transferring her forces to the Far East, and by strengthening her war preparations in the East begun as early as in late February. It was an evident preparation to attack our forces. Her unfriendly attitude was also revealed by the notification expressing her intention to abrogate unilaterally the Neutrality Pact with Japan. Denunciation of the Pact was a political attack on Japan in the same manner as the speech given by Marshall Stalin last autumn and was considered as another preliminary step toward participation in the war.

It was believed Soviet Russia would enter the war during summer or autumn because that would be about the time when American and English Forces would invade our Homeland, Southern Korea and North-Central China. In addition, owing to climatic conditions in Manchuria operational aims would have to be achieved before the coldest season started in December.

Although estimates of the number of Russian troops and time required for their transfer to the Far East differed, it was believed a redeployment of a force consisting of 40 rifle divisions as a nucleus (superior in tanks and airplanes) and with their necessary war supplies would take at least from four to five months. Since Russia began to transfer the above-mentioned forces late in February, it was calculated they would be concentrated in the strategic areas in East Russia by the end of June or July. As some of the war supplies needed by these forces had already been accumulated in East Russia and troop movements could be speeded up, it was expected they could be completely ready for action by August or September even though one or two months would be necessary for attack preparations.

After considering the activities of the Russians and the unfavorable trend of battle on Okinawa, the Army General Staff realized the necessity for hastily strengthening defense preparations in Manchuria and Korea. On 30 May, Army General Staff issued battle orders for the Kwantung Army, modifying present duties and adding two new missions. In carrying out present duties (defense preparations against Soviet invasion), the Kwantung Army commander was to prepare to secure the strategic area east of Dairen-Changchun Railway and south of Changchun-Tumen Railway and conduct a prolonged war of resistance in order to support overall Japanese military operations.

By the same order, the Kwantung Army commander was directed to crush any American invasion of Southern Manchuria or North Korea. In addition, directions were given for defense preparations in North Korea against Soviet invasion. To do this, the Army commander was authorized to locate necessary units under his command in North Korea and to control the Korea Army Administrative District commander in so far as operations against an American invasion and anti-Soviet defensive preparations were concerned. In localized matters pertaining to security and maintenance of peace and order in North Korea, however, the Korea Army Administrative District commander was authorized to control Kwantung Army units located in North Korea. Only limiting factor involved in the latter case was that he must not hinder operational preparations for the Kwantung Army's basic missions.

Since the picked divisions forming the nucleus of the Kwantung Army (1st, 8th, 9th, 10th, 12th, 23d, 24th, 28th, 29th and 71st Divisions and 2d Tank Division) had been diverted already to battle fields extending over the Pacific area, China, Formosa and the Nansei Islands, forces in Manchuria at the close of 1944 had been depleted to about one half the total strength on hand at the end of 1943. Air, signal and engineer units, especially, had been affected. In addition, forces in Manchuria were in poor condition due to a lack of officers, particularly junior officers, who had been transferred back to the Homeland for the purpose of strengthening defense there. Equipment of units and war supplies were in poor condition, also. Fighting power of the Kwantung Army was pitiably weak in both men and materiel.

The Army General Staff, on 16 January 1945, had ordered an emergency mobilization of eight divisions (121st through 128th) and four mixed brigades (77th through 80th) according to the previously mentioned plan to strengthen military preparedness in Manchuria. These units were organized from the 3d Cavalry Brigade, Border Garrison Units, etc. However, as discussed previously, this was a more or less artificial increase. This had completed the defense organization of the northern boundary. In the meantime, four picked divisions (11th, 25th, 57th and 1st Tank) were redeployed to the Homeland and three divisions (111th,

112th and 121st) to the Korea area. At the same time one third of the ammunition and some officers had been transferred to the Homeland.

It was decided on 5 May to relocate one Army headquarters (34th Army headquarters in Hankou) and four divisions (from China) in Manchuria. On 12 May, the organization of Kwantung Army headquarters was strengthened to prepare for the coming battle. A special construction brigade was activated to take care of construction of fortifications and roads and demolition of airfields in Manchuria. Studies were carried out to increase the Kwantung Army troops strength from 450,000 men to 90,000 men by mobilizing civilians in Manchuria.

Summary of Operations June 1945 to End of War

During this phase the Army General Staff tried to accelerate preparations for Homeland Operations and at the same time reinforce our positions on the continent, especially in the North. Special importance was given military preparations for Kyushu and southern Korea. The date for supplying equipment to newly mobilized units was advanced. It was planned to shift, gradually, the disposition of Air Forces to western Japan.

Enemy air raids on the Homeland became more and more violent destroying cities, factories, military installations, communication lines, harbors etc, and making a planned conduct of war by the government and army very difficult. To overcome this difficulty, with the co-operation of the government, the Army General Staff provided a logistic structure for each Army which would establish its ability to fight without outside help.

Transfer of Soviet Army Troops to the Far East was increasing gradually. Along the eastern border of Manchuria, preparations for offensive operations were started by them in July. To make our operations easier, the Army General Staff strengthened the Kwantung

Army command system and planned a total mobilization of manpower and materiel available in Manchuria and Korea. The transfer of four divisions from the China Theater was speeded up to strengthen operational preparations in the North, especially Southern Manchuria and North Korea. With the deployment of forces from Manchuria, priority was given in Korea planning for strengthening positions on Saishu (Quelpart) Island. It was considered important in the defense for the Homeland and Japan Sea.

The USSR declared war against Japan on 9 August and the Soviet Far Eastern Army invaded Manchuria. Although the Army General Staff ordered the Kwantung Army and other units to open hostilities against the Soviet Forces in accordance with the "Anti-Soviet Defense Plans", superior enemy force gradually advanced in Manchuria due to our inferior fighting power in Manchuria and our lack of preparation in the southern Manchuria area.

The termination of the war was announced on 15 August.

Homeland Operations

18 divisions which were activated during the Third Group Operational Army Mobilization Preparation in June, were placed on active service on 19 June. The 50th, 54th and 59th Army headquarters were organized and placed under command of the 11th (Northeast), the 13th (East coast), and 15th (Central) Area Army headquarters, respectively. Zentsuji and Hiroshima Divisional District headquarters were reorganized into Shikoku and Chugoku Army Administrative District headquarters.

Order of Battle for the Tokyo Defense Army which was placed under the 12th Area Army headquarters command was issued on 23 June. Instructions were given to strengthen capital defense positions. The Imperial Palace and important sectors of the capital surrounding the Imperial Palace were to be firmly secured.

In order to carry out this plan, a part of the force was to strive to destroy the enemy forces on the outskirts of the city. With the beginning of No 3 "Ketsu-Go" Operation, the following units were to be placed under command of the Tokyo Defense Army: two or three field divisions (to be assigned from troops outside the 1st General Army's command); 1st AAA Division (less the main body and consisting of approximately one regiment); and, other units (one independent tank brigade, two heavy field artillery regiments, one independent field artillery regiment and one independent mountain artillery regiment, etc to be assigned from troops other than those under command of the 1st General Army).

The enemy was to be denied use of all facilities including harbors outside of above-mentioned sectors by their being destroyed after being stripped of equipment and materiel necessary for our operations before the enemy invasion. The National Volunteer Fighting Units in the vicinity of the Capital were to participate in the early stage of operations to defend the Capital under command of the Tokyo Defense Army commander. Fortification of underground positions was to be carried out during operational preparation. These operations were expected to last for one year. The greater portion of ammunition needed for these operations was to be shipped from other areas and underground facilities were to be equipped to handle the same. The 1st Imperial Guard Division could be used if operation preparations did not interfer with the primary duties of guarding the Imperial Palace.

Air Operations

Enemy air raids on the Homeland by B-29's from their Mariana Base increased gradually during the early part of 1945. At first, their chief objectives were munitions production installations. Starting in March, they turned to large scale indescriminate attacks inflicting heavy damages on our cities. It was impossible to stop the raids because of our weakness in aerial defense units and facilities to combat night bombings. These raids increased further after the Okinawa Campaign. At the end of June the enemy was using approximately 2,000 airplanes against the Japanese Homeland, 700 of which were based on Okinawa, 300 on Iwo Jima and 1,000 (mostly B-29's) on the Marianas. The estimated increase of the United States' Air Force strength was as follows:

Time	Total Strength which could be used against Japan	The Strength able to Attack our Homeland					
		Sea Plane	Fighter	Light Bomber	B-24	B-29	Total
Sep 1945	10,200	120	1,500	480	650	1,150	3,900
Dec 1945	11,200	120	1,775	830	1,200	1,500	5,425
Mar 1945	11,200	120	1,950	1,090	1,400	1,500	6,060

The Army General Staff had intended to preserve its air combat power until the beginning of the "Ketsu-Go" Operation. However, in late June, this plan was revised by a decision to use the principle air forces in the Homeland in air operations against B-29's, at least for the time being. The Air defense divisions (formerly under operational control of ground force commanders) were placed under the centralized command of the Air General Army commander. He was in charge of all air defense operations in the Homeland.

Checking of operations by B-29's was to be done in the following way:

    1. The Air General Army commander was to direct air defense operations in close co-operation with the Navy. There was considerable discussion and study made as to the proper objectives for our air defense operations which involved whether to concentrate on shooting down enemy planes or to throw up a tight defensive screen around important sectors and installations. The former was established as the policy

and emphasis was placed on shooting down large-type bombers. Air defense units were to be deployed so there would be four fighter regiments in the Eastern Districts; four fighter regiments in the East coast and Central Districts; and from one to three fighter regiments in the Western District. These units could be redeployed to other areas when necessary. In addition to these specifically assigned air defense units, a mobile reserve (as strong as possible) was to be maintained which could be concentrated effectively when needed to destroy the invading enemy.

Counterattack measures were to be taken against even a signal enemy bomber (larger types). In general, the main protection of the important sector and installations in the Homeland would be handled by AAA ground force units. Interception was not to be carried out against an enemy fighter attacking singly unless it was easy prey or when its destruction was necessary.

2. Cooperation in carrying out the afore-mentioned operations, would be given by the First and Second General Army commanders co-ordinating with the Air General Army commander. Searchlights were to be located and operated to help in air battles.

The previously mentioned operations were carried out after 10 July, but were not as successful as was expected. Lack of strength and night air battle equipment and the fact that land-based fighter units from Iwo Jima and carrier-borne fighters were escorting the enemy bombers in their raids caused the objective to be difficult.

Anticipating the possible outcome of air operations during the "Ketsu-Go" preparations which would probably be the last phase of the campaign and presuming that the enemy undoubtedly would invade Western Japan, Army General Staff sped up air operation preparations in accordance with the following Army-Navy Central Agreement concluded in mid-July. The enemy was to be destroyed at sea by concentrating our entire fighting strength of Army and Navy Air Forces. If that failed, we would annihilate his landing units with the cooperation of our ground forces. Activities of anti-aircraft and anti-submarine operations in and around our Homeland were to be increased. Chief aim of air Operations directed against an enemy invasion of our Homeland was to destroy enemy transports through suicide attacks.

In order to carry out these plans we would place importance on preparations in Kyushu, Shikoku and Southern Korea; immediately establish operation positions and strengthen them later; meanwhile, equip operation positions in other areas, especially in the Kanto Districts, reconnoiter enemy bases and operation lines and make advanced estimates of enemy plans; concentrate and display full fighting power during a short period (approximately ten days) at the start of an enemy invasion; carry out persistent attacks day and night and destroy enemy transports before or immediately after they entered the anchorage; check the activities of enemy task forces through tactical attacks; and co-operate with the ground operations according to the progress of the situation.

Enemy Naval bombardment was to be stopped by attempting with part of our forces to destroy enemy Navy craft prior to the invasions, and/or attacking them with our main forces after our ground counterattack has started, making our ground activities easier. Against enemy attacks on isolated islands in the vicinity of the Homeland (Goto Retto, Tanega Shima and Izu Shichito Islands), we were to destroy enemy transports. However, only a limited amount of strength was to be used in order to avoid upsetting any of the planning for the decisive battle in the Homeland. In event the enemy attacked Saishu Island and Southern Korea, we were to counterattack them with the necessary forces.

Anti-aircraft and anti-submarine operations prior to Operation "Ketsu" were to be strengthened. The Army would concentrate interceptor units to carry out tactical operations against enemy bombers raiding our Homeland. The Navy was to co-operate eith the Army. Both the Army and Navy were to attempt surprise raids on important enemy bomber bases, especially in the Mariana, Iwo Jima and the Okinawa area. The Navy was to check enemy submarine activities in the Japan Sea area. The Army was to co-operate with the Navy. The Army and Navy would co-operate in checking enemy attempts to drop mines in important harbors of our Homeland.

Part of our forces would inflict as much damage as possible on the enemy attacking Nansei Islands other than Okinawa, Ogasawara Islands, and Central China before his landing on the Homeland.

Disposition and utilization of places from the Air General Army and the Naval Air Force are shown on Charts 20 and 21.

The Army and Navy as a rule were to co-operate in all operations. Top commanders of the Army and Navy Air Forces were to remain at one location during operations to direct close co-operation between the Army and Navy.

As a result of strengthening our air power by equipping suicide attack units and their bases, our fighting strength was kept pretty high despite the fact that B-29 raids continued to increase in intensity. However, the decrease in airplane production and lack of fuel became more and more evident as the days passed by giving us a dull outlook in the future.

Disposition and Utilization Plan of the Air General Army

Air General Army			
	1st Air Army (Mainland East of Suzuka)	Approximately 600 Special Attack Planes	1. Reserve forces of the 6th Air Army in case of an operation in Kyushu and in Shikoku. 2. Main force for the operation in Kanto.
		Approximately 500 miscellaneous planes	Concentration of fighters for intercepting the enemy bombers attacking the Homeland.
	6th Air Army (Mainland West of Suzuka; Shikoku and Kyushu)	Approximately 400 miscellaneous planes	
		Approximately 1000 Special Attack Planes	Main body of the Air General Army as a nucleus for the operations in Shikoku and Kyushu.
	5th Air Army (Main Force in Korea and a part in Manchuria and Northern China)	Approximately 200 miscellaneous planes	1. For either front line fighting or as a reserve force of the 6th Air Army in case of an Operation in Kyushu and Shikoku.
		Approximately 500 Special Attack Planes	2. Main force for the Operation in Southern Korea

Note: This plan was to be altered to fit the situation 500 to 1,000 additional Special Attack Planes were to be readied during July and August. Miscellaneous planes included fighters, reconnaissance planes, assault planes, and bombers, for orthodox tactical use.

Chart 20

Disposition and Utilization Plan for the Navy Air Forces

- 12th Air Fleet (Hokkaido) ----- No plane, only air base units ------- Responsible for the defense of Northeastern area.

- Combined Fleet ---
  - 10th Air Fleet (All Mainland)
    - (1,070 planes for attacking task force)
    - 30 intercepters
    - Reserve force for the 3d and 5th Air Fleet.
  - 3d Air Fleet (Mainland east of Suzuka Mt Range)
    - (1,140 planes for attacking task force and landing convoy)
    - 40 reconnaissance planes
    - 470 intercepters
    - 1. Main force for the operation in Kanto.
    - 2. Reserve for the 5th Air Fleet.
  - 5th Air Fleet (Mainland west of Suzuka Mt Range, Shikoku and Kyushu)
    - (1,765 planes for attacking task force and landing convoy)
    - 100 reconnaissance planes
    - 530 intercepters
    - 1. Main force for the operation in Kyushu.
    - 2. Reserve force for the 3d Air Fleet.
  - 4th Fleet (Truk Island) ---- 80 planes for attacking task force -- Responsible for the defense of South Sea Islands.

Note: The number indicates the planes on hand.

Chart 21

The greater part of the air units as shown below redeployed at the end of June from the South to Formosa, to facilitate operations there and in the Homeland.

Place of Redeployment	Formosa			
Original Units	3d Air Army	5th Air Div	7th Air Div	9th Air Div
Units Redeployed	35th Air Brig Hq 204th Air Regt (Fgtr) 12th Air Regt (light bmr)	50th Air Regt (Fgtr) 8th Air Regt (light bmr)	13th Air Regt (Fgtr) 61st Air Regt (Heavy bmr)	21st Air Regt (Fgtr) 24th Air Regt (Fgtr) 26th Air Regt (Fgtr) 58th Air Regt (Heavy bmr) 71st Air Sq (Fgtr)

The 7th and 98th Air Regiments, formerly under tactical command of the Navy, were returned to the command of the Sixth Air Army in June. Operation units of the Air Training Divisions in the Homeland were reorganized and the 11th Air Division (formerly under the First Air Army) was placed under direct command of the Air General Army. At the beginning of August, it was planned to redeploy all air units stationed in Formosa to the Homeland, but termination of the war was announced before this could be carried out.

Operations After Fall of Okinawa

The main body of the 32d Army had been 1st in the Okinawa Campaign on 19 June and the main battle field shifted to our Homeland. On 20 June, Army General Staff ordered the 10th Area Army commander to crush the enemy attacking Sakijima Islands and Formosa and to harass their air and navy bases in the Nansei Islands. This was designed to aid our general overall operations on the Homeland. Operational boundary between the 10th Area Army and the 2d General Army was changed to the boundary line between Kagoshima and Okinawa Prefectures.

Instructions in the order received by the 10th Area Army commander further stated that he was to assist the China Expeditionary Army with his air forces, in operations against American and British Units in Chekiang and Fukien. The Takao Naval Guard District commander was to be under the 10th Area Army commander in regard to operations. After consulting with adjacent Army commanders, the 10th Area Army commander could dispatch units to other Army's operational sectors and place them under other Army's command if he found it necessary.

After the fall of Okinawa in June, enemy submarines ventured into the Japan Sea and seaplanes began to attack our ships in the Korea Strait and Japan Sea. Considerable damage was caused and transportation of units and munitions from the Continent to Japan became increasingly difficult. In order to facilitate transport of necessary units and munitions to the Homeland, the Army and Navy on 28 June worked out a plan to secure the Japan Sea.

Objective of the Central Agreement was to stabilize and secure the Japan Sea through joint cooperation. All efforts were to be made to transport the maximum amount of essential war materiel in the minimum amount of time. Initially, main effort of escort, anti-submarine and mine-sweeping operations was to be directed in the Tsushima Strait. Later, in line with developments, it was to be shifted to the inner Japan Sea. To prevent infiltration of enemy submarines in the Japan Sea and to strengthen protection of shipping, a tight defense and patrol system was to be established in Tsushima, Soya, and Tsugaru Straits. Shipping navigation control was to be imposed when necessary to obtain maximum efficiency in navigation and transportation. This was to be a joint operation of Army and Navy forces and close liaison was to be maintained regarding intelligence information. In carrying out the operation (designated "Nichi"), every effort was to be made to make the most efficient use of fuel.

Continental Organization Revisions and Operations

After June, Russia appeared to have speeded up her operation preparations aiming to complete them by the end of August and to start war against Japan early in Autumn. She seemed able to concentrate forty sniper (infantry) divisions by the end of August and increase these to fifty divisions by the end of September. Following preliminary completion of the troop movement of front line units, tremendous numbers of vehicles and supporting units were being transported into the area. She was also deploying units and storing munitions in all areas along the border paying special attention to the Suifenho (Pogranichnaya) area from which, presumably, they would launch their main offensive.

The Kwantung Army reorganized its forces in Manchuria according to previously mentioned situations and existing defense operations plans. One Army headquarters, eight divisions, and seven Mixed Brigades were mobilized. Third Area Army headquarters (formerly located in Tsitsihar) was moved to southern Manchuria to take charge of the operations there. Under the Third Area Army commander, the 30th Army headquarters was activated in July to take charge of construction duties in the fortified areas. Defense in northern Manchuria was transferred to the 4th Army headquarters. The Kwantung Defense Army was redesignated as the 44th Army on 5 June with defense duties in western Manchuria. Altogether, approximately 250,000 out of 400,000 reservists residing in Manchuria were mobilized on 10 July. This did not include some 150,000 men assigned to civil transportation and other duties.

The following units were organized: eight divisions (from the 134th through 139th, 148th and 149th Divisions); seven Mixed Brigades (from the 130th through 136th Brigades); and, a few Line of Communication Units. In addition, it had been planned to organize the

158th Division.

While the 34th Army headquarters (redeployed from China) was engaged with defense preparations in Northern Korea, the Army General Staff on 13 July issued an order concerning actions to be carried out by the 34th Army when the Soviet attacked the Central Sector between the 34th Army and 17th Area Army. Main objective was to be destruction of the attacking Soviet forces in the important regions of North Korea. If this failed, the Army was to use its main force in checking an enemy advance toward Pyongyang and part of its strength in protection of Seoul.

On the same day, the Army General Staff issued the following order to the 17th Area Army concerning operational conduct for the Saishu Island.

1. Operation objective on Saishu Island would be to foil enemy planes to establish air and naval bases. Major efforts were to be made during initial stages to crush enemy landing efforts when first attempted.
2. The 17th Area Army commander was to keep one division in southern Korea in readiness to redeploy it to Saishu Island to strengthen the 58th Army in case an enemy attack against the island seemed probable.

The China Expeditionary Army, contracting its front in the Hunan and Kwangsi areas, redeployed the 3d Tank Division to Inner Mongolia to strengthen preparations there and dispatched four divisions from Central and North China to Manchuria and Korea. These divisions were placed under the Kwantung Army commander in order on dates indicated as soon as they passed through the border: 63d Division on 19 June; 117th Division on 25 June; 59th Division on 19 July; and, 39th Division on 21 July.

The China Expeditionary Army gradually contracted its front in southwestern China resorting to counterattacks against the

Chungking Army which was pursuing it. The 11th Army headquarters withdrew from Kweilin on 28 July. Contracting of the fronts, generally, was carried out successfully. Enemy pursuit was very slow.

The Army General Staff planning to complete strengthening of our defense preparations on the Continent before July was concerned with reexamining plans of operations there especially the chain of command for Manchuria and Korea, important areas to be secured to the last and redeployment of troops from China in the light of estimated possibility of Soviet entrance in the war about the beginning of fall.

It was decided that while resorting to delaying actions in Manchuria we would engage in decisive actions against the enemy in Korea, especially in southern Korea. If these operations were not up to expectations important sectors in southern Manchuria (east of the Dairen-Changchun Railroad and south of Mukden) and in southern Korea must be secured. As many units as possible were to be redeployed from northern China to sectors in Manchuria and Korea.

Future operation plans in China during the period until the end of 1945 were to be based on the contraction of fronts in Hunan and Kwangsi Provinces in order to redeploy as many units as possible (as a nucleus, approximately ten divisions and ten brigades) to Manchuria and Korea. At the same time, important sectors in northern China were to be secured against combined US and Soviet attacks. This would aid the general operations of Japanese Armed Forces.

Operational Conduct Following Soviet Entry in War

Before the above-mentioned decision was wholly materialized, the Soviet Goverment entered the war on 9 August. Soviet Forces invaded Manchuria (from the eastern border and the Manchouli area to the west) raiding strategical sectors in Manchuria and Korea. The Kwantung Army commander in preparing the general operations counterattacked the enemy with units stationed along the bordering areas.

The Army General Staff issued an order on 9 August stating that troops along the border were to check the enemy advance. The Army General Staff would prepare for general operations. The 17th Area Army on 0600 of 10 August would be placed under command of the Kwantung Army. The Kwantung Army commander was to counterattack with units stationed along the bordering areas and prepare for the general operations. In doing this, he was to bear in mind the following objectives: operations of the Kwantung Army were designed to protect and secure Korea against Soviet invasion; and, he would prepare to resist an American invasion of southern Korea with the minimum number of troops. The China Expeditionary Army commander would prepare to send part of his forces and equipment to southern Manchuria holding off troops. The China Expeditionary Army commander would prepare to send part of his forces and equipment to southern Manchuria holding off Soviet attacks with remaining units. Operational boundary between Shanhaikuan through Tachengtzu, Dalidor to Yujul Temple. The boundary line, itself, was to be included in the operation sector of the China Expeditionary Army. The Kwantung Army commander would place troops in the sector, transferring them to the China Expeditionary Army command. The 5th Area Army commander was to carry out its original duties of repulsing enemy attacks with units in the bordering area and preparing for subsequent general operations.

Though there was no declaration of War against Russia, the Army General Staff deciding to break down the inordinate ambition of the Soviet on 10 August issued the following order:

1. While carrying out major operations against US Forces, Army General Staff would begin general operations against Soviet Forces in order to break down their inordinate ambition and crush their forces thus protecting the Imperial Homeland.

2. The Kwantung Army commander, directing the main effort against the Soviet, would crush the invading enemy and protect Korea.

Following the above order, Army General Staff issued orders to the China Expeditionary Army commander that he would direct his operations in such a way as to assist the Kwantung Army's operations in Southern Manchuria and Northern Korea. At the same time, he was to dispatch part of his strength (six divisions and six brigades with ammunition sufficient for six large engagements of one division) to Manchuria and Korea.

Due to superiority in air power and armored forces, the Soviet Far Eastern Army's invasion of Manchuria was carried out with unexpected speed in spite of stubborn resistance by our troops in the bordering area. Within one week, the enemy advanced to the Mutanchiang Plain in the east, Sunwu in the north, the peak of Tahsinganling Mt Range in the northwest, and Paicheng and Taonan in the west. Owing to the existing situation in the Pacific we were unable to send Air Force reinforcements from the Homeland or from other areas. While this situation prevailed termination of the war was announced.

South Burma and Philippines Operations

The Southern Army concentrating the Burma Area Army in southern Burma (south of Sittang River) ordered it to recapture Rangoon. However, it was not able to fulfill its missions with its depleted strength. In accord with the changed situations in Burma, the Army General Staff readjusted the duties of the Southern Army commander by ordering him on 26 July to continue resistance in southern Burma and Sumatra as long as possible firmly securing at the same time important sectors in Indo-China, Thailand and Malay.

At the end of June, the enemy was in full control of the Cagayan Valley with paratroops descending at Apali and the American-Filipino Army in northern Luzon. After the 14th Area Army headquarters withdrew to Pacdan in mid-June there were practically no communications between the Army General Staff and the Area Army. It seemed to have concentrated in the retrenchment area north of Pulog Mountains in northern Luzon. The 19th, 23d and 105th Divisions plus a part of 103d Division, the 2d Tank Division and Line of Communication Units totalled approximately 45,000. This included Japanese residents.

Line of Communication (Logistical Support) During Fifth Phase

Measures concerning Line of Communications during this phase of war were not carried out in the outer areas at all and only in part of the Homeland zone. Preparations for the Homeland Operations were accelerated in light of the general situations which was aggravated by the beginning of the Okinawa Campaign. Although we tried to complete preparations in Kyushu earlier than scheduled and organized transportation of equipment from the Continent in spite of violent air raids, termination of the war was announced before we could accomplish our task.

In the attempt to establish independent self-supporting organizations in each Army Administrative District, central supply depots (which were established originally to supply overseas units) were reorganized and placed under command of the local Army Administrative District commanders. They were instructed to protect production of ammunition by dispersing manufacturing plants and stockpile munitions as much as possible. Although the Army succeeded in the stockpiling of munitions, production decreased greatly due to violent air raids. Also, affecting production was the lack of food and communication facilities. Under these circumstances, it became necessary to have each Army Administrative District commander control and assist production elements in his area of responsibility. A part of the munitions mobilization operations was placed under him as directed by higher Army authorities. Each Army Administrative District commander made every effort to repair and restore to operation all damaged production facilities and to produce agricultural equipment in order to establish a self-supporting system. However, not much success was achieved.

Although attempts to transfer materiel to the Homeland started in April, due to increased activities by enemy submarines in the Japan Sea since June, transportation became very difficult. Not much was brought over. This fact coupled with the low production rate in Japan and with lack of ground communications made the whole prospect of waging battles in the Homeland look very gloomy. Duties of the Army had increased greatly because of the necessity of helping repair and restore damaged civilian installations. It was also necessary to help such civilian work as agriculture and transportation because civilian labor supply and transportation facilities had been reduced greatly by the successive Military Mobilizations. As a result, much difficulty was encountered by the Army commanders in making their operational preparations.

Termination of Hostilities

Around the beginning of August, all Army forces were making every effort to complete operational preparations for "Ketsu-Go". In Kyushu, it was believed these preparations would be completed by mid-September. The Army General Staff estimated that an Allied landing surely would made there first, during late September or soon thereafter. It was the conviction of the Army that any such landing could be defeated convincingly, at least the first wave. On the basis of the estimate regarding potential enemy operations, the Army General Staff had about decided to send its last reserve force (main elements from the 36th Army) to the 2d General Army area.

In spite of the Army's confidence in achieving victory in a Kyushu Operation, the dropping of the first Atomic bomb on Hiroshima (6 August) and the Soviet entry in the war (9 August) caused deep concern among leading Japanese statesmen and high government circles, including the Emperor himself. The first decision to accept the Three Powers' Declaration made at Potsdam on 26 July was arrived at during a Council in the Imperial Presence on 10 August. A clause was included in the acceptance which was intended as a protective effort to maintain the traditional Japanese form of government as represented by the Emperor.

The Allied answer regarding this proviso clause caused further discussion and argument. The Foreign Minister insisted Japan should be satisfied with the reply (a restatement that the government of Japan would be established by the freely expressed desires of the people). The War Minister, Chief of Army General Staff and Chief of Navy General Staff strongly objected. Their opinion was that to follow the Foreign Minister's suggestion would mean the loss of Japan's traditional form of government as represented by the Emperor. They also argued that by continuing the war more favorable terms could be obtained. This was based on their confidence in the Kyushu Operations. At this critical point, the Emperor expressed his earnest desire to terminate the war quickly and asked members of the Council for immediate cooperation in agreeing with his desire. The foregoing discussions took place at the Council in the Imperial Presence on 14 August which had been insisted upon by the Emperor, breaking tradition with the normal method of joint agreement by members of the Council prior to convening a Council in the Imperial Presence. By this method and meeting, the dissenting elements (War Minister, Chief of Army General Staff and Chief of Navy General Staff) agreed and the decision to end the war finally was reached.

Following this, the Army General Staff on 15 August issued orders to all Army forces to suspend all offensive actions. The next day, another order was issued to cease all hostile activities.

Just preceding the convening of the decisive Council in the Imperial Presence, the Emperor summoned the three oldest ranking officers of the Army and Navy to appear before him. The Emperor requested their help in transitting his true thinking to the Army and Navy. Those attending this meeting included: Field Marshall Sugiyama, 1st General Army commander; Field Marshall Hata, 2d General Army commander; and, Fleet Admiral Nagano, member of the Board of Marshalls and Fleet Admirals (not a Fleet commander). They were summoned as senior officers of the Army and Navy and not as field commanders or fleet commanders.

Immediately following the Council's decision, a meeting of Army personnel was held attended by the War Minister, Chief of Army General Staff, Inspectorate General of Military Training, 1st General Army commander, 2d General Army commander, and Air General Army commander. The meeting agreed upon faithful obedience to the Imperial Decision. To make the agreement more binding, a written statement was prepared and signed by all attending the meeting. It stated, "The Army will act in obedience to the Imperial Decision to the last."

On the afternoon of 14 August, a similar message as mentioned in the preceding paragraph was sent by telegram to all field commanders who were immediate subordinates of the Army General Staff. The telegram was sent over the joint signature of the War Minister and Chief of Army General Staff. Except for some elements which attempted uprisings during the night of 14 August, all Army forces quietly obeyed the Imperial Decision.

When Japan received the reply from the Allies in answer to the conditional acceptance of the Potsdam Declaration and it was revealed to some of the field grade officers in the War Ministry, they drafted a plan to maneuver a coup d'etat and establish a Military Government to continue the war. This plan was presented to the War Minister in an effort to obtain his approval. He did not commit himself at the time. Later, on the morning of 14 August just before the last Council in the Imperial Presence, the War Minister held a conference with the Chief of Army General Staff regarding the proposal which had been presented. The Chief of Army General Staff did not approve. Thus, the plan was dropped.

However, extreme elements in the field grade officer group in the War Ministry created an uprising during the night of 14 August in spite of the final decision for unconditional acceptance of the Potsdam Declaration. They killed the Imperial Guard Division commander who rejected their demands. An order was counterfeited for the Divisional Guard units to assemble and isolate the Imperial Palace. The immediate objective of the move was to find the Imperial Rescript recording which was to inform the Japanese regarding the termination of hostilities. It was to be broadcast at noon 15 August. The intent of the faction mounting this uprising was to prevent the broadcast and gain time to achieve a reconsideration by the Emperor. The search efforts were unsuccessful. Meanwhile, elements of the Imperial Guard Division began to feel suspicious of the orders involving them in such an assignment. The incident was settled finally on the morning of 15 August when the 13th Area Army commander entered the Palace, took command of the situation and declared his will to obey faithfully the Imperial Decision.

SUPPLEMENT I

Chronology of Major Events during Greater East Asia War

1941 October 18 -- Third Konoye Cabinet resigned and Tojo Cabinet was formed.

　　　November 26 -- Hull Note issued.

　　　December 8 -- Outbreak of Pacific War.

　　　　　　　　　　　Military Agreement was concluded between Japan and French Indo-China

　　　　　　　11 -- Japan, Germany and Italy agreed on Non-Separate Peace Treaty.

　　　　　　　21 -- Offensive and Defensive Alliance Pact was concluded between Japan and Thailand.

1942 January 2 -- 14th Army captured Manila.

　　　February 8 -- 14th Army's attack on Bataan temporarily suspended.

　　　　　　　15 -- 25th Army captured Singapore

　　　March 8 -- 15th Army captured Rangoon

　　　　　　　9 -- Dutch Forces surrendered in Netherlands East Indies.

　　　April 3 -- 14th Army's attack on Bataan resumed.

　　　　　　　9 -- 14th Army occupied Bataan.

　　　　　　　18 -- First air raid on Japan was made by US task force.

　　　May 7-8 -- Naval battle of Coral Sea.

　　　June 5 -- Naval battle of Midway.

　　　　　　　7 -- North Seas Detachment landed on Kiska and, on the 8th, on Attu.

　　　July 1 -- Navy forces landed on Guadalcanal.

　　　August 7 -- Allied landing on Guadalcanal and Tulagi.

　　　　　　　20-21 -- Ichiki Detachment's counterattack on Guadalcanal.

　　　September 5 -- South Seas Detachment captured summit of Owen Stanley Mt Range.

　　　　　　　12-14 -- First general attack by Kawaguchi Detachment on Guadalcanal

　　　　　　　26 -- South Seas Detachment began withdrawal from Owen Stanley.

	October	
	24-25 --	Second general attack by 2d Division on Guadalcanal.
1943 January	20 --	Japanese withdrawal from Buna Sector
February	1-7 --	Japanese withdrawal from Guadalcanal.
March	3 --	Bismarck Sea Battle.
May	12 --	Allied landing on Attu.
June	30 --	Allied landing on Rendova Island, Solomons, and Nassau, New Guinea.
August	1 --	Declaration of Independence by Burma. Signing of Japan-Burma Alliance Pact.
September	4 --	Allied landing at Hoppoi east of Lae.
	8 --	Italy surrendered.
	22 --	Allied landing at Finschhafen.
	28 --	Decision made to establish Munitions Ministry.
October	14 --	Declaration of Independence by the Philippines.
	21 --	Establishment of Provisional Government of Free India.
November	1 --	Allied landing on Torokina.
	5-6 --	Greater East Asia Convention held at Tokyo by leaders of Japan, Manchukuo, Nanking Government, Philippines, Thailand and Burma.
	21 --	Allied landing on Makin and Tarawa.
	23 --	Cairo Conference.
	28 --	Teheran Conference.
December	26 --	Allied landing on Cape Gloucester
1944 February	1 --	Allied landing on Kwajalein.
	17 --	Allied task force struck at Truk.
	18 --	Allied landing on Eniwetok.
	23 --	Allied task force struck at Marianas.
	29 --	Allied landing on Admiralities.
March	8 --	Imphal Operation started.
	30 --	Through 3 April Allies struck at Palau and Hollandia.

April	18 --	First phase of "Ichi-Go" Operation started.
	22 --	Allied landing at Hollandia.
	27 --	Allied landing on Biak.
		Second phase of "Ichi-Go" Operation started.
June	15 --	Allied landing on Saipan.
	19-20 --	"A-Go" Operation (Naval Battle off Mariana).
July	8 --	China-based B-29's first raided Kyushu.
	22 --	Tojo Cabinet resigned and Koiso Cabinet formed.
	29 --	China-based B-29's first raided Manchuria.
September	15 --	Allied landing on Peleliu and Morotai.
October	12 --	Through 16 October, Air Battle off Formosa.
	20 --	Allied landing on Leyte.
	24 --	Through 26 October, Philippine Sea Battle.
November	9 --	President Roosevelt elected for the fourth time.
	10 --	China Expeditionary Army occupied Kweilin and Liuchow.
	24 --	Allied Saipan-based B-29's raided Tokyo area for first time.
December	15 --	Allied landing on Mindoro.
1945 January	9 --	Allied landing at Lingayen Gulf.
February	19 --	Allied landing on Iwo Jima.
March	9 --	Southern Army began to occupy French Indo-China with armed forces.
	9-10 --	First Allied air raids on Tokyo using incendiary tactics.
	26 --	"Ten-Go" Air Operations commenced.
April	1 --	Allied landing on Okinawa Main Island.
	5 --	Soviet declared her intention to abrogate Russo-Japanese Neutrality Pact.
	7 --	Koiso Cabinet resigned and Suzuki Cabinet was formed.
	3 --	Rangoon lost to the Allies.
	8 --	Germany surrendered.

July   26 -- Three Power Joint Declaration issued at
                  Potsdam.

August.   6 -- First atomic bomb dropped on Hiroshima.

             9 -- Soviet entered war.

                  Second atomic bomb dropped on Nagasaki.

SUPPLEMENT II

Chronology of Major Liaison Conferences during Greater East Asia War

1941 September 6 -- Council in Imperial Presence decided to make further effort for Japanese-American Negotiation, while initiating war preparations in a resolution to fight US, Britain and the Netherlands in event of failure in diplomatic negotiation.

November 5 -- Council in Imperial Presence decided to concentrate effort on war preparations, while still seeking to break deadlock by diplomatic means.

15 -- Liaison conference decided on outline of objectives which was titled as "Tentative Plan to Expedite the Termination of War with The US, Britain, China and the Netherlands".

20 -- Liaison Conference decided on outline of administration of occupied Southern areas.

23 -- Liaison Conference decided on measures to be taken toward Thailand.

December 1 -- Council in Imperial Presence resolved to open hostilities against US, Britain and the Netherlands.

1942 March 7 -- Liaison Conference adopted "General Outline of War Direction Policies to be carried out in the Future", main point of which was consolidation of occupied regions in the South.

December 10 -- Council in Imperial Presence agreed upon "Matters pertaining to control of military operational demand in view of the present national materiel power, and measures to increase national fighting power".

21 -- Council in Imperial Presence agreed upon "Basic policy toward China in order to carry out the Greater East Asia War".

1943 May 30 -- Council in Imperial Presence decided on "Outline Plan for the Direction of Greater East Asia Political Strategy", main point of which was to accelerate independence of Philippines and Burma.

September 30 -- Council in Imperial Presence decided on "Outline Plan for the Direction of Future War", in which the Council decided on absolute zone of national defense as submitted by Imperial General Headquarters and also decided to increase aircraft production.

1944 August 5 -- Liaison Conference reorganized into Supreme Council for the Direction of War.

	19 --	Council in Imperial Presence decided on "Outline Plan for the Direction of War", in which Council decided to fight the war vigorously.
1945 January	25 --	Supreme Council for the Direction of War decided on "Outline of Emergency Measures to Support the Decisive Battle".
June	8 --	Council in Imperial Presence adopted basic policy for preparation of Homeland decisive battle.
August	10 --	Council in Imperial Presence agreed upon acceptance of Potsdam Declaration with an understanding concerning status of the Emperor.
	14 --	Council in Imperial Presence agreed upon unconditional acceptance of Potsdam Declaration.

SUPPLEMENT III

Chronology of Major Actions & Decisions by the Army General Staff

1941 mid-September -- Issued orders concerning preliminary war preparations, organizing operational forces and dispatching them to South China, Formosa and French Indo-China.

November 6 -- Issued orders of battle for Southern Army, 14th Army, 15th Army, 16th Army, 25th Army and South Seas Detachment. Ordered them to carry out preparations for Southern Invasion Operations.

15 -- Issued preliminary order to carry out Southern Invasion Operations, but D Day was to be set by separate order.

25 -- An agreement was reached regarding division of responsibility for military administration of occupied Southern Areas between the Army and Navy.

December 1 -- Issued order setting D Day for 8 December.

3 -- Instructed Kwantung Army to avoid any border dispute with Soviet. Also instructed China Expeditionary Army to strengthen anti-Chungking blockade with present position to weaken Chungking's will to continue war.

late-December -- Decided to advance Java Invasion Operation by one month.

1942 January 4 -- Ordered South Seas Detachment to occupy Rabaul.

14 -- Ordered transfer of 48th Division from 14th Army to 16th Army.

22 -- Ordered Southern Army to expand operations in Burma to capture all important areas.

February 2 -- Ordered South Seas Detachment to capture important points in British New Guinea and Bismarck Archipelago.

7 -- Ordered Southern Army to capture Andaman Islands and authorized it to operate in the Portuguese Timor.

10 -- Ordered 4th Division to come under 14th Army to strengthen Bataan offensive.

mid-March -- Tentative plan for direction of subsequent military operations following completion of Southern Invasion Operations was established, main point of which was consolidation of occupied Southern areas and reserve fighting power.

March	20 --	Beginning on this date, issued orders successively to transfer a part of air and ground forces from Southern Army to Manchuria, Homeland and China.
late-March	--	Began studies on New Caledonia-Fiji-Samoa Operations and Western Aleutian Operations on the basis of a tentative agreement between the Army and Navy to carry out these operations.
early-April	--	Issued a plan to settle the China Incident suggesting an intention to launch an attack against Chungking.
April	20 --	Issued order of battle for Borneo Garrison Army.
	30 --	Ordered China Expeditionary Army to capture air bases in Chekiang Province.
May	5 --	Issued orders of battle for Ichiki and North Seas Detachments and assigned them the mission to capture Midway Island and the Western Aleutian Islands, respectively.
	18 --	Issued order of battle for 17th Army and assigned it a mission of invading Fiji, Samoa and New Caledonia.
June	27 --	Placed 14th Army under direct command of Army General Staff.
	29 --	Ordered Southern Army and 14th Army to stabilize and secure occupied areas. Army-Navy Central Agreement was concluded regarding defense policy and defense responsibility in the occupied Southern areas.
July	4 --	Activated 1st and 2d Area Armies, Armored Army and 2d Army under Kwantung Army to strengthen war preparations in the North.
	10 --	Activated 3d Air Army under Southern Army command.
	11 --	Cancelled New Caledonia-Fiji-Samoa Operation Plan and ordered 17th Army to capture Port Moresby and mop up Eastern New Guinea.
August	13 --	Assigned an additional mission of recapturing Guadalcanal and Tulagi to 17th Army.
	29 --	Issued order to strengthen 17th Army with the reinforcement by the 2d Division.
	31 --	Issued order directing 17th Army operations with priority to recapturing of Guadalcanal.
September	3 --	Ordered China Expeditionary Army to carry out preparations for Chungking Operation.

November	16 --	Issued orders of battle for 8th Area Army and 18th Army. Instructed 8th Area Army to strengthen Southeastern area operations and recapture Guadalcanal. Effective date 26 November.
December	10 --	Cancelled order regarding preparations for Chungking Operation.
	31 --	Army and Navy General Staff decided on new operations policy to withdraw units from Guadalcanal and re-established the front line in the Southeastern area to the Northern Solomons--New Britain Island--Eastern New Guinea line.
1943 January	4 --	Issued orders to 8th Area Army in compliance with the 31 December decision.
	7 --	Activated 19th Army under Southern Army to strengthen war preparations in North-of-Australia area.
	30 --	Ordered China Expeditionary Army to occupy important points in Raichow Peninsula and French Leased Territory along Kwanchow Bay.
February	11 --	Redesignated Northern District Army as Northern Army giving it status of operational army.
late-February--		Established a plan to direct Southwest Pacific area operations during the year 1943.
March	27 --	Activated Burma Area Army under Southern Army to strengthen command system in Burma.
April	12 --	Took first step to strengthen ground operational preparations in Central Pacific Area by dispatching 1st and 2d South Seas Defense Units (Army) there.
May	20 --	Issued order to withdraw units from Western Aleutians.
June	19 --	Issued orders to dispatch 7th Air Division and 1st Raiding Group to New Guinea for contemplated Bena-Bena Operation.
July	28 --	Activated 4th Air Army under 8th Area Army Command to strengthen air operations in Southeastern area.
August	30 --	Issued order to re-establish main defense position in New Guinea from Lae-Salamaua to Finschhafen area.
September	15 --	Army and Navy General Staff decided on new operations plan to establish a firm national defense line extending from Banda Sea area to Marianas through Western New Guinea and Carolines.

	30 --	Ordered Southern Army to strengthen operational preparations in North-of-Australia area, also ordered 8th Area Army to shift to a delaying action.
October	29 --	Ordered transfer of 2d Area Army headquarters and 2d Army headquarters from Manchuria to North-of-Australia area to strengthen operational preparations there. They were ordered to assume command there from 1 December on under direct command of Army General Staff.
November	15 --	Took first step to strengthen operational preparations on Ogasawara Islands by dispatching 1st and 5th Independent Mixed Regiment there.
December	10 --	Issued orders of battle for French Indo-China Garrison Army and Thailand Garrison Army.
1944 January	7 --	Approved execution of contemplated Imphal Operation by Southern Army.
	15 --	Activated 28th Army under Burma Area Army to strengthen operations in Akyab area.
		Activated 29th Army in Northern Malay to strengthen war preparations there.
	24 --	Ordered China Expeditionary Army to carry out Hunan-Kwangsi ("Ichi-Go") Operations.
February	15 --	Activated 5th Air Army under China Expeditionary Army command.
	25 --	Activated 31st Army in Central Pacific area to consolidate operational preparations there and placed it under command of Combined Fleet.
early-March	--	Began studies for "A-Go" Operations with the Navy.
March	14 --	Issued order to transfer 18th Army and 4th Air Army from 8th Area Army to 2d Area Army. Effective date 25 March.
	16 --	Redesignated the Northern Army as 5th Area Army and activated 27th Army in Kuriles under 5th Area Army command to strengthen operational preparations there. Effective date 27 March.
	22 --	Issued orders of battle for Formosa Army and 32d Army and directed them to strengthen operational preparations on Formosa and Nansei Islands respectively (Battle Preparations No 10).
	27 --	Activated 7th Area Army at Singapore under Southern Army.

	27 --	Placed 2d Area Army and 14th Army under Southern Army command to simplify command system in the South. Effective date 15 April.
April	11 --	Activated 33d Army in Northern Burma to strengthen operations there.
early-May	--	Issued order directing "Battle Preparations No 11" to strengthen war preparations in the Philippines.
May	2 --	Ordered Southern Army to contract first line in Western New Guinea to Manokwari-Sorong-Halmahera line.
	4 --	Ordered Homeland Defense commander to strengthen defense of Homeland and placed Eastern, Central and Western District Armies, and Air Defense Divisions and Brigades in the Homeland under his complete command.
	9 --	Ordered Southern Army to contract first line in Western New Guinea to Sorong-Halmahera line.
	12 --	Ordered transfer of 2d and 4th Air Divisions from Manchuria to the Philippines to strengthen operational preparations there.
June	15 --	Activated four divisions in the Philippines and placed them under 14th Army command.
	26 --	Issued order of battle for Ogasawara Group under direct command of Army General Staff.
July	4 --	Directed Southern Army to discontinue Imphal Operation.
	11 --	Placed 32d Army under Formosa Army command.
	18 --	Ordered China Expeditionary Army to capture important points along the Southeast China coast.
	21 --	Organized 36th Army under direct command of Army General Staff to strengthen the defense of Homeland.
	24 --	Issued order regarding battle preparations for "Sho" Operations.
late-July	--	Compromising measures were taken to unify operations of Army and Navy Air Forces in various local areas.
August	4 --	Redesignated 14th Army in the Philippines as 14th Area Army. Activated 35th Army under 14th Area Army.
	26 --	Activated 6th Area Army under China Expeditionary Army to support Hunan-Kwangsi Operation.

mid-September	--	Ordered Kwantung Army to defend Manchuria by general delaying tactics.

Ordered Southern Army to secure Southern Burma in carrying out future operations in Burma theater. Withdrew intention to cut off Burma Aid Route.

September 22 -- Decided to prepare No 1 "Sho" Operation (for the Philippines area) with top priority.

Redesignated Formosa Army as 10th Area Army.

October 18 -- Ordered execution of No 1 "Sho" Operation.

November 1 -- Issued order to push the execution of No 1 "Sho" Operation.

mid-December -- Took measures to exploit a more effective use of Continental Railways.

December 26 -- Activated 6th Air Army to strengthen air defense operations in the Homeland.

1945 mid-January -- Decided on a new outline plan of decisive operations to protect strategic sphere around the Homeland.

January 16 -- Ordered Kwantung Army to mobilize eight divisions and four mixed brigades.

22 -- Ordered China Expeditionary Army to shift its main efforts from anti-China operations to anti-America operations and to speed up operational preparations along Southeastern China coast.

26 -- Ordered transfer of 6th Army headquarters from Manchuria to China to strengthen command system in lower reach of Yangtze River.

27 -- Ordered Southern Army to direct its operations so that the Army should obstruct enemy advance toward China and Homeland.

early-February - Ordered China Expeditionary Army to mobilize three divisions, 12 mixed brigades and seven independent garrison units.

February 3 -- Ordered 10th Area Army to secure Formosa and Nansei Islands, and repel advance of enemy air and sea bases there.

6 -- Issued order of battle for Homeland Defense Army and, under its command, activated 11th, 12th, 13th, 15th and 16th Area Army headquarters and four mixed brigades in the Homeland. Also activated Civil Defense Forces. Redesignated Korea Army as 17th Area Army and Korea Army Administrative District. Activated two divisions in Korea.

Issued orders concerning air operations in East China Sea area ("Ten-Go" Air Operation).

             26 -- Decided on General Mobilization Plan for Homeland Defense, calling for mobilization of 42 divisions, 19 mixed brigades and six tank brigade in three groups.

             28 -- Issued order for 1st Group Mobilization

                  Ordered Southern Army to occupy French Indo-China with armed forces, if necessary.

March   1 -- Army-Navy Central Agreement regarding Air Operations for the 1st half of 1945 was concluded and issued.

             19 -- Placed 6th Air Army under Combined Fleet command.

             20 -- Disclosed rough draft plan of "Ketsu-Go" Operations to chief of staff of each Area Army.

             31 -- Issued order to transfer four divisions from Manchuria to the Homeland.

April   2 -- Issued order for Second Group Mobilization

              8 -- Activated First and Second General Armies and Air General Army in the Homeland. Homeland Defense Army was abolished. Effective date 15 April.

                  Declared "Ketsu-Go" Operation Plan for defense of Homeland and Korea.

             18 -- Ordered China Expeditionary Army to assemble four divisions in North-Central China from South China.

May   5 -- Decided to transfer one Army headquarters and four divisions from China to Kwantung Army.

              8 -- Instructed 5th Area Army to direct its main efforts on the defense of Hokkaido Main Island. Also gave the Army an outline plan for anti-Soviet defense.

             10 -- Issued order to transfer 40th Army headquarters from Formosa to Kyushu.

             23 -- Issued order for Third Group Mobilization.

             26 -- Returned 6th Air Army to Air General Army command.

             30 -- Ordered China Expeditionary Army to withdraw from Hunan-Kwangsi area and strengthen strategic positions in North-Central China. Also ordered transfer of four divisions from China to Kyushu.

	30 --	Issued order of battle for Kwantung Army. Instructed the Army to prepare for anti-Soviet defense operations with main objective of securing Southern Manchuria. Also authorized the Army to dispatch a part of its forces in northern Korea and to control Korea Army Administrative District in regard to operational preparations.
late-May	--	Decided to prepare for Homeland battle with priority on Kyushu.
June	23 --	Activated Tokyo Defense Army under 1st General Army.
	28 --	Took measures to maintain sea transportation in Korean Strait and Japan Sea.
	30 --	Returned all air defense units (flying units) to Air General Army command from General Armies' command. Instructed Air General Army to strengthen anti-B-29 air defense operations.
July	10 --	Effected total mobilization in Manchuria and mobilized eight divisions and seven mixed brigades.
mid-July	--	Issued Army-Navy Air Agreement for "Ketsu-Go" Operations.
July	26 --	Directed Southern Army to hold Southern Burma and Sumatra as long as possible, while firmly securing Malay, Thailand and French Indo-China as central sectors in the South.
August	9 --	Ordered Kwantung Army and 5th Area Army to prepare for an all-out defense operation against the Soviet.
		Ordered 17th Area Army to come under Kwantung Army command.
		Ordered China Expeditionary Army to send six divisions and six brigades to Manchuria.
	10 --	Ordered Kwantung Army and 5th Area Army to commence all-out defense operations.
	14 --	Instructed all the Army forces to faithfully obey the Imperial Decision to end the war.
	15 --	Issued order to suspend all attack operations against Allied forces.
	16 --	Issued order to cease all hostile activities.

SUPPLEMENT IV

Guide to Designation of Units, and Their Purposes and Normal Size

Designation	Purpose	Normal Size	Example
Independent Mixed Regiment	Defense of isolated island or isolated point	3 inf bns 1 arty bn 1 engr co	4th Indep Mixed Regt
Border Garrison Unit	Garrison of border in Manchuria	3 to 10 inf bns 3 to 10 arty bns 1 to 4 engr cos	5th Border Garrison Unit
Detachment	Combat team for general purpose (Temporarily organized)	2 to 3 inf bns 1 arty bn 1 tank co 1 engr co	South Seas Det 5th South Seas Det Kawaguchi Det
Defense Unit	Defense of isolated island	3 inf bns 1 arty bn 3 tank cos 1 sig co	1st South Seas Defense Unit
Independent Garrison Unit	Garrison of railroads in Manchuria	4 to 6 inf bns	1st Independent Garrison Unit
Expeditionary Unit	Unit temporarily organized from units stationed in Manchuria and Korea to reinforce troops in Central Pacific	3 to 6 inf bns 1 to 2 arty bns 1 to 2 engr cos	1st Expeditionary Unit
Mixed Infantry Group	Combat team for general purpose (Temporarily organized)	3 inf bns 1 arty bn 1 engr co	56th Mixed Infantry Group (Sakaguchi Det)
Brigade	Garrison of occupied area	3 inf regts 1 engr unit 1 sig unit	65th Brigade
Cavalry Brigade		2 to 3 cavalry regts 1 tank unit 1 arty unit 1 engr unit	1st Cavalry Brig
Independent Tank Brigade	Defense of the Homeland	2 tank regts 1 machine cannon unit 1 maintenance unit	1st Independent Tank Brig
Amphibious Brigade	Unit specially organized for landing operation	3 mobile inf bns 1 tank unit 1 machine cannon unit 1 engr unit	1st Amphibious Brig
Independent Mixed Brigade	Combat team for general purpose	3 to 6 inf bns 1 arty unit 1 engr unit	68th Indep Mixed Brig

Fortress Unit	Defense of fortress	1 to 2 hvy arty regts Some inf units 1 AAA unit 1 engr unit	Tokyo Bay Fortress Unit
Cavalry Group		2 cavalry brigs 1 sig unit	3d Cavalry Group
Division		1 inf gp hq 3 inf regts 1 rcn (cavalry) regt 1 arty regt 1 engr regt 1 sig unit	1st Division
Tank Division		3 tank regts 1 inf regt 1 rcn unit 1 arty regt 1 AAA unit 1 anti-tank gun unit 1 engr unit	2d Tank Division
Group	Common name of such units as division, tank division, cavalry group, independent mixed brigade, etc. Commander of a group was a general and he had one or more general staff officers.		
Army	General purpose of operations in the field.	Varied according to the operational needs. Normally composed of one or more divisions, other combat units and necessary line of communication units.	1st Army Mongolia Garrison Army
Garrison Army	Garrison	Varied according to the needs. Normally composed of garrison units and military administrative organs.	Borneo Garrison Army Thailand Garrison Army
Armored Army	Armored Army was established, in 1942, with 1st and 2d Tank Division as its nucleus.		
Area Army	General purpose of operations in the field.	Varied according to the needs. Normally composed of one or more armies, other combat units directly assigned and line of communication units.	2d Area Army Burma Area Army

District Army	Homeland defense and Home Depot works	Varied according to the situation	Eastern District Army Korea Army Formosa Army
Army Administrative District	Civil defense in the Homeland and Home Depot works.	Varied according to the situation.	Eastern Army Adm Dist Korea Army Adm Dist Formosa Army Adm Dist
General Army		Varied according to the situation	1st General Army Kwantung Army China Exped Army
Independent Air Unit	Reconnaissance and direct support	2 to 4 indep squadrons	21st Indep Air Unit
Air Brigade	Air Operation	2 or more air regts or indep air units	1st Air Brig
Air Division		2 or more air brigs, and air regts directly assigned.	1st Air Division
Air Group	Redesignated as Air Division		
Air Corps	Redesignated as Air Army		
Raiding Brigade		2 parachute regts 1 glider regt 1 machine cannon unit 1 tank unit 1 engr unit	1st Raiding Brig
Raiding Group		2 raiding brigs 1 transport brig	1st Raiding Group
Naval Landing Unit	Landing operation and ground defense	1 inf bn Necessary supporting elements.	Sasebo 5th Landing Unit

www.ingramcontent.com/pod-product-compliance
Lightning Source LLC
Chambersburg PA
CBHW060231240426
43671CB00016B/2906